BODY LANGUAGE

*Writers on Identity, Physicality, and
Making Space for Ourselves*

**Edited by Nicole Chung
and Matt Ortile**

Catapult New York

ISBN: 978-1-64622-131-8

Cover design by Nicole Caputo
Cover illustration by Sirin Thada
Book design by Laura Berry

Library of Congress Control Number: 2021947048

Catapult
New York, NY
books.catapult.co

Printed in the United States of America

10 9 8 7 6 5 4 3 2 1

Contents

CONTENTS

CONTENTS

CONTENTS

Introduction

Nicole Chung and Matt Ortile

We talk a lot about bodies: from their right to safety and respect to how they take up space, from their sizes and shapes
and shades to what each is able to do, it's a conversation
that's both constant and ever evolving—especially in our
new decade, as we've become hyperaware of the ways we
physically navigate our world, whether in close proximity
or six feet apart. To recognize and celebrate human bodies
in their myriad beauties and braveries, we offer this mosaic:
Body Language, a wide-ranging anthology of essays about
the stories our bodies tell, and how we move within (and
against) expectations of race, gender, health, and ability.

Since its founding in 2015, *Catapult* magazine's goal has
been to elevate writers who move cultural discussion forward through telling the stories that matter most to them.
As a digital publication, *Catapult* is committed to publishing literature that fearlessly explores the areas where human identities intersect, while providing a free, welcoming
space for a diverse, curious, and growing readership. This
anthology is an extension of that project. *Body Language*
features an astonishingly talented and diverse group of thirty

writers—including Black writers, Asian writers, Latinx writers, trans and nonbinary writers, disabled writers, immigrant writers—whose stories document their lived experiences, help to bridge the gaps between us, and add needed perspective and nuance to personal and political conversations around human bodies.

Bodies are beautiful: Natalie Lima documents the ways men fetishize her fat and powerful body; A. E. Osworth chronicles their transition through thirst traps. Bodies endure: Jenny Tinghui Zhang confronts her eating disorder in the harsh landscape of Wyoming; Destiny O. Birdsong tackles what she calls "Karen Medicine," the broken and often biased U.S. healthcare system that Black women must navigate. Bodies need care: Melissa Hung eases her chronic headaches with swimming; Jess Zimmerman reframes what we consider "pain," especially after the trauma of 2020—which Gabrielle Bellot beautifully describes as our "year of breath." Most importantly, bodies carry us through our one life: Bryan Washington writes about playing high school football as a Black teenager growing up in Texas; Bassey Ikpi returns to Nigeria and considers the different stories skin can tell; s. e. smith pays tribute to the small beauties of funeral sex, in defiance of grief—after all, as the late Nina Riggs writes in her essay "The Crematorium," "Dying isn't the end of the world."

As has been said, our bodies are wonderlands, but they can also be battlefields. And we all have one—for better or for worse. It would be impossible to include every experience, every argument, every kind of body in one anthology. *Body Language* is meant to be a tribute to the human body's multitudes, as well as a conversation starter, a challenge to the ways in which many of us were taught to understand our bodies and what they can be. What these essays all have in common is that they are by writers speaking their truths for themselves, for their own bodies and individual identities, as opposed to submitting to society's expectations about what bodies should look like, what they should do, or how they must behave.

BODY LANGUAGE

The Crematorium

Nina Riggs

We are following two black-suited undertakers across the one-hundred-degree parking lot out to a windowless metal building—my dad; my brother, Charlie; his wife, Amelia; me. My husband is at work, our kids at school. It is the day before my mom's memorial service. My phone is buzzing in my pocket with texts of flight arrivals and last-minute arrangements.

We are all frazzled by the heat and the events of the past week, but I think I look the most haggard. On top of my mom's cancer and final days, I have been lugging the weight of my own breast cancer around with me for the past eight months—a sneaky aggressive kind that has made everything feel deeply off-kilter since the day I was diagnosed. The hair on my head is a patchy fuzz following months of chemo. I am one-breasted from a mastectomy last month, my T-shirt sagging off my body on that side like a sheet on a windless clothesline. I'm facing another three months of chemo scheduled to start the Monday after the memorial.

"Dammit," my mom had said a few weeks ago, when she was still coherent. "I can't believe I'm going to die right when you're in the middle of all this. It's killing me." One of her wry smiles.

The bulk of me is standing here in grief—in that unhinged and unpredictable way we are led toward things after a loss—but I have to admit that part of me is here for some kind of morbid test drive, death hitching a ride in my chest from my mom's sickbed to this parking lot behind the funeral home.

In the far back corner, in the corrugated metal building: the crematorium. *The uglification of America*, my mom used to say when she would see this sort of cheap metal structure going up along some rural North Carolina highway, quickly announcing itself as a Dollar General or a liquor store. Now, inside one, her body awaits its final moments.

We know they'll have her in the hundred-dollar cardboard cremation casket we'd picked out at the funeral home. What we don't expect is that it will look like a large white cake box.

The morticians seem uncertain about us for wanting to be here—like it's *we* who are the creepy ones. Honestly, I'm not sure we want to be here, either, but Charlie feels strongly that we should see this through to the end, and we have agreed to try to support each other through whatever twists and turns our mother's death takes us.

We kept vigil at her bedside until she died. We kept her body in the house for several days after she was gone—taking turns sitting with her, watching her change and become increasingly less her.

And now.

This is the end, I think to myself.

———

Three days earlier we'd sat in the funeral home office with a different mortician—our next-door neighbor, Joe, a friend and the new father of a baby girl born the very week my mom died—and asked about observing the cremation.

"Uh, sure, that can definitely be arranged," Joe said. Two of his great gifts: tact and kindness.

On the glossy mahogany table in the funeral parlor was the flowered canister we'd brought from home—her stash can. "And can you put her ashes in this?" Charlie asked. "Sorry—it has kind of a strong smell. It's where she kept her pot."

"Oh, definitely," said Joe, nodding without blinking. "Not a problem."

I was actually relieved this was the container we'd shown up with. When I'd picked up my dad for the funeral home appointment, he climbed into my car holding the orange Tupperware pitcher we'd been mixing powder lemonade in since the 1970s. "Will this work?" he'd asked.

"I don't think so, Dad," I'd said. "Maybe something— not from the kitchen?"

When he ran back inside to get a different vessel, I'd snapped a photo of the pitcher sitting in the passenger seat and texted it to my mom's number. *Please come back*, I'd written. *Dad wants to put you in this.*

The first of a million non-replies.

Inside the Uglification of America, it is one hundred degrees hotter than the hundred-degree parking lot. It looks like a garage, with a large cooler and an even larger oven. The oven is, it seems, preheating.

"Do you want to see the body first?" one of the under-takers asks us.

She's been in their refrigerator for five days. There is a sheet covering her face when they lift the cake box lid. Of the whole thing, I like that part the least. The undertaker pulls it back with some fanfare, and the four of us lean forward and peer in at her.

She is no longer my mother—and that, I think, is part of what I'm supposed to understand by visiting her here in the metal box. Although I knew it already. I knew it the moment my phone rang at 3:00 a.m. and Charlie said, "I think you should come," and I tripped into two different sandals and put my shirt on backward and ran both of the stop signs between our houses, and I knew it when I skidded into the driveway and a startled rabbit in the grass by the gate stared back at me—unflinching, unmoved—as I slammed the car door and ran past it. I knew I was too late.

She isn't decomposed or anything like it, but her coloring is distinctly orange and waxy now, and her face is covered in beads of condensation. Only her hair looks like her—lovely wisps of graying brown swept back from her forehead. The purple flowers we'd strewn on her the morning she died are wilted and browning like a discarded corsage. Her eyes are sewn shut—uneven stitches between her eyelashes that look like the doll dresses she helped me sew in third grade. Her mouth is sewn shut as well.

"She would definitely not like that!" I whisper to my dad. He squeezes my shoulder.

The other undertaker turns to my dad. "Do you want to press the button for the incinerator?" he asks, as though my dad is the birthday boy at a special party. He starts showing him the levers and the different dials. My dad, who is usually game for just about anything but who I can tell in this moment is going along with the undertaker's shtick just to avoid further interaction, presses the green button.

The oven door starts to open and then lurches suddenly, and someone else's leftover ashes plume briefly into the air like a thought bubble or a dream about how little we belong here. We all jump back, and I can almost hear my mom yelling at my dad, "Jesus Christ, Peter—what are you trying to do to me?"

When the door fully opens, they close the box and slide it in on a short conveyer belt, and the oven door clanks shut with my mom inside. There is no window. Somehow all this time I had imagined there would be a horrifying little window like on a potbelly stove. There is only a thick metal door and she is on the other side of it and we cannot enter and she will not return.

The cremation itself will take four or five more hours to complete.

"Okay, I'm good," I say almost immediately. I'm lightheaded and annoyed at whatever made me think this might be a reasonable thing to do. Outside, I need to squat down on my knees on the blacktop while my eyes adjust to the sun. My dad comes out with me and rubs my back. Charlie and Amelia stay inside a few minutes longer, but soon emerge.

Charlie is ten years younger than I am—not yet thirty. Growing up, we never really fought with each other, or our dad—it wasn't part of the architecture of our childhood— but we fought a lot with our mom. For a long time, that was what Charlie and I had in common. Me, maybe, because I'm so much like her—impulsive, demanding, emotional. Mom and I even got cancer together. Charlie, maybe, because he is her opposite: he can be hard to connect with, and she took that personally sometimes. He is kind and smart and sensitive and disarming—but he can be hard to read, and he lives in his head. Amelia already understands him far better than the rest of us ever did.

"Sorry about that," says Charlie, cry-laughing, Amelia leaning her head against him as we all walk arm in arm back to the car. "I don't know if that was okay or horrible."

"It's okay," says my dad. "Let's just not ever do that again."

"Dying isn't the end of the world," my mom liked to joke, after she was diagnosed as terminal. I didn't really understand it until, suddenly, I did—when my breast cancer became metastatic and incurable. There are so many things that are worse than death: old grudges; a loveless life; insufficient self-awareness; severe constipation; a lack of curiosity; no sense of humor; this grim parking lot.

After the cremation the rest of the afternoon is airport runs and phone calls, and the evening is soup and beers on the back patio with music and family and friends. An old best friend pulls into the driveway on her motorcycle, driven that day from New York. Amelia's parents are here. My mother-in-law walks through the gate. The neighbors bring dessert. All through this, the oven is at work in the back of that parking lot on the other side of town.

———

The cremation was not, it turns out, the absolute end. It will be a couple days before we receive the ashes because, as Joe tells me one morning in the driveway, after the incinerator, there is the cremulator—a high-speed blender of sorts that grinds the cremated bone fragments into approximately four pounds of rocky sand.

Two days after the memorial service, Joe rings the door-bell holding the stash can. He's home from work for a quick lunch, the hearse crowding the narrow driveway between our houses. His wife, Josie, is home full-time with the baby, and Joe is trying to get back to working a regular schedule. His eyes are raw with the shock of parenting. I can hear the sound of newborn cries through our open windows at all hours.

"These are for you," he says when I open the door, hand-ing me the container. Four pounds.

"Thank you," I say, holding it awkwardly with both hands, wanting to put it under my arm, but knowing that would not be right, either. "I hope you guys are doing okay over there."

"We are," he says, smiling. "Tired—but she's so great."

Fifteen minutes later I peer out the dining room window. The driveway is empty. I discover I'm still holding the canis-ter, balanced on my hip and in the crook of my arm. I've let the dog out and straightened the couch cushions and made a grocery list, but I haven't put it down. Through the screens, I can hear Josie humming and cooing to the baby—that mind-less meandering tune of comfort and companionship—the loveliest of music, one of the first sounds I imagine I ever heard.

When Your Body Is the Lesson
On Art Modeling
Rachel Charlene Lewis

The most awkward part is that I don't begin naked. At first, the students think I'm maybe a new classmate, the result of an add/drop, maybe a new teaching assistant. They look at me the way you look at new classmates, disinterested or dismissive—or sometimes hopeful, like maybe they imagine we'll be friends, lovers, more. It's how I look at them, too, despite knowing that I'm here to make money.

The art professor arrives late. She approaches me where I sit on a paint-splattered metal table shoved against the wall. She says hello, asks if I'm the model, and introduces herself. I decide I like her when she gestures to where I'll spend the ninety-minute class and I glimpse a soft poof of copper armpit hair. It makes me feel better about the fact that I didn't shave for this, less worried that my body hair is something I should have rid myself of before being naked in the presence of other bodies. My body hair makes me feel less beautiful.

My beauty has always been the way I pay my way into spaces I don't feel I deserve to inhabit. I've been trying to deconstruct this in my everyday life by not wearing makeup, not shaving, not panicking when my drawn-on eyebrows smear against my partner's face during sex. I'm trying to be more bodily and more okay with who I am. This gig is a part of that.

As the professor speaks to her students, she points to the closet across the room, and I go where I'm directed, grabbing my bag and stepping around stray book bags and extra sets of charcoal. I find the light switch in the closet and shut the door. As I change into my robe, I am surrounded by abandoned paintings and charcoal drawings—rejected bodies, drawn before mine. I wonder if my image will end up in this closet, too.

After I change, I turn off my cell phone. My mom and I normally talk once or twice a week during her lunch break, but I didn't tell her about my new side gig today. When I told my partner, she asked if I wanted her to take me shopping for a robe. I imagined a red satin one, the type that I could re-purpose for sex, one that would make me feel beautiful—but I picked one made of thick white cotton instead. I decided in the aisle of Walmart that I didn't want to be masturbatory for the sake of my own ego or anyone else's.

I leave the closet and head over to the "stage," which is composed of two metal tables pushed together, with a thin white canvas thrown on top. I spend a few minutes stretching to try to look like I know what I'm doing, but I don't and it's apparent. All of this makes me feel vulnerable, a feeling I'm not used to. In my everyday life, I am unabashedly sexual, unapologetically queer, pro-Black and fighting the patriarchy. I imagine myself at age thirty working as a sex ed teacher during the week and at a sex store on weekends. I text my friends reviews of new sex toys I've tried and have one-night stands with ease.

Being nervous up here makes me feel like a fraud. I crawl onto the stage and stand, still in my robe. The professor explains that I'll start out doing quick poses ranging between ten and thirty seconds, and that over the course of the hour and a half I'll begin holding longer poses—a few for ten minutes, a few for fifteen. I'm to come up with the poses as I go. If I get stuck, she'll throw some ideas out. I can sit, or stand, or lie down on the tables. It's up to me.

Whenever I'm ready, she says.

This is a midlevel graduate course, so the class is more diverse than the ones I took in undergrad. Still, many of the students are white boys of a specific type, the sort I probably would have had a crush on growing up if they'd popped up in a mediocre romantic comedy or a movie about vampires. But I'm not interested in boys these days. It makes this a little easier for me; I imagine that if I don't find these white boys sexual, they won't find me sexual, either.

I know it doesn't work that way, but I pretend it does.

I've been naked around other people before, and have been so for purposes of art as well, but never like this— under bright classroom lights and surrounded by strangers. When I drop my robe, some students know not to look away. They hurry to copy the pose down, eyes flicking between me and their easels as if a half-second glimpse is all they need to understand my body. One white guy, in particular, looks me over several times in a way that feels sexless but still noteworthy, still new to me, a first-time model.

In practice, this gig is easier than expected. I don't like when people make me pose for pictures, but this is different. I pose and pose and pose, twisting and rising and lowering again. I learn which poses cause my muscles to cramp with fatigue and which I can easily breathe through. The brainstorming of a pose every ten seconds, and then seeking a single pose I can hold for ten minutes, is the second most stressful part of this job.

It's my mind that throws me off. I'm fine with the practical aspects of the job—*stand on a table, be naked, pose*—but am less comfortable with it in theory. I still don't know what it means to make money with my body like this. I know I support sex workers, but I don't know how to categorize this work I'm doing, and it bothers me to not know how to define this moment in my life. Is this a bad thing I'm doing? A good thing?

Everything about this feels like a gray area to me. Because it seems like the only way to be comfortable up here, to not be sexualized, is to drop my humanity. Once I'm on the stage, I don't shift my expression, or speak, or show discomfort, even when my legs feel like they may give out and deposit me in a clump on the floor. As the minutes pass, I begin to dissociate from myself, focusing on the sound of charcoal scratching away at paper, breaking myself down as the dozen or so students build me up. I become little more sensual or human or alive than the thin white cloth beneath me, splattered with paint and now dusted with my skin cells and stray hair. I de-animate, and time passes.

An hour in, I get dizzy and remember my fear of heights, and it's a snapback into my own body. Suddenly, standing

on two metal tables in front of all these people feels ridicu-
lous. I crave both feet together on the ground. I look out the
window and again locate myself on the third floor of a large
concrete school building. As I sink back into my skin, it over-
heats. I focus on feeling my feet, wiggling my toes. I think of
my fingers in my hair, the fat on the backs of my knees, my
tongue in my mouth.

The more I come back to myself, the more human I become, the more I think of how these students have been
taught to view me as an object. If I fall, will it cause any
more commotion than the sheet billowing and stuttering in
the breeze from the fan? Would it take them a moment to
recognize me, a body, not an object, bleeding and bruised
before them?

I wonder what they'll do with my body in their sketches.
I realize they know nothing about me—that my queerness,
potentially even my Blackness, is something I feel so deeply
but isn't always read. As the students flip their pages back in
favor of new blank space, I catch glimpses of myself on their
pads: There is no key, no way for a viewer who catches sight
of my body in charcoal, to know of these aspects of my identity. I am little more than a half dozen lines on paper, some
curls if the artist even attempts my hair. Most don't, leaving
a bald circle where my hair should be. It's odd being stripped
of these parts of myself. If I am, for them, only what I'm
perceived to be in a handful of lines, does my identity even
matter? Does it lose its value? Do I?

I inhale. I try to remember that this is just another small
thing, just a work of art. I breathe out. I feel my stomach
grow round. I stretch my fingers and toes and hear my bones

pop. It helps me calm down. The professor requests a final pose, and I lower myself until I am seated, stretching my legs out before me. I listen to the sound of pages flipping, paper crinkling and being brushed flat again. I let my feet flop and lean my weight back on my hands. My mind feels quiet. My anxiety behind me, I watch the art students try to create me one last time.

(Don't) Fear the Feeding Tube

Kayla Whaley

Before we figured out why I lost the ability to swallow solid food, Mom kept warning me about feeding tubes. If I didn't start eating, she said, the doctors would have no choice. As a teen, she'd been in a car accident that left her intubated in a burn unit for months, so I believed her when she said, "You don't want that."

With every bite I forced down—and especially every bite I couldn't force down—I imagined latex-gloved hands pushing a tube up my nostril, imagined gagging as it slimed down the back of my throat and farther, past where I could track its progress by feel. Feeding tubes were scarier to me than anything else, largely because they were concrete, tactile in a way my other fears (of cancer, of surgery, of death) were not. Even after we discovered the cause of my swallowing issues and I switched to a liquid diet, feeding tubes seemed to present a threat. If smoothies and soups weren't enough, I knew what would come next. Or I thought I did.

When I posted in a feminist Facebook group looking for smoothie recipes, a woman I'd gone to summer camp with as a child messaged me. She invited me to join a Facebook group for people with muscular dystrophy. She said the members would have plenty of suggestions about nutrition since many had similar swallowing issues. "And if it comes to it," she said, "don't fear the g-tube. It was one of the best things I've ever done for myself."

I'd never heard of a g-tube before, but context suggested it must be a feeding tube. She confirmed it was and described hers as "like a belly button piercing." A small incision is made through both the abdominal wall and the stomach wall. A silicone feeding tube is threaded through and held in place by a "balloon" that anchors the stomach against the abdomen. There are variations in the details according to the patient's body and the doctor's preferences, but essentially: a hole is made and an object (jewelry—a feeding tube) is placed in its new home.

My body flooded warm at her explanation, skin tingling so hard I thought the outer layer of me might shake itself loose. An adrenaline spike—an instinctive response to a sudden precipice, body prepped for either flight or fall, certain of neither, convinced of both.

Before gastrostomy tubes (g-tubes) were developed in the nineteenth century, nutritional enemas of broth, milk, or brandy were the go-to method when patients couldn't nourish themselves orally. It was partly because we knew so little about how digestion works; while autopsies led to some understanding of the organs involved and the path from mouth to rectum, it was impossible to see what happened during the process of digestion. Did the stomach mechanically chew food, like a second set of teeth buried among our innards? Or did some slurry of juices dissolve what we ate before passing it off to the intestines?

These and other questions were finally answered in the 1820s and 1830s thanks to Alexis St. Martin, who, after being accidentally shot at close range, had a permanent hole (medically known as a fistula) that opened directly into his stomach. St. Martin's doctor, William Beaumont, studied and experimented on St. Martin for over a decade. The fistula acted as a literal window into the main site of digestion, an area doctors had been unable to explore prior. And explore Beaumont did, often in painful and gruesome ways. In addition to simply watching St. Martin's food break down in his stomach, Beaumont dangled hunks of meat on a string in the hole, sampled vials upon vials of stomach acid, slipped spoons or other objects into the opening, and even once licked the inside of St. Martin's stomach to determine whether there was an acidic taste (there wasn't, so long as no active digestion was happening). His findings revolutionized gastric medicine and paved the way for the future of gastrostomy.

The earliest recorded surgical gastrostomy (the medical creation of an opening into the stomach) happened in 1849. Over the next several decades, doctors performed more surgeries, without much success. As Gayle Maynard discusses in her history of feeding tubes, most of those early patients died within hours. A few lasted days or a month. One little boy, the extreme exception, lived nearly twenty years by chewing his food before inserting it into his feeding tube. The real breakthrough came in 1894 with what is now known as the Stamm gastrostomy, named for its inventor. Unlike its predecessors, this procedure included the creation of an artificial sphincter around the newly inserted tube to prevent any stomach leakages. Apart from a few minor tweaks, the Stamm gastrostomy is still one of the most commonly used techniques today.

I couldn't contain myself after my brief conversation with my former fellow camper. As soon as Mom got home from work that day, I gleefully, almost wonderingly, said, "You were wrong! About feeding tubes. You were wrong."

A few months later I was wearing a hospital gown, all jewelry removed, lying uncomfortably in a hospital bed, ready for surgery. I was still drinking my smoothies, but not as easily. I didn't need a g-tube yet, but both my doctor and my friend assured me it's better to get one earlier rather than later. Anesthesia is dangerous for me, so I would be going under twilight sedation instead. I'd technically be awake throughout, but the drug would ensure I had no memory of being so. The anesthesiologist said its proper name was propofol. Like a schoolkid excited to know an answer before his classmates, Dad said, "Oh, like what killed Michael Jackson!"

The woman smiled politely at the familiar response and assured me this would be nothing at all like Michael Jackson. She gave me small amounts in ten- and fifteen-minute increments. She and the surgeon wanted me unaware, but only to a point—too much sedation and my lungs could give out.

(The earliest gastrostomies were performed under chloroform anesthesia, a popular method despite the high risks, including respiratory failure.)

"How do you feel now?" she asked after each incremental ratcheting.

"No different," I said for a few rounds. Then I suddenly felt very different, and then I felt nothing.

My first, slurred words upon returning to my consciousness were spoken through a raw throat and a cold haze: "I'm so glad I didn't die." The people filling the operating room—at least ten, maybe fifteen—laughed. Probably because, though all surgery carries risk, my wide-eyed awe was disproportionate to the risk of this routine outpatient procedure.

I wasn't talking solely about the surgery.

In the worst moments of that summer, I'd had the fleeting thought that maybe things would be better—easier, certainly, if I died. I didn't want to kill myself, not in any active way. I had no plan. I had hurt myself, yes: scratching my chest so hard I tore off a patch of skin that later became infected, biting my knuckles hard enough to leave indents for a few hours, pinching the back of my hand, clenching my fists until the muscles seized. These seemed like small things. A way to release the anger and fear that coursed through me like a new bloodstream circulating parallel to the original, emotional toxins building up and up and up with every heartbeat until my skin felt inadequate to contain the pressure. The small hurts opened small valves. I wasn't suicidal. But maybe if my body simply decided to shut down on its own . . . that might be okay.

My body didn't respond well to the propofol. I got home from the hospital and spent the next eighteen hours nauseated, alternately breaking into cold sweats and hot to the point of feeling faint. Every thirty minutes or so I would grab the puke bucket (an old brown mixing bowl that's never been used for cooking). Saliva would fill my mouth, stomach and diaphragm clenching in preparation—only for the sensation to pass without incident. The cycle continued until morning. Neither Dad nor I slept. (Mom was on a cruise she'd booked a year in advance with my sister.)

I think the stress and exhaustion of that night is why we didn't solve the problem of transferring me out of my wheelchair until later. The sling I use to get in and out of my wheelchair has straps that slip under my thighs and crisscross in front of my stomach—right where my new fistula was. The pain of those straps digging in was unbearable. We did the only thing we could think of: skip the crisscross when transferring, and skip transferring at all wherever possible. For five days and five nights, until we realized we could simply belt my knees together, I slept in my chair.

Wheelchairs aren't made to be slept in. After five days, my body was in pure, constant pain. I hurt too much to brush my teeth. I hurt too much to even consider showering. I dreaded having to pee. I dreaded trying to sleep. *Arm* and *leg* and *torso* became meaningless descriptors, because my body was no longer a collection of parts hinged together by joint and sinew; my body was whole in its pain.

The one exception was my tube. The site itself was as my friend had said: sore, but not terribly so. And I was fascinated by my new appendage. It snaked out of me, fully sixteen inches visible. A nurse taught us to spin it once a day, "Like when you get your ears pierced," she said. She showed us how to check the contents of my stomach before every feeding. Thin, cloudy liquid pulled through the transparent tube and into the waiting syringe. After the acid was replaced ("Whatever you take out, you put back in"), we started pumping me full of formula. I felt it enter—all the way in my chest, like it had traveled against gravity, retracing the steps it should have taken from esophagus down. Not a painful sensation, just exceedingly strange.

When not in use, we curled the tube up and around, arcing under my breasts and across my ribcage, held safely against my skin until I needed it.

The first night I truly slept, ten days after surgery, I was in bed for fifteen hours. I woke once, around two o'clock, and couldn't feel my body. I had lost sense of my boundaries, couldn't define my physical form in the dark and warm. I didn't want to, either—I didn't want the pain to come flooding back. I wanted this respite to extend forever.

Maybe this no-feeling is what would have come on the operating table if my body had chosen not to cooperate with the anesthesia. I thought suddenly about the movie *Secretary*, which I had seen the year before. At the end of the film, Maggie Gyllenhaal's character has spent days sitting in a desk chair, unmoving. She is exhausted, soiled, in pain; she's trying to convince the man she loves that their (Dominant/submissive) relationship is good, healthy, loving, worth pursuing. He comes to get her, carries her gently from the desk to his home. He bathes her, massages her, soothes and comforts her. She relaxes into his careful touch, her body in painful, blissful recovery.

Lying numb in my bed, that scene appeared in my mind, and I willed myself back into my aching body. At first my fingers didn't respond, like the signal had been misplaced, but when I found their edges, I drummed them against the bed until sensation tiptoed along the rest of me. In slow stages, I felt the cradle of mattress beneath me, the support of a firm pillow, the tender softness of flannel sheets, the weight and warmth of a faux-down comforter. I hurt, and I knew the pleasure of pain temporarily relieved.

Even after recovery, I rarely used my feeding tube. For months I kept forcing down smoothie after smoothie, conceding to take one tube-fed meal per day. I said it was because I liked the smoothies (which I did) and because I could manage (which I couldn't). Drinking them got invariably harder. I was exhausting myself in trying to keep myself alive: the exact problem surgery was supposed to solve.

"Why did you get the g-tube if you aren't going to use it?" my doctor asked during the six-week post-op appointment. A reasonable question. One I felt an unreasonable anger at being asked, because questions expect answers, and I was unwilling to offer any.

After my research and conversations, I hadn't feared getting the g-tube. But now that it was an irreversible part of my reality, I feared relying on it in any meaningful way.

Whenever Mom spotted me struggling to get down my soup or smoothie of the day and asked if I'd rather—

"No," I'd say before she could finish.

My feeding tube could make my life unbelievably easier and quantifiably better, but a visceral, inexplicable shame pulsed through me when it came to actually using the thing.

The daily ritual of "sucking out" (as we started calling the process of checking for issues with the tube) continued to fascinate me, though. Every day was different. The color, amount, even texture of the liquid we pulled from inside changed for no discernible reason. This was normal, we were assured, so I was free to be intrigued without worrying. The human body excretes plenty of various fluids and substances all the time, so maybe my delight was uncalled for. But snot, saliva, urine, feces, and sweat are mundanities, not only in the daily nature of their presence, but in the fact that all humans experience them. Not many people can whip out their stomach's contents on a whim. A strange party trick, to be sure, but one I was proud of, as if I'd gained some new and exciting talent. More than that, knowing what was inside felt like sharing a secret with myself. Seeing inside my gut, learning to recognize its patterns and moods, felt intimate in a way that was wholly unexpected but altogether a joy.

So why was I so reluctant to put anything in? Why should there be any difference between my wheelchair as an assistive device and my feeding tube as an assistive device? The sensation was weird, yes. If we went too fast, my stomach would slosh for ten minutes after we finished, like I had a mini tide pool at my core. And I was more paranoid than was warranted that something was going to pop loose or pull free. But neither of those, together or separate, were reason enough for me to be so averse to putting this new tool to use.

Maybe it was resentment, then. I missed food. I would have traded a year of my life, *Princess Bride*–style, for a cheeseburger with cheddar topped with ketchup and mayonnaise. When my parents cooked sausage and potatoes, or pizza, or spaghetti, or chicken and rice, the desire for those once-familiar flavors, for the heat, for the texture, drove me to swipe baby oil over my top lip to try to drown out at least some of the scent. Sautéed onions alone were enough to make me involuntarily growl, some animalistic instinct come alive. Formula-filled syringes couldn't possibly compare. The shake of the small box in preparation of each feeding just reminded me of what I could no longer have.

If that resentment was part of why I resisted, though, I refused to voice it aloud. I wouldn't play to the stereotype. I wouldn't be a bitter cripple.

But wasn't I one? I felt like one. Weren't the juices I pulled from within myself bitter? An acid designed to corrode, to convert all manner of matter into fuel. Bitterness swirled sharp and newly familiar inside me.

But being bitter isn't the same thing as grieving. And grief isn't the same thing as denial. I was under no illusion about the ways my life had changed: I would never again have that cheeseburger. Never again face the challenge of a plate of barbecue with all the fixings. No more tuna melts or biscuits and gravy or simple turkey sandwiches. Spring would no longer mean boxes of Samoas and Do-si-dos. I was in denial, but not about the food—about the optics.

———

Whenever a parent murders their disabled child, the narrative is always the same: those poor parents, under so much stress, having to care for someone who couldn't care for themselves. When describing the murdered child, there's usually the same litany of physical limitations. They couldn't walk. They would have needed to be bathed, toileted, dressed for the rest of their life (had they been allowed to have one). They were on oxygen or would have needed to be eventually. They weren't even able to eat on their own; they were forced to use a feeding tube. How horrible.

On average, one disabled person a week is murdered by a parent or caregiver. The articles that cover those once-a-week deaths as mercies are, for all intents and purposes, describing me. Hard not to let that get at you, even if you're able to articulate the many fucked-up angles of that particular argument. Even if you believe all those arguments are particularly fucked up.

Before, I could eat. Now, I couldn't. Now, I needed a feeding tube.

Hard not to hear all those voices in all those articles covering all those murders over all those years echoing in your mind.

I wouldn't tell my doctor why I refused to use my feeding tube because I was ashamed of the answer. I'm supposed to be a proud disabled woman, one who has built a career on exploring and dismantling ableism. I could barely admit to myself, let alone to anyone else, that I had this festering pool of the stuff inside me. I should have rooted it out by now. I shouldn't be this stunted.

I didn't tell my doctor the truth, didn't tell him much of

anything. But his question prompted me to ask the same and
more of myself—and to recontextualize my answers. My bitterness, for instance.

Maybe it wasn't about the food or the admittedly significant change to my life, but was rather directed at those voices
ringing so steady and so loud in my head, telling me that a
feeding tube is anything other than a tool, telling me my death
would be a mercy. Maybe my bitterness, like the stomach
acid I was now on intimate terms with, was useful after all,
converting the bullshit presented as truth into simply bullshit, into something worth fighting against wherever it might
be found—including inside me. Matter into fuel. If feeding
tubes and wheelchairs were tools, maybe bitterness and pain
could be, too.

View from the Football Field; or, What Happens When the Game Is Over

Bryan Washington

1.

I'd never touched a football before I turned ten. Didn't have a favorite team. No Cowboys posters on the wall. But in the first week of September in my last year of high school, I sat in the locker room at Rhodes Stadium just outside of Houston, with my ankles taped and my wrists taped and my arms and my legs extended in down dog. Giddy like a bee, or a newborn kitten.

It was our last season, the only one that matters. We took the field in waves, ball carriers and quarterbacks first. Next came defenders, and everyone who couldn't catch. The kicker and his backups made up the third wave, already leaning toward spring for that other holy *fútbol*. That left the rest of us in the room, splayed out like dead things waiting to dance.

We huddled at the exit, palming a finger-worn doorway. We jogged through the awning, under the blow-up, onto the turf. We mumbled the Pledge of Allegiance, palming each other's shoulder pads during the national anthem, slapping the hell out of them on the *brave*, until the captains swaggered forward for the coin toss—and then we huddled up, shouting *motherfuck* and *fuck you* to set the mood, all under the lights, all under the crowd.

We took the first snap.

We spent ninety minutes colliding like dogs, broken up with rare moments of grace: a plié across the sideline, an extension to fondle the shitty pass. Exhilarating, all of it; but absurd, all of it. Pointless, at the end of it, but beautiful if you're in it.

And we did it until it was done. Until it was done with us. We found intramurals, adult leagues. Fantasy drafts. But we didn't get it back.

2.

Lately it's been in vogue to disparage the sport. Possibly because we have unraveled the layers of the game, deconstructed some of its ironclad lore—but maybe just because of the way the thing was designed; it couldn't help but show its ass eventually.

There's the question of the brutality, the long-term damage. There's the question of sponsoring domestic violence as routine. There's the stout homophobia and the misallocation of national attention and, maybe, most significantly, the deification of men—some of whom have no business being anyone's role model, let alone their god.

If you're a devotee hearing these issues discussed in mixed company, there's denial. My personal response is always a clench of the gut. The clipped inhale. Because there's no denying any of it; I have yet to hear a credible refutation. But it's also hard, sometimes, to sip your beer and agree. There's the conciliatory *yes*—and then also your *but*.

Because it was different, if you were there. You think if you could just show it to them, they'd believe you.

3.

Or maybe this is just to say I'm finding it harder and harder to justify, to quantify that *but*.

It's hardest when I look at my brother, R. He, too, lives in Texas. He's growing up in a place that puts pigskin on a pedestal higher than God. A place that could, ultimately, give a shit about boys like him, unless they're out on the field, running a ball, in which case there's nothing on earth that could be holier.

But when we talk about football, often, we don't talk about that. We don't talk about the repercussions. We don't talk about *after*.

R: You see this highlight? You see this move he put on him?

Me: I saw it. You sent it to me.

R: I'm putting that on someone next season.

Me: Sure. Okay. But if it happens to you, I'm calling 911.

R: You're sleep. Not in your life. But look at this one—that's sick.

Me: You're right, it's not happening. You're right, that's pretty sick.

4.

I recently moved to a new city. On the eve of the preseason, fans don face paint along with their usual wares; whole platoons of children strut around rocking their jerseys. It's strange to watch what you thought was small-town mystification grab a whole city by the heels. You look up, and it's everywhere.

But it wasn't until I was in the chair with my barber—a woman with tattoos of, among other things, notable Saints players—that the full effect of football's social dominance hit me square in the beans. Her enthusiasm struck me because I'd evicted myself from that world; easing back into talk of tackles and dominance and projections and stats wasn't a seamless transition.

We started off with small talk: She asked if I watched the sport at all. Smiled when I began the test with the correct answer. Moving on: My favorite team?

I told her I didn't have one; I watched whoever was winning.

It was then, for the first time in a decade, that a hairdresser clipped my ear. She apologized immediately. Chalked it up to a long day. We moved on to other topics, the changing weather, the price of gas. After another lull, she asked me, grinning, where I planned on watching The Game.

5.

Here's a literary mystery: no one's written the Great American Football Novel.

There's no obvious reason for this. Every yard on the field holds a lifetime. Football's a narrative within many narratives, same as any other sport; you could call it our nation's very own literary device. It is a void, and it is a mantelpiece. The standard and the *otra*. We've even got in-house heroes: Brett Favre. Aikman. Moss, Faulk. Sayers and Ditka. Bradshaw and Elway. Lewis. Manning. White and Marino and Deion.

But something else occurs to me: In order to write the Great One, or even a Very Good One, then, statistically, objectively, your protagonist would have to be Black. Or at least he probably wouldn't be white.

I suppose the possibility of a Black man as the star of the Great American Football Novel is about as dim as the possibility of a football novel to begin with.

6.

Who's to say that everyone on the field isn't living their own odysseys already?

I was living somebody else's. The same way a lot of us are, maybe even more so when we're younger. I was stuck in Ben's and Sean's stories. They were my confidantes on the team, these two guys I looked up to. They were our protagonists.

They were both the same age, generations apart when it came to cool. While Ben was effortless—tall and lanky and goofy—Sean was his opposite: short where the other was tall, curt where the other was affable. Ben had skin like dull oak. Sean wore his light, like creamed coffee.

They scored most of our points. No one else on our side did shit. We were a suburban school, hot on academics but broke when it came to athletic depth. Which is also to say we weren't overburdened with Black people. Part of it came down to district demographics, but chalking it all up to that would leave out layers of intent: the boosters, the grooming, the drawing boards in the coaches' offices. Even if Sean and Ben didn't look the part, initially—hampered by the rest of us, dropping screens and scuttling tackles—by the third game in the season, there wasn't any question who we leaned on. Ben caught the ball, and Sean ran it in.

Sometimes I got to touch it. Mostly I blocked for my friends. I didn't like blocking, but I did it well; I picked people up and set them down elsewhere, while my friends looked more and more like the heroes our team needed them to be.

7.

Sean was short, stocky. A thoughtful asshole. The first boy I knew to go into town and come back with a half sleeve (angels up and down his arm, cradling his mother's initials) and also tight pants, revolutionary for Katy, Texas. He had the quickest feet I've ever seen. During one practice, in the heat of August, he pointed out a player on the defense—someone decent at his position—and told me exactly how he'd put him on his ass. Then he slipped on his helmet, took his stance, caught the ball, and did it.

If Sean was steel, Ben was butter. Jokes were his way of life. When he finally made it around to cracking on you, you couldn't get mad, because that's who he was. He was also the laziest human being I'd ever encountered.

But! When he caught the ball!

I'd have to draw you a picture to help you understand. Or maybe I could just say that every catch was the climax of a very short play, a little Locrian rink-a-dink, one you couldn't recognize until you finally saw it. Ben plucked the ball from the sky like a daydream. He took care of the rock like most parents do their children: no one else was touching it, you had to work to even look at it, and if you did sneak a peek, he was probably already on his way past you, out of sight, out of mind. Despite the sloth, despite the things we sometimes hated him for, Ben could catch the hell out of the ball, and no one was taking that away from him.

8.

R: Look at this one. You see what he did here?

Me: Knees don't do that. Knees aren't supposed to go there.

R: If he'd come correct, he wouldn't be the one on the ground.

Me: How long you think anyone will remember that?

R: Doesn't matter. Long enough. The guy on the ground will.

Me: The guy on the ground is done. His career could be over. This was the last day in the league for the guy on the ground.

R: You're not making any sense—no one makes it in the league. But look at this one. Look what he does here.

9.

We lost the first few games, but then we started winning. We started winning because Sean and Ben started being themselves. When Sean ripped off a twenty-yard sprint, our defense remembered their cues. Ben stretched out for a pass behind the end zone, and all of our kicks went in.

There's this thing that happens in sports—when it's going well, the only future is the one right in front of you. The next play was what mattered, because that's what led to the next one. And when all the plays had run up, we had practice to look forward to. And after practice, we had the game, because the game was what we worked for; and who cared what came after the game, after the rainbow we'd forsaken every other prospect to reach?

Ben and Sean moved the ball up and down the field, because that's what they knew they could do. They knew that, if nothing else, was possible. And because there wasn't a readily available model of any other brand of Black achievement (not in our town, not where we were coming from), it was widely assumed that after the season (our glorious season!), our local stars would be transplanted from the field of the last game to the field of some college or another. They would go on to play college ball and be at least moderately successful.

Ben, for all of his laziness, had a momentous season. He broke our school's record for reception yards. Sean, as predicted, followed suit, running in and by and around his pursuers. We made it to the playoffs. We won one game and got stuffed in the second.

10.

Most of us got started settling into future prospects. Ben and Sean didn't go on to play college ball. They didn't, as far as I'm aware, go much of anywhere.

And that didn't bother us. They were celebrities in our lives. Where they were going after, and what they were sacrificing to get us there, wasn't something we ever thought about. That was tomorrow, and any athlete will tell you that tomorrow is a lie.

11.

One night about a year ago, a friend and I slipped into a bar in Houston just after the game-day crowd had dispersed. The conversation turned to the people sitting around us, and whatever film was plaguing charts that weekend, until we ended up at the police shooting the week before.

Which shooting specifically doesn't especially matter—and that's sad, that I don't even have to tell you for you to get the gist—but, my friend concluded, it was the most Black people he'd seen on the news in his lifetime.

We thought about that. We sipped from our drinks.

Except, he said. Except for Katrina. Maybe. But it's definitely been the most as of late.

I told my friend he was wrong. He'd forgotten about sports.

Ah, he said.

The silence that followed was a little deeper, a little longer. We ordered another round.

12.

If I've experienced any real joy in my lifetime—pure, unfiltered bliss—it's been on the field. If all of this stupid sport's faults emerge from this metaphor, this summation, then surely all of its merits do, too.

Let me tell you about it: A cool night in November. Crisp, Southern cold, just enough to make you flinch. Halftime of a game I haven't played in, and I am a junior, and the match is so fucking tight—close enough to punk both sides into believing. In an arena seating something like ten thousand, every seat is full and everyone is standing. A wall of white on one side, a sea of blue on the other.

All of a sudden, a collective roar.

After one boy has leaped over someone else's child, pure silence—an entire town willed to nothing by a moment of art, a glimpse of ballet. And then, again, the roar. When he hits the ground running. When he's slammed into the sideline. When he jumps right back up.

Maybe I've gotten close to what I felt then. Maybe drugs could inch me close. Maybe those seconds after sex are closer. But a coach looked at me then, just after the jump, the two of us representing entirely different levels of involvement, and, as if we really understood each other, he asked if I'd ever seen anything like it.

I told him I had not.

This, he said, was magic. There was nothing else like it.

13.

R: Next season will be the big one.

Me: Next season's always the big one.

R: Don't be spiteful.

Me: I'm being serious. I'm just thinking about afterward.

R: I am, too. But not everyone makes a problem out of a game.

Me: I'm not making problems.

R: You're looking for them.

Me: I'm waiting. I'm waiting for your next season.

R: You should be. It's gonna be wild. Y'all don't even know yet.

14.

I know the price is too steep. Sometimes, though, it almost feels worth it.

Around this time last year, my father and I drove to a scrimmage way out in the middle of nowhere to watch my little brother, who is taller than me, who is funnier than me, who has it in him to believe in a thing I will not always believe in. My folks live in a small town just beyond the city. For whatever reason, the destination in question was even more remote. A smidgen of Nothing in the Everything of Texas.

We got lost twice. Both teams were already stretching when we finally reached the field from the back roads—and I hardly had time to tell my brother to be careful, to not get his ass beat, before he told *me*, with a flick of the wrist, to go into the stands and watch the master do his thing.

And it came again, that giddiness. For the first time in years.

My dad and I sat with our elbows on our knees. The sky was a chalky red. When halftime came, he slipped me a dollar to get us some snow cones, and on my way back to the stands I saw a couple of kids tossing their own ball around. Other parents sat behind us, most of them white, but the color of their subject was the team in front of us. Everything was the team. Who'd end up starting that season. Which opponents needed scouting. Which weekends they were having family down, and whose child had just recovered from a traumatic injury. After a particularly gruesome collision, the lady behind me, in a straw hat and white sandals, asked if it was my brother who'd made that hit.

I won't say I was happy or conflicted—just warm—when I told her it was.

Smother Me

Natalie Lima

I was at an upscale sushi restaurant in West Hollywood, staring at an extensive sashimi menu, the first time a man asked
me to sit on his face and smother him.

"Did you notice there's bluefin tuna on the menu?" he
added, pretending not to be glancing my way as he waited
for a response.

I did not know what to say exactly. Because I've always
been a large woman—at that time weighing about three hundred pounds. Many men I'd dated had confessed that my
large size made them feel like I'd be a less judgmental person,
someone they could share secrets with. So I wasn't exactly
surprised that my date came out and confessed his fantasy,
but what were we talking about here? Smother like you do
with a pillow in a Lifetime movie? So I asked.

"What do you mean by smother? Like, where you won't
be able to breathe?"

My date—let's call him Richard—reached over and
rested his hand on top of mine. "Yes," he said. "I know it
sounds a little weird. But you can keep your underwear on. I

just want to feel the pressure of you on top of me—you have the perfect body for it."

I gently pulled my hand away, picked up the menu again, and eyeballed the prices. Even though I wouldn't be drinking alcohol, I knew that he was bound to drop a pretty penny at this place. Our two previous dates had been equally nice, lavish. He had only taken us to restaurants I couldn't afford and had told me to order whatever I wanted each time.

"Okay," I said, nodding. "It sounds fun."

We sat in silence while I continued staring at the menu. It was only a few unoccupied seconds, but it was long enough to think about all the mediocre men I'd had sex with in the past, after less-refined dates. I thought about the one time, in college, I'd jerked a dude off in the back seat of his Honda, next to the empty bucket of fried chicken we'd just eaten. I thought about all the times I'd been fucked, quietly, by a grown man in his mother's house (because he still lived there). Richard had treated me kindly thus far. His face was easy on the eyes, and also looked okay for straddling—smooth, soft pillowy cheeks, no sharp edges. Also, at twenty-five, this was a rare opportunity to be the boss. And who doesn't want to be the boss sometimes?

Eventually I spoke up. "We should skip dessert."

I'll never forget how his face beamed, the first time I'd seen him smile with all his teeth.

Heinrich Lossow was a classically trained nineteenth-century German painter and illustrator. He was also a pro-lific pornographer. He came from a family of artists, the son of renowned sculptor Arnold H. Lossow. Much of his work was PG and included subject matter you might expect from that time—ladies petting cats and carrying children, flying baby angels flapping their wings, rich ladies in frilly dresses and giant hats, rich ladies napping, rich ladies looking at nature, and all types of portraiture.

But I am captivated by the porn. Or what intellectuals call "erotic iconography." I'm intrigued by the divisiveness around porn, among feminists and folks who consider themselves open-minded and progressive. Is it sex-positive or not? Intellectuals debate the issue frequently; there are a plethora of academic articles arguing one way or the other. With the rise of the Stormy Daniels scandal and other sex scandals, it has become a topic of discussion in the media. And frankly, I'm not sure whether it's sex-positive or not, either. What I do believe, regardless of the consensus, is that porn and unconventional sexual tastes will be around forever. There will always be dudes like Richard. And there always have been.

Lossow's erotic work mostly consists of men and women having sex. But there are two particular pieces that I return to. The first is an illustration of a strong, plump woman sitting on an almost fully dressed man's face. The curves of her ass and the muscles in her thighs are pronounced. Her breasts are large, hanging at an angle, the way big breasts do. And she holds the man's penis confidently in her right hand, like she's done this before. She knows exactly what she wants.

The second work is a painting—oil on canvas—called *The Enchantress*. In a garden, a burly statue of a classical Greek sphinx and a man kiss while embracing. The sphinx is clearly the alpha in the image; she hovers over the man and wraps her hulky arms around most of his body. The man, on the other hand, sits in the more submissive position on a bench, beneath her, clearly entranced, but letting her take the lead.

If these images are any indication of a pattern, it's that the large female form has been a curiosity lusted after for ages. Plus, it's no secret that the larger female physique was revered throughout history. We see this all the way back to at least 25,000 B.C., with the Venus of Willendorf figurine. She is a cute round thing and looks a lot like I do in the nude. I'd bet my next paycheck that several millennia ago, fat ladies like the Venus of Willendorf sat on plenty of eager, smiling faces.

The morning after the sushi date with Richard, my thighs were a little achy. I'd happily done exactly what we'd discussed at the restaurant; with my dress and panties still on, I had straddled his face and smothered him with my ass and thighs. For a few seconds at a time, I asphyxiated him, then lifted myself back up when I felt inspired to do so (being mindful of not actually suffocating him). It was easy, and I liked having control, but the whole time all I could think was *I can't believe this turns him on*, and, *This is actually kind of boring*, and, *I'd rather be eating a sandwich right now.*

I sent him home that night panting and smiling.

When I received a text from Richard a couple of days later, asking to meet again, I pulled the *New phone, who dis?* act on him. I love a free sushi dinner, but though his request had been fairly painless, there hadn't been any real pleasure in the experience for me. It seemed transactional. I felt like I was this person living in a somewhat niche body—but a body with a cult following—and I was getting shortchanged by my fans.

I felt like I should be asking for more. Though I'd physically been in the dominant position that night, it was still all about *him* and *his* fantasy. It was a one-way street. In retrospect, I wondered, *If this isn't about making each other feel good, then shouldn't I be getting compensated somehow?*

On today's popular porn sites, fat women have a giant, devoted audience and are often referred to as BBW (big beautiful women, not basketball wives). Smothering has its fair share of fans as well. And the two are often combined. If you're on the hunt online for videos of some version of BBW smothering, the results are endless, and subgenres vary.

There's face-sitting: young college BBW face-sitting, SSBBW (super-size BBW) face-sit, BBW face-sitting outdoor, ethnic videos BBW girls face-sit.

And there's smothering, where you cover your partner's mouth or face with a part of your body, typically your ass or genitals: latina BBW smothering, ebony BBW smother, BBW Asian smothering, monster ass BBW smothering.

Squashing—literally crushing a person until they're unable to breathe—is also a thing: BBW squashing women, two BBW squashing unlucky man, BBW squashing lesbians, awesome BBW squash face-sitting.

And wrestling: curvy BBW wrestling and sucking cock, BBW fight club, BBW wrestling grappling, BBW oil wrestling.

And finally, long live The Queen, in which a woman sits on a person's face as though she is a queen on her throne: dominant mature SSBBW queening young guy, BBW queening brutal, young BBW queening dude in park, BBW queens man and suffocates him.

Ad infinitum.

My weight has fluctuated my whole life. Now that I'm in my thirties, and long past Richard, I know that when my weight rises and my body expands, so do the kinkier requests that come in. I am so used to the fetishization and immediate sexualization of the fat on my bones that I wait for the invitations like clockwork, like a surprise party that you knew was coming all along.

At a convenience store, a young man—college aged—who was maybe a little drunk, recently stood too close to me in line, so close I could feel the warmth coming from his sweaty skin. He whispered in my ear that he's always loved big women, and that he'd give anything to go home with me and feel my body on top of his all night. I told him that if he didn't stop talking like that, I was going to grab his phone and call his mother. I paid for my sparkling water and split.

With each clothing size I go up, the dudes get bolder with the advances, more honest with their confidential desires. Which is something I don't mind if he and I have shared, say, a few meals together and a fart or two in bed. I often write about sex, so I certainly don't mind talking about fantasies or kinky interests when we've built that rapport. When it's consensual.

But, from strangers, without warning, these yearnings seem way more appropriate for Reddit forums than my inbox. When foisted on me by a man I don't know in line behind me at the convenience store, these secret cravings are totally fucking gross and can be scary.

Not long ago, a man in Colorado messaged me on a dating site: Are you open to wrestling? I am willing to travel down to Tucson, if so.

Tell me more, I wrote back. So far, he'd been respectful, so I was, at the very least, intrigued.

He sent me a link to a video on YouTube, said, Look, this is essentially what I want. There's no sex or nudity involved, he assured me. He'd pay $400 for a half hour of my time, and an extra $200 if I won the match. Winning meant I pinned him onto the ground for ten whole seconds. I wasn't sure where the thrill was for him, but it seemed simple enough for me to execute.

I watched the video. A blond SSBBW—somewhere between 350 to 450 pounds, I'd guess—stands fully clothed at one corner of a room, empty but for a few bookshelves that line the walls. My solicitor—a forty-year-old man with a bodybuilder's physique—stands at the diagonal corner. A timer from a cell phone blares and the two lunge toward each other, with more obvious effort coming from her. They grab each other, but really, she grabs him. It's as if he's not trying at all, having obviously curated this experience. She tosses him to the floor and pins him down.

This is the moment when the mystery was solved for me—my curiosity about what part of the encounter aroused him, since no genitals are involved in the action. In the grand finale, her entire body cocoons him as he lies on the floor, grinning madly, rocks off.

I considered his offer seriously because my car needed four new tires. And, as a current graduate student, my funds are tight. I can be quick to fantasize about all the ways to make seemingly easy money, short of robbing pawn shops or selling a limb. I thought about agreeing to his offer, but only if I could bring my dog to the hotel with me (though that seemed like it might be confusing for my dog, watching me wrestle with a stranger, and I didn't want to traumatize her). I thought about bringing a friend—the kind who would take this secret to the grave with them.

But after a few days of rolling the scenario around in my head, the offer felt too heavy, there was too much at stake for me—my safety, but also my mental and my physical well-being (I have a bad back)—and so I declined, and charged the new tires to my credit card.

In my bedroom hangs a photo of one of my favorite sculptures by Fernando Botero, the Colombian artist. A woman sits with her head turned just over her right shoulder, reaching for her hair with her left hand. Botero, widely known as "the painter of fat ladies," has been painting and sculpting corpulent bodies for decades now. When asked about his fascination with large bodies, he is quick to explain that he is not obsessed with fat women but with "volume," that everything he paints is volumetric.

And though his supposed motivation for rendering his large-bodied muses is underwhelming (he claims to have only been "attached to three women, all of them skinny"), I

still know him as the artist who has normalized the presence
of fat women in paintings that I've seen in home after home
my entire life. The fat woman always takes center stage in his
work. She prevails. She is infinite.

What I have found jarring over the years is not that kinks
like this exist, but that folks either pretend, or don't know,
that big women have always had an immense following, in
real life and online. When I see the way plus-size women are
still portrayed in Hollywood films, as jesters to buttress the
narrative of the conventionally hot, superstar female lead,
I wonder why all of pop culture has yet to catch up with
reality. When will everyone start getting truthful about the
demand for big, sexy bodies?

The more I see big bodies like mine in film and music and
art, the more excited I get for the girls coming of age today,
for the fat girls who spend their Friday nights pussy-popping
to Lizzo until their legs cramp. I follow a couple dozen plus-
size models and influencers on Instagram. I follow young
illustrators who exclusively paint lush, corpulent bodies.
I follow photographers who only capture bodies as big as
moons. The secret of the beauty of our bodies is slowly starting to get out, becoming less and less niche each day. And I
hope it moves faster.

When I think of the night with Richard and the many
other men I've encountered since, I think of the fat body as
royalty. How the big body is coveted—yes, as a fetish, but
also as beauty. Teenage me had never pictured a time where
the fat body would be seen as modern art. And I may never
fully understand wanting to be smothered or squashed or
wrestled and pinned, but I do understand the power and
worth of a body that blooms.

Don't Let It Bury You

Eloghosa Osunde

I know the sound of my mother's voice better than I know anything else. As a child, I didn't like the way the soft and smooth of it could explode into a growl in sudden seconds, shouting and overheating the house, sending my small anxious heart darting through my body, displaced. I never liked how it fractioned my breathing and slowed my movements into a drag. But I liked that it always prepared me for trouble, at least. I like that it helped me get ready.

So, one Saturday, when I was nine years old, I followed that voice downstairs and found it in the kitchen, bursting out of my mother's mouth and screaming at the maid, Irene, who had worked with us for four years.

"Pack your things and leave this house right now!"

I stood pressed against the door—body like a whisper, barely there, hidden in all the noise and the smoke. From what I could tell, Irene had been rude to my mother. Their eyes remained on each other so stubbornly I was afraid they would never separate. Then Irene's nose started flaring, her fists bunched up at her sides, and I knew she was trying not to cry or trying not to punch my mother. I had seen that look before when no one else was there. I was so afraid for her. Then my mother's jaw moved like she was chewing all her own teeth.

"You bastard!" my mother yelled. She pulled Irene outside by her shirt, and I followed them.

"Don't let me warn you again. You know me; you know that if I deal with you the way I want to, you will never forget it in your life!" My mother meant it, so I stood still, trying not to fan her anger into a small hellfire. It was better to remain unseen by angry eyes.

They searched Irene's bags, which is what they do whenever a member of staff leaves our house. It's just to make sure. Her two black suitcases and one Ghana Must Go were splayed open on the concrete blocks. My mother was sitting on a white chair, her blue boubou spilling over its arms. Two security men dressed in all black were on standby, and the second maid was picking clothes out of the suitcase for my mother to see, one by one.

You see, Irene hadn't expected to leave, so she had no time to hide anything—and Irene was a thief. So that's how they found my mother's gele, my mother's gold bracelet, my father's dollars, my brother's shoes, and, at the bottom of the suitcase, some clothes I had secretly given her, others I had no idea she had taken. When they got to one of the pieces I secretly gave her, Irene pointed to me, with her eyes still on my mother, and said, "She gave me all these ones." It didn't take me long to make up my mind to say no, it was not me, what exactly is she talking about, I don't know what she is talking about. I already felt my blood congeal as I prepared to betray her there, but it was because I wanted her to look at me, even if in anger.

"You liar," my mother said in disgust, and I let my head fall, anticipating the heat from a slap. But my mother wasn't talking to me, she was talking to Irene, directing the rage at her.

"Mummy, but—" Irene replied before my mother cut her off. The word jarred me because it only occurred to me then that Irene calling my mother Mummy—a choice she was never coerced into—made it easy for everyone to assume she saw me as a little sister and saw my younger brothers as her own. Why would anyone squint at her or wonder what else she had tried to take from me? How would they ever find out? She knew that all the eyes in the house would have to be around and awake and alert at the same time to truly see her. It was hardly possible.

"I will believe my children one hundred times over before I ever consider believing a liar, a thief," my mother told her. "God forbid that I ever believe you over my children."

There is a saying that you must never allow a child to become comfortable with lying, because liars—if they are not stopped and straightened in time—will surely become thieves. So if you catch a thief red-handed, it only makes sense not to believe a word they say, because one must take that first step to get to the second.

Every item Irene stole was taken back from her, and then she left. She left and the day went on as normal until the night.

I was asleep, alone, in my room and it was midnight, dark except for a dull light beating against the other side of my yellow curtain. I woke up, rose from my bed, and walked to my window, shifting the curtain to let the light from the moon touch my shoulder. I closed my eyes and breathed, feeling a draft of cool air from the air conditioner above. The urge to dance started slowly: a sway and a twirl, then my feet became light, moving by themselves, spinning my head, shifting my arms up in a surrender until I fell to the floor, breathless. I began to cry—not because of the carpet burn on my knees and elbow, but because of what had happened. Irene had been there, in our house with us before that night, and after what happened that morning, she wouldn't be there anymore. I was crying because grief had woken and shaken me, had twirled me around without asking for permission. It had caught me unawares, lured me and pushed me to the ground.

Before she was asked to leave, Irene molested me every day for two years in our home, where life was supposed to be safest, and made me keep it a secret. They found everything that she took, but of course, they didn't find the one thing I wish they had. Nobody found my body, stolen. She didn't look back at me when she was leaving, for that reason; she just faced the gate, bag in hand, shame at her back, which made me feel sorry for her and annoyed at myself. I felt trapped, confused, unsure of how to reclaim what had been taken from me, how to retrieve the thing nobody could see—my now intangible, invisible body.

That night, I learned that when you dance, when you shift the weight of your body from one foot to another, when you shake to the sound of the night breeze and to the thrum of your own grief, when you continue the private practice of movement, you will be reminded of the fortunate (or unfortunate) fact that your body is real. Your body, even after betraying you, will carry you. Sometimes mercifully, sometimes mercilessly. But it will carry you. And sometimes, dance is the gift in all that rubble. Dance is the gift in all that mess. Dance is the conjuring.

Over a decade later, I sat on a therapist's couch for the first time. One of the things she told me was to stop believing that there are two responses to stress. There are three, she said: fight, flight, or play dead. "When terrorists go to a crowded space, the victims most likely to stay alive aren't the ones who cry or fight or beg, ironically. It's the ones who get kicked, punched, stabbed and lie there—still and unresponsive."

I got it. When someone thinks you're already dead, they know that they can't kill you again, so they leave you alone. That's a great way to survive traumatic situations, she said, but that's no way to live a life. "You have been playing dead all your life," she told me. "It's the right thing for your brain to do for as long as the trauma keeps occurring, but when it's over, you have to get up and start remembering how to live."

Therapists, I realized, do not know everything. If they did, then she would've known that there's a difference between playing dead and dying. I know, because I've done both. The former suggests that you are wearing another reality you can strip off when you're ready. That you can just take it off and go back to your regular life. Playing dead is what I was doing when I was still a devout Christian in university, refusing to move my body in a way that would remind me that it was alive and desiring, or worse still, remind other people that I was alive and desirous. But dying is different. Dying is all of depression's many hands pressed against your throat at the same time. It is the only reality, is the flesh and blood and bone and sinew of you, is entirely overwhelming and correct. Dying is what I was doing even as I sat in front of her.

There was a time when I had no words for God, when I could not pray at all, because I was too angry and heavy inside. So instead, every morning, I woke up before 5:00 a.m., before the sun, to dance. Even if I forget everything, just from those years, I will always know how to express anger with my body, how to bend to gratitude, how to cry and grieve without my face, how to show joy with my back and hands, how to express my own inner peace. I know how to talk to God from inside the flesh I was encouraged to deny. God knows my body and all the ways I have tried to keep it alive, loves me in this way, accepts the way my body moves as worship, knows my (in)flexibilities by name. God knows my victory dance, my war cry; because dance is my prayer itself, and dance is the amen that follows.

When I was a teenager in secondary school, trying to figure out how to carry a burgled body with grace, I reclaimed myself through dance. When the prefects called my friends and me into a classroom, called us loose, sluts, whores— over rumors they hadn't actually confirmed—and dared us not to answer, we did, even though we knew those were not our names. And because that happened at a time when being shamed was a small crucifixion, we left there crying, but it didn't stop us. We still whined our bodies tirelessly against boys, pressed our backs into their starving hands and their sweating bodies that stayed still against the white walls. At those school discos where "Will you dance with me?" was a question asked with a hand already on your waist, we still danced as apology, danced as desperation for approval because we wanted somebody to love us, to call us worthy. Dance back then was a plea, an I-beg-you-please-see-me.

But dance is also a coming-to-know of one's spirit, the fullest view, the best way to behold oneself. After the cluelessness had worn off, after many heartbreaks and unutterable things—in an unspoken agreement, my friends and I stopped dancing with boys we didn't want to touch us. We were germinating comfort in our own bodies, so instead, we formed circles of friends where no boys could enter except by invitation, where all unholy hands would be met with blazing rage. The boys stayed away. They couldn't break or enter our fortified circle, and they knew it. Dance is power. Dance is a fortress.

I have known the lasting salvation of dancing in a group of women who are not there for men, who are there to affirm one another, to say, I see you, I see your body, you are beautiful and you are marvelous in my sight, despite what you've been through. I learned this again last year, when I was remarkably depressed and needed to be out every night. I had to avoid stillness. I was afraid every day that my body would disappear into nothing if I didn't move it aggressively. I was hanging over death, falling slowly into the slick black of it. If I'd found myself in the wrong circles back then, I know it would've been done and my life would have slipped away.

Instead, I was in the belly of Lagos, surrounded in those clubs by living women who loved me fiercely, who moved their bodies in a way that was redeeming. If there is such a thing as playing dead, then there must be such a thing as its opposite. Next to them, dance was that for me. I shook my body into every painful morning, dancing to the loud music in my chest where my heart should have been, to the alcohol pumping through my veins where blood should have been, and all those things were me playing alive. Dance was second flesh, a vicious mask, my whole disguise.

Last year, after my Christian ex-boyfriend assaulted me and then suggested that we both pray for forgiveness, of course I danced to survive. The back of my eyes was full of a dizzy hunger—I was starving for my own blood. I continued my routines. I wrote, I dressed up and went out, I showed up. I took care of the house—serving my father food, keeping an eye out for my brothers, mothering my mother. Meanwhile, my body was disappearing, as in numb, as in dead, and again, nobody noticed, not because they weren't looking, but because I'm excellent at acting fine, at playing perfectly alive.

I moved countries after that. I chose my new home strategically, because I thought being in my favorite city would shake me alive. But still, I walked past Mercato Centrale each morning thinking about how I couldn't feel the rest of my body, how my head was the only alive thing. I was not a person. I was a bobblehead with a dumb numb body and a heavy, restless head, something my therapist later referred to as depersonalization, as dissociation: "When a mind becomes dangerously overwhelmed with stress, it can begin to isolate itself from the body." In Florence, I survived by sitting through my lectures, going home, napping for hours, drinking a glass of wine (or too many), then getting dressed and going dancing.

I would stand outside of myself, back pressed against the railing, watching my own unreal body make an altar out of us. My unreal body would get bathed in red and blue light, in a club full of strangers, bodies intertwined, gravitating desperately toward me. But when I moved, I moved entirely alone, sweat pouring down my face, into my clothes, soaked in my own stubborn insistence on staying alive. Sometimes it took hours, other times it took days, but dance and the ache that lay in its wake reminded my body that it was still alive, that the illness was the lie, that I was and I am—aren't I, despite everything—still alive.

When I got discharged from the local hospital in Florence after a frightening breakdown, I went dancing at a club called Space. The bouncers had stopped questioning me a long time ago. From the moment I stepped out of the taxi, it was routine, how they moved me to the front of the queue and ushered me in, never asking me to pay a thing. It was enough that they knew me as the girl who came alone and often, to dance as revenge, to dance as assertion, to remind herself of her own hereness, and I felt welcome there. Dance and the bodies that know how to wield it well are valuable currency.

These days, when I feel the anxiety buzzing at the back of my neck or the depression curving my spine forward or the dissociation distributing me between more realities than

I can count at once, I make myself get up. I remember that that is what power is—to be experiencing what I experience and still be able to bend entirely to the bass. After all, when it came to it, apart from writing and writing and writing, dance was one of the things I listed as a reason to stay alive. It was one of the reasons that worked.

So it doesn't matter if no one else is moving. Even when the entire room is sitting, even when I am self-conscious and my body is peppered with goose bumps, even when I am afraid what they will think of me, I get up. I look straight ahead and tell myself that this moment is for me. Every moment is for me.

I throw my hands up, let my hips move where they deem fit, use my hands to frame my moves, to take up space. I sway forward in a line, I circle around a willing stranger, let the beat hyperventilate on my waist. I unknot the room all by myself, until the space around me becomes a crowded dance floor full of strangers who know nothing about my secrets or my joys, who just know because of how well my body moves that I am something to stop and watch, that my freedom and desperation for the music are some things to aspire to.

I am aware that the dance floor will close. When I see the crowd thinning and the lights changing, I encourage my body to slow down and remember the truth: there is healing in movement and music, but also in the standstill, in the heart's beat, in the truthful feeling of something, anything— as long as you don't let it bury you.

Writing My Truth as a Deaf Queer Writer
Ross Showalter

Days before spring break ended, my laptop lit up with an email notification. I was a creative writing major at Portland State University, studying fiction writing. I was about to start my last quarter before graduation, and I had signed up for a fiction workshop with Leni Zumas.

Leni had sent over the syllabus for the workshop. She asked me what she could do to ensure the classroom was accessible to me; as a Deaf person entering her classroom, I would work with ASL interpreters as I had done every quarter.

When I went through the syllabus for Leni's class, my heart leapt. Leni had assigned the first act of Ilya Kaminsky's *Deaf Republic* as reading. I read that line in the class schedule over and over, a smile growing on my face. Work from a deaf writer was in a class. Work from a deaf writer was part of a class I was in.

A deaf writer on Leni's syllabus felt like encouragement. I had made it a personal goal to read d/Deaf and disabled writers whenever I could. Those readings were always in bed, in the hour before sleep. Now, I would be moving past that.

I wouldn't just be reading a deaf writer. I would be studying him. My peers would be studying him.

Even the thought came as a shock. I had assumed I would be the only person in the room to write about deafness and think about deafness, because I was the only Deaf person in the program and, by extension, the only Deaf person in every classroom.

Whenever I think about Portland, I mainly think about my second and last year. During my second year, I was writing what I liked, and with that came the exhilaration that I was saying something only I could say.

My first year was an exorcism. My first year, I regurgitated the stories I'd read before, and it was only during spring quarter of that year that I looked down at my story being workshopped and realized I hated it.

I hated that I'd written another story that revolved around abled straight people discovering disability and queerness. I wrote stories of discovery and uncertainty when I was further down the road: I was comfortable in my skin as a Deaf queer person. But hearing straight people told me that those stories about deafness and queerness, soaked in uncertainty, were what they knew. Those stories were important, people claimed, whether they were about two men struggling with their attraction to each other or about an abled person who was unsure of how to behave around a disabled person. People said those stories came from important writers, serious writers. I wanted to be taken seriously, and I had followed in those writers' footsteps.

After my workshop that day, I hid in the bathroom. I waited for the feeling of defeat to drain out of me. It didn't.

The teacher in that workshop, Gabe Urza, gave me an A on the workshopped story, an A I was confused by. I felt like I didn't deserve it for a story steeped in clichés. I felt like I didn't know what I was doing. I wanted to ask him why he'd been so generous—the closest I came was asking about a class he would teach in the fall.

"It's research for writers," he explained. "We spend one quarter developing one fiction story. It's a lot of fun."

I nodded. I didn't give him an answer then, but I emailed him my final project for his class with a postscript: *I signed up for your research seminar, so I'll see you then.*

I had stumbled, but Gabe saw something in my stumbles. I wanted to take another class with him to learn how he looked at fiction, where he was looking, and how I could get there.

In that research seminar, months later, I saw what I could do. I could write about Deafness if I pulled from our history, our trauma, our community. Surrounded by hearing peers, I wanted them to read what I knew instead of writing something they knew and expected.

In order to move forward as a writer, I had to reject the idea of hearing approval. I had to move away from writing stories that were in line with what people expected. There are already plenty of stories about abled discomfort, and I didn't have anything to add to those conversations. I could be taken seriously, I learned, without writing what was already there.

When Gabe gave me an A for the work I did in the

research seminar, I felt accomplishment instead of confusion. The next quarter, in a workshop with Janice Lee, I got a story back with so many check marks I felt disbelief. I knew I was on the right track, but I had expected a course correction, a suggestion, or a fine-tuning toward where I was supposed to go.

When I admitted this to Janice in a one-on-one meeting, she chuckled. The ASL interpreter behind her suppressed a smile.

Janice grew serious as she talked: "You just need to keep going. You're not writing the stories typically told. You're not writing for the straight white men out there"—the ASL interpreter, a straight white man, suppressed another smile as he interpreted—"and people may want you to explain things. It's not necessary. You're not writing for them."

I left the meeting with warmth cresting in my chest. I felt empowered in a way I hadn't before.

Before, I had dreaded workshops simply because I was bringing in stories about Deaf people to a room full of hearing people. Participating in writing workshops means you are introduced to other people's perspectives, their minds, and their traumas, which are all part of their stories. It also means that you are introduced to their prejudices, their pet peeves, and their assumptions. I submitted my stories, and people responded in the ways they knew how. Peers' biases showed up in their annotated copies and their critique letters.

In one critique letter, a peer wrote, "Maybe you shouldn't write these stories." I felt small and uncertain as I read her words. I wondered if she couldn't understand or if I hadn't been clear enough about why I wrote what I did.

Even as I physically set peers' workshop letters aside, I couldn't shake them from my mind. If creative writing programs are representative of the literary industry, I would be in an industry where people like me are rarely given space. Janice's words in our meeting felt like permission to trust myself—but in my lowest moments, I wondered if it was worth it to ignore those words if I was the only Deaf person in the classroom, if no other Deaf people were critiquing my work. I wondered if it was worth it to ignore my peers' feedback if they were saying they would never understand my work.

By my final quarter, I was writing the stories I wanted to write. I couldn't control what people thought of them, but I could control how it affected me. I could stop writing, or I could keep going.

I kept going.

When Leni Zumas walked into the classroom on our first day, she caught my stare and smiled. I felt a flush of embarrassment but smiled back. I felt anticipation, more than I ever had before. I was excited for a class that included reading from a deaf writer. I was excited for a class where I wasn't the only deaf writer that would be read.

When the day to discuss *Deaf Republic* came around, I brought in my book. My peers pulled printouts out of their backpacks and folders. As we discussed it, I could feel eyes on me; my peers were watching me, waiting on what I would have to say about this deaf book by a deaf writer.

I remember us talking about syntax, about the fact that

this was a story about rebellion and love; I remember us talking about the signs illustrated in the book, the way it dissected embodiment and language.

What I took away the most from that discussion was that people could analyze my work and talk about it, just as they do any other book. While context and content matter, so do the choices you make. The choices to invent. The choices to explain. You only have to put in the work to make sure someone who does not share your experience can enter the world you create. If the reader refuses to enter, you cannot do anything. But if the reader encounters a barrier, you must decide if that is part of the path. If the work cannot be understood or felt, it only becomes something to admire rather than something to engage with. Conversation can't come from admiration. Conversation comes from understanding.

The best thing a teacher can do for a marginalized writer in their classroom is to include texts by people who share their identities and write about it. Ilya Kaminsky and I are both deaf. Ilya is not similar to me. Our forms of deafness are different. Our relationships to English are different. Our voices and forms are different.

But we both write about deafness. Including a deaf writer and making sure I could participate in a conversation about his work made people pay attention to me like never before. I wasn't only a peer, but someone who understood this book in ways they couldn't. I was someone who could understand and continue the conversation Ilya had started. More than any other class, on any other day, with Ilya Kaminsky's words before me, my goal of being a writer, a Deaf writer, felt tangible and possible.

———

That spring, at the end of my last year, at the end of my time at Portland, I was striding forward, moving toward a space I could call my own. *This is my space, this is what I have envisioned*, I could say now. *This is what I know, and this is what I will write about.*

I think of my time in Portland now as both a learning of craft and a preparation for the responses I would receive on my writing. Since I graduated from my program, I continue to write and publish the stories that feel true to me, and I've learned over and over that reading is never a neutral act, and abled people project their ideas of disability onto disabled people constantly. Abled people's responses have nothing to do with me and everything to do with their preconceptions of me. And the best thing that writing can do is to replace a shallow illusion with something more nuanced and closer to the truth, to my truth.

Writing is often a solitary act. It does not have to be lonely. A piece of writing invites comparisons, experiences, ideas, responses—conversations. In the process of putting my own ideas to paper and letting other people, hearing people, criticize them, I often felt like I was saying something people wouldn't listen to.

The knowledge that there were disabled and d/Deaf writers out there was what kept me going in a space where I was the only Deaf person. The discovery that there were writers, like Ilya, who were given close attention and study within a creative writing class thrilled me. Because I saw my peers studying a deaf writer, being moved by a deaf writer, I could see my voice having impact as well. I could see myself as part of a conversation that progresses. At Portland, I learned to look beyond abled people and their approval to imagine only what I wanted and then write it. I hope for the disabled writers who come after me to do the same. Conversations about us, by us, are being written. What we see now is only the beginning.

A Variant of Unknown Significance

Taylor Harris

The answer, you should know, is *no*.

Genetic testing did not help me see my son, Tophs, more clearly. Whole-exome sequencing, the most advanced test available to us, which examined over twenty thousand genes and took four months to process, did not help me find the boy behind those deep and wide umber eyes.

I had been searching, with the help of his pediatrician (and Google, if I'm honest), to find the source of my son's frightening hypoglycemia, short stature, carnitine deficiency, and developmental delays since he was two years old. What I wanted more than any diagnosis, though, was to understand what made him tick.

Kids are all mystery, and mine are no different, but the unknown has especially marked my son—from his lower birth weight to the way his body can't tolerate heat or cold to the way he didn't express basic feelings, like hunger or thirst, as a preschooler. It's because of him that I've googled the terms "carnitine deficiency" and "Russell-Silver syndrome" and "motor planning." He's why I know that AST stands for the enzyme aspartate transaminase. How I'm certain a perfectly round-cheeked toddler can eat pizza and ice cream one night and barely wake up the next morning. And that a person's blood sugar level can drop into the twenties without warning.

What's misleading about Tophs is that you have to look closely, take your time before you realize he's wired differently than you first assumed. As a parent, sometimes I'm tempted to declare I've made it all up. I'm noticing too much. Then, inevitably, there's a blip on the radar—a medical emergency, his inability to find a common word—and I have to remind myself that I'm not in the business of fabricating nuance. My boy is who he is.

At five years and five months, my son looks like he's three. He's skinny but well-proportioned and has a certain swag, even with a front tooth missing. Or maybe it's *because* of the lost tooth, paired with his left dimple and long lashes. You'll often find him in his skinny Gap jeans, distressed at the knees by him—not by a stylist—a soft T-shirt, and Velcro sneakers. On most days, he'll give you a fist bump. (He thinks it's hilarious to offer you a high five if you ask for a bump, and a bump if you ask for five.) If you play Common and John Legend's "Glory," he might break into contemporary dance, his pants revealing a plumber's butt as he bends low and moves like he's lifting heavy air with his arms. If you play his favorite Christian hip-hop artist, he will perform a combination of isolation dance moves and dabs. Even if he's forever in need of a shape-up, the boy is smooth. You'll leave him feeling like you've met somebody.

At one point, I thought genetic tests could sever the rope from around my waist, let me walk free from the load

I'd dragged behind me. If the doctors found mutations in Tophs's genes, we'd be forced to look back to conception, even pre-conception, even to God, who is way bigger than any mistake I might have made as his mother. Was it the time he fell off the bed? Had he missed too many feedings as an infant? If his challenges were present in the beginning, then I'd be free to respond, rather than atone.

Two years ago, my husband, Paul, and I visited the pediatric geneticist's office with Tophs. On the simplest level, we wanted answers. We followed the path of referrals and showed up to appointments, because that's how the system works, but what we really wanted was more than we could explain on any intake form. We wanted to understand just who our boy was. Not whether he'd grow up to be a firefighter or a dancer or a prophet—but how we could best find him inside that little body. How we could know him, and him us. Tophs's lack of growth, his drops in blood sugar, his delayed speech—they weren't disconnected from the boy behind those deep-set eyes.

My chief concern as his mother was this sense that I couldn't consistently get through to him—as though he was a place, and I was an eager but frustrated traveler who might never reach it. We hoped that by sending off his DNA we'd be able to map him out, to discover what made him slow to respond to pain or his name. To know why he could eat from a buffet one night and need an IV drip by morning.

We'd entered the geneticist's office looking for the very boy we'd brought with us.

Shelley, tall with an Elsa-like braid, had greeted us that morning before taking her seat at the computer. Her eyes

were Disney-clear blue and direct, but not unkind. I'd resisted
her at first. She was young and engaging, but she wasn't the
geneticist. And the only thing worse than not knowing how
to tell your son's story—how to relay the scope of puzzling
issues without getting lost in details—is muddling through
that story twice in one appointment.

But Shelley wasn't a resident or medical school student;
she was a genetic counselor, guiding families, by way of Pun-
nett squares and lab orders and test results, through what
genetics had to say to them. In this way, she wasn't entirely
unlike a pastor, consulting her source and caring for whoever
walked through her doors, no matter the circumstance.

"Is there any chance you two are related?" she'd asked
Paul and me.

"Uhhh, we don't think so?"

It strikes me now that the question Shelley really asked us
was: "Are the odds stacked against your child?" Beneath that
question, there lurks another I frequently ask myself: What
were my expectations—of my child and his body, of myself
and my body? Had I expected easiness, perfection even? And
what about the man I married—did I expect him to be free
of misspelled genes?

She would send our samples away, alongside Tophs's, to
be interrogated. If something was awry in our son, the science would first look to us, his parents. And if that same
thing was awry in one of us, we'd be left to add a second
layer of interpretation, one Shelley couldn't possibly help us
with. One that would beg us to parse guilt from faith, and
science from predestination, and what we *can* know from
what we can't.

Maybe I hadn't paid close enough attention to how the test worked. I'd talked to Shelley, signed consent forms, and taken home a copy of the lab's whole-exome sequencing patient guide. It contained paragraphs of text, along with figures and drawings—an electric turquoise X for a chromosome, a glowing orange cell and nucleus, a blue double helix winding its way down and across white space.

I thought the scientists, whose faces I would never see but whose brains I trusted, would superimpose my boy over maps of these normal cells and nuclei discussed in the pamphlet, and he would either line up exactly or not. I assumed it would work like one-to-one correspondence.

The results did tell us *something*. It's not like the lab over-promised or falsely advertised.

Four months after Shelley sent our samples away, on the Monday morning after Thanksgiving, I held a pregnancy test in my hand, waiting and scolding myself for wasting ten dollars at Target. The chances were so slim, and my hands were already so full with my daughter and Tophs, and—the faintest pink second line didn't care about any of that. It timidly stretched across the test's window, as though gathering courage, and I was pregnant with our third child. My hands *were* full, as men who held doors open liked to remind me.

When Shelley called that afternoon, my pulse quickened, and I walked into the kitchen, away from the kids. "We have the results of Tophs's genetic testing," she said. "Is this a good time?"

"Only one kid's screaming, so it's great," I joked. I grabbed a piece of paper and pen. If anyone was going to get to the bottom of this, I knew it would be her.

"So there are three results I want to talk to you about."

The world was on fire but I didn't know it. I wrote to not miss anything. I wrote because what else would I do?

The first mutation was found in a gene that causes a recessive disorder, meaning Tophs would need two changes to develop the actual disorder, in this case glycogen storage disease. But he only had one change, so he didn't have the disease. "Not found in me or Paul," I scribbled in parentheses. No blame here. We didn't cause this quirk. *De novo,* they call it, literally meaning "of new."

According to what Shelley and science knew at this point, Tophs's single mutation did not matter clinically. He was a carrier and should consider his status before having kids, but his particular misspelling wasn't known to cause symptoms. One down.

Shelley described the second finding: the lab detected two mutations in a gene known to cause a recessive disorder related to bone size. One mutation came from Paul, one from me. "We haven't seen this particular misspelling before," she explained. "It could be a benign familial change." She used the words *variant of unknown significance,* and I wished I had paid better attention to that pamphlet. A VUS means there's a change in a genetic sequence, but science hasn't yet determined whether that change is potentially harmful or benign. It could carry a risk of disease, or not. Tophs's short stature could be related to this mutation, or not. Genetics has a way of being completely specific—pinpointing the exact erroneous sequence within the exact gene—and still not locating you in time and space and significance.

Shelley's voice signaled she was winding down. We would

not solve this case today. She paused, and I assumed I'd mis-understood her, there were only two results. Or maybe the two mutations, one from Paul and one from me, counted as separate results. "The last result is actually a secondary find-ing," she said. "Do you remember how you and Paul agreed to have us look at those actionable genes?"

Actionable genes. Like cancer genes. Things you might have time to prevent. A chance to cheat death. "Wait, who is this about?"

"Yeah, I know this is a bit scary." Shelley's voice was a tonal apology. "Have you heard of the BRCA mutation? We found that your son has this mutation, and so do you."

What is it called when we have every right to fear?

I knew exactly what BRCA was. Lindsay, my best friend in middle school, whose mother survived breast and ovarian cancer, had both breasts removed in her twenties because of it. As Shelley talked, I envisioned the cemetery up Route 29, across from the Target Tophs loved so much. Is that where I would be laid to rest?

"The BRCA2 mutation is associated with an increased risk of breast and ovarian cancer." And as though she'd read my mind, she said, "This doesn't mean you have or will get cancer."

What did this mean for my son, who had no breasts or ovaries, who still peed in a pull-up and watched *Daniel Ti-ger*? Daniel visited the doctor for X-rays or shots, not to discuss his predisposition to certain kinds of cancer. "This won't change Tophs's care now, but he will need certain screenings in the future."

And his big sister?

"She has a 50 percent chance of having the mutation. And so do your siblings . . . One of your parents must carry it . . ."

"Shelley," my voice the wing of a dragonfly, "I guess I should tell you now. I took a pregnancy test this morning, and it was positive." Had I just confessed or asked for help? Either way, I hid within my throat, calling out to Shelley and science and God that I hadn't been given the chance to not conceive a baby. It was too late. This seed, this baby, I just knew she was a girl. She had no breasts yet, and I was already threatening to take them away. How do you excise ovaries that don't exist?

"This is so much to process in one day," Shelley said.

I told her I didn't want to hear the numbers yet. Turns out, when it's about my health, I want less information. I don't want to google. I agreed to take a day before coming to see her.

"I know this is hard to imagine," she said, "but remember, this mutation isn't new. You've always had it. You were born with it. We're just finding out about it now."

I hung up. Everything in my life had prepared me for something other than this. Every scary circumstance or medical test had eventually come with a release valve: Tophs didn't have fragile X syndrome; my heart palpitations were nothing to worry about; my firstborn's pneumonia resolved with antibiotics.

I couldn't protect myself, couldn't protect my children, couldn't promise them Mommy wouldn't get sick. Every single bit of my fear was deserved. A terrifying and lonely place, this corner of the world, this corner of the mind, where you can't rationally talk yourself out of darkness. I showered and wondered if my breasts were poison.

Tophs and I walked along a new road—was it a detour or always the planned route?—as a mother and her boy, one oblivious to danger or lack, the other shouldering parts of both bodies, hers and his, that no one could promise were healthy. I didn't have two working copies of a gene that suppresses tumors. If my one good copy were to mutate, for any long list of reasons, my lack, or genetic vulnerability, would be the perfect soil for an abundance of abnormal cells. Even if genetics figured Tophs out one day—*Genetics is moving so quickly*, Shelley said—I could already be gone.

"It's not a guarantee you'll get it, but a *risk*."

The only guarantee is I am high risk. The only guarantee is that we don't know.

On the Camino de Santiago
Andrea Ruggirello

I slid a needle and thread into my own skin at a hostel in Paris. Sitting on the bottom bunk, I poked a sterilized needle through my first blister, which had appeared somewhere between the Louvre and the Sacré-Coeur, and liquid oozed out. *Relief.* I left the thread in as the blogs I'd read had instructed, allowing it to continue draining.

The Camino de Santiago, which I would start the next day, stretched five hundred miles ahead of me. Since the Middle Ages, pilgrims have traveled the eight-hundred-kilometer route across northern Spain to Santiago, where Saint James's bones are said to be buried. There are dozens of churches and cathedrals along the way. Three-quarters of the way, at the Cruz de Ferro, pilgrims lay stones at the base of a cross upon which many have recorded the things or people or burdens they wish to leave behind. And at the end of the road, the Cathedral of Santiago waits for the pilgrims who will jump, cry, hug, or collapse in the plaza below, having completed their journey for whatever reason led them to the Way of St. James in the first place.

For many, that reason is God. Not for me. I was raised Catholic but am no longer practicing. I'd once believed that *something* was out there—a guiding hand, a benevolent being that cared for each of us—even if it wasn't the God I'd grown up hearing about. But by the time I took to the Camino, I'd been slipping toward atheism for years, prompted by a series of family crises. I was no longer able to imagine there was meaning in the pain and death of people I cared about.

The loss of faith was hollowing. For me, the Camino was an escape after a painful year—a journey away from trauma, not toward anything. Or so I thought.

Three months before I began my hike, a friend from my writing group had killed herself. Those of us left behind emailed and called each other, crying, shocked. One night I lay awake, thinking about life, death, the seeming impossibility of the divine, my own restlessness, my friend's shy smile. She was one of the youngest people I'd ever known to die.

And then I remembered another: Sasha, who I'd done an AmeriCorps program with years earlier, who had thanked me for helping her write her college application essay. She would have been the first in her family to go to college. Her death was an accident, and she'd left behind a beautiful little girl. So many young lives, shattered. So many twists and bends in our life's path, sometimes at our own hands.

Eventually, I did fall asleep, only to awaken suddenly at 3:30 a.m. Nothing seemed out of place. I drifted off again. The next morning I checked my phone and saw that I had a new email. It was from Sasha. For a moment, I panicked. How could she be emailing me? Why now, of all times?

As it turned out, the email contained nothing but a suspicious-looking link. I wanted to click it but feared a virus, so I just stared at Sasha's email address. The time stamp on her email read 3:30 a.m.

A few weeks later, I learned about the Camino from a friend who'd watched the movie *The Way*, which follows Martin Sheen's character on the pilgrimage after his son dies attempting it. It felt exactly right for me: meaningful, relatively inexpensive, physically demanding, an ocean away from home. It would be over a month of simply putting one foot in front of the other and thinking.

Many people prepare for years for the Camino. I believed my young, healthy body could handle it with just a few miles a day of walking to and from work. Just two and a half months after I first heard of it, I was on my way.

A week and a half after that first blister, my feet had their worst day of the Camino. It was Day 8, and I was supposed to walk 30.1 kilometers from Logroño to Nájera. My blisters were most painful near the ball of my right foot, close to the toes. I tried needles and thread again. I tried Compeed, Band-Aids, Vaseline. I carefully snipped bits of dead skin away—sometimes right there on the trail. It's common to see Camino pilgrims sitting by the side of the road, caring for their feet, and I had no shame about doing it wherever I needed to. My shoulders were used to the weight of my pack. My breathing came easily, even up steep inclines. Every muscle was growing stronger, but my feet were falling apart.

I first made contact with Kat, a fellow pilgrim, as I sat

soaking my feet in a stream. We were on the *meseta*, the several-day stretch across flat, brown nothing. The sun beat down on us, unrelenting. Water lapped around my red, swollen feet as Kat called down to me from the path, "Good idea!" We had alternated passing each other all day, another common occurrence on the Camino. Like a small-town community, you constantly run into people you recognize and embrace those you haven't seen in a few days as if it has been years.

Kat wore a purple bandana with all of her hair tucked up underneath. Her backpack was blue, and the yellow mouthpiece of her water bladder bobbed near her cheek. She grinned at me, looking like a person made for this type of trek—comfortable and at home on the road. I smiled back at her and told her the water felt great. She continued on her way.

We met again in Nájera, outside the municipal *albergue*, or hostel, where pilgrims could stay for five euros. We were told there were no more beds. The woman at the front desk directed us to a gymnasium filled with mattresses across town. Kat was cheerful; I pressed a smile on over my pain. We walked by the main dining area next to the river, where other pilgrims drank wine and relaxed, secure in knowing where they would rest their heads for the night. I envied them deeply.

Kat's cheery attitude was infectious, and soon we were chattering away like old friends. She was from Serbia and was on the Camino for a vacation, or at least that was the reason she chose to share. Our conversation was easy—the first easy part of my trip, really. It felt like she'd arrived just in time.

By the time we arrived at the gym, having lost our way twice, it was nearly seven o'clock. The woman at the front desk led us into the large gymnasium with its blue-painted walls, wooden floors, bleachers, and a heaping pile of mattresses. We chose the least stained ones from the pile, two each, and set them up near the bleachers. "Homey," Kat said, her voice echoing.

We showered and changed, intending to head back to the waterfront for dinner. But my feet were throbbing intensely by then, and I told Kat I didn't think I could make it. I could barely hobble out to the lobby. Kat insisted she would help me find a doctor, and when we stepped outside she looked to her right and laughed. We had ended up right next to the town hospital.

I felt surprised—and something close to blessed—as I looked up at that neon-green cross. That feeling grew when the doctor patched me up and told me I was fine to continue walking if I wanted to. In the hospital lobby, the receptionist waved me away. "No charge," she said.

You could chalk this up to human kindness, a superior healthcare system. Or to the laws of probability: after so many bad days, surely there had to be some good. As a nonbeliever myself, that's how I view it. All the same, as I emerged from the hospital to find Kat sitting outside, smoking while she waited and ready to greet me with a big smile, I felt a surge of healing and hope I hadn't felt in months.

I lost Kat after Nájera, after deciding to take the bus to give my feet one day's rest. She walked and perhaps decided to go on ahead farther than I did. I kept looking for her in the days that followed, but I never saw her again.

Carrión de los Condes to Calzadilla de la Cueza was approximately 17.5 kilometers, the shortest hike of my trip. It was a flat stretch through brown, open fields, with no villages or cafés to stop in on the way. There was only one lean-to more than halfway between the two towns. That morning, nearly three weeks in, started off with a drizzle but became a torrential downpour within the hour. The "waterproof" rain jacket I wore was soaked through by hour two. I pulled the strings of the hood, tightening it around my face like a bonnet. I hoped the rain cover on my pack was actually waterproof. There was no stopping to check. There was no point in stopping at all that day because there was no cover for miles.

My feet were soaked, too. The blisters that had forced me to ride the bus, had driven me to the doctor and the pharmacist for every remedy they had, were secondary to the cold, driving rain. I felt the water squish up between my toes and cursed the salesman at REI who suggested the lighter-weight non-waterproof boots. Not for the first time on my hike, I felt vastly unprepared and inexperienced.

By the time I reached the lean-to, a few kilometers out from my destination, my red jacket was translucent—I could practically see the goose bumps on my arms through the fabric. A group of pilgrims huddled beneath the structure, arms wrapped across their chests, shivering. Like commuters on a train, we stood in close quarters and commiserated. *A few more miles to go. Doesn't seem to be letting up. Where are all the trees?*

Finally I left and walked onward. I knew the town was

just a few kilometers past the lean-to, and I picked up my pace. It didn't register that my feet had stopped hurting as I flew past other poncho-clad pilgrims. I didn't reflect on how far I'd come, what I'd seen, who I'd met. Who I was. I could only think of a warm shower, my sleeping bag (hopefully still dry), and a roof over my head. I walked quickly, and I walked alone.

Like many Camino towns, Calzadilla de la Cueza appeared suddenly. At the top of a hill, like magic, I spotted the bright yellow sign for the municipal *albergue*, a rainbow painted on the side of the otherwise plain white building. A woman I'd met earlier, Nancy, had injured her foot and took the bus ahead; now I saw her waiting just outside of the *albergue*, smiling as I approached. "I saw your smile from a mile away," she said as she hugged me.

The rain had let up, I realized, now that I'd arrived—of course. I hadn't been aware of my grin, but Nancy told me it was the biggest and brightest she'd seen yet on the Camino.

The next morning, as I prepared my feet for the day's walk, I realized they were healed. The skin was soft and new— the old, hard flakes washed away, the burning spots calmed, softened. It felt as if I'd been given a second pair of feet, as if my body remembered it'd had a spare set in the trunk the whole time.

Can you believe in miracles without believing in God? There's so much we don't know, so many explanations we have yet to discover. Why did the email from Sasha arrive just when I'd been thinking of her? Why did I end up staying next to the hospital, with a friend, just when I most needed both? Why did it rain so hard, for so long, that day on the road to Calzadilla de la Cueza?

When we don't have explanations, we might use words like *miracle* or *divine*, turning each significant moment into a warm hand guiding us through life and providing for all our needs. To me, God is the 98 percent of the universe we have yet to explore. So many answers are still hidden in those dark pockets that are, for now, untouched and undiscovered. We find those miracles in the human body, too—in its ability to learn, to heal, to overcome in ways even doctors don't fully understand yet. My body had surprised me in its weakness; it startled me with its sudden strength. Some would tell me my healed feet were proof of God. To me, they were proof that our bodies are as unknowable as the rest of the universe. But a lack of religious faith doesn't make these moments, these rare gifts, any less beautiful. Months after returning home, I would look back on my experience on the Camino and feel warm and well cared for. Even loved.

I looked at my new feet for a long moment. Then I took out the medical tape I had been using for gauze patches to cover my blisters. With my Swiss Army knife, I cut long strips and wrapped my feet, covering both from ball to heel, like mummies: this miracle was one to protect. I pulled on my boots and headed out, ready for another long walk.

In Certain Contexts, Out of Certain Mouths
A. E. Osworth

I mean, you would be surprised how many women like getting fucked by an unclassifiable monster. [Relax: I'm reclaiming the term. I like it. I mean, when uttered in certain contexts out of certain mouths. Must I justify everything?]

—*Confessions of the Fox*,
Jordy Rosenberg

In California, it is month two of lockdown and I'm early on testosterone—about four months—so I'm breaking two cardinal rules: we, the trans mascs, don't talk about early transition because it will be embarrassing for my people and eventually for me; we, the writers, don't talk about the pandemic because everyone is talking about the pandemic.

And here I sit, extremely proud of myself that I finally thought to turn on the timer to take a photo of myself with my phone. That without asking anyone, or admitting that I would like to reproduce an image of my body, I thought of filling a jar with water and propping my phone against it. I took a whole-ass armchair out onto the porch, which is really a balcony, but which I call a porch because "plague porch" makes for good alliteration. The sun sinks into evening; the people who occupy the plague porch above me are smoking weed. The scent curls around me like a settling dog.

I am locked down with one cis person in an apartment that isn't mine, having been on the West Coast before the pandemic struck us all down and now stuck here after. I usually live in New York City. I am extremely sad. And somehow all I want to do is take photos of myself in which I look hot and send them to other people to show them how hot I look. That is a thirst trap: it initiates desire, one's own and others'. A deeply horny act in the face of global tragedy. I can't really explain the cognitive dissonance away.

I search for theory. Theory is a category of reading I've been able to keep up with, even as the pandemic depletes my ability to pay attention. I feel like I only understand a quarter of it at the best of times, so nothing has changed. I look for the theory that explains the thrill of thirst trapping, that contextualizes my transness in my desire to artfully examine the shapes I make in physical space. A newfound ability to look at my own body and an obsession with doing so. When I chopped my tits off, I could finally look in a mirror. Never before have I wanted a photographic record of what I saw there.

I cannot find any scholarly papers on the taking of thirst traps and the trans body. I turn, instead, to Susan Sontag.

I oscillate wildly between wishing Sontag were alive to write about Instagram and being very glad that I don't have to read Sontag's *On Instagram*. Instead, what I think I will use to process my newfound obsession: "In teaching us a new visual code, photographs alter and enlarge our notions of what is worth looking at and what we have a right to observe." It is from the first essay in *On Photography*, titled "In Plato's Cave." I am reading it in the bath.

There are plenty of other seemingly relevant nuggets, of course, from that essay and others. Things that seem to speak from the past to right now, that use the new buzzwords: "What is surreal is the distance imposed, and bridged, by the photograph: the social distance and the distance in time." I should be fixated on those, as well.

What I actually cannot stop thinking about: Sontag's writing about Diane Arbus's "thing" for "the Halloween crowd." People Sontag calls freaks. People about whom she writes: "Do they see themselves, the viewer wonders, like *that*? Do they know how grotesque they are? It seems as if they don't." Even a cursory look at Arbus's body of work answers the question—yes, me and mine would be included in "the Halloween crowd." I don't love thinking of us this way; also, I do. The freedom from normality gives one permission to do anything. To break any rule.

4 26 20. The date is stamped on the subject's inner thigh, directly on the subject's body hair. The subject sits on a fluffy blanket, the pile of which is clearly synthetic. It is gray, which contrasts the blue-stitched red boxers nicely. It puts the subject's wide-legged seat—a crotch-bearing seat, honestly—squarely in the foreground. It is, perhaps, where the eye goes first. Directly between the legs, though only one leg is visible. The other falls out of frame. The subject's arms rest behind the head, elbows arcing up toward the sky—the

elbows are very pointy. The subject wears glasses and smirks at the camera, stares directly at it, with fingers resting softly on the neck. The subject has a massive, visible chin zit. The faintest shadow is present above the lip; essence de mustache.

The subject's gender is indeterminate.

In California, I text friends from the plague porch in the dark. Friends whom I know very well and to whom I send my thirst traps; acquaintances I only casually know from the internet to whom I do not send my thirst traps. All trans, all with vastly different understandings of their bodies, their genders, all also staying at home but in very different circumstances— by themselves, with cis people, with other trans people, with partners or friends or roommates they cannot stand.

They thirst trap in different ways. They do it for the internet, for romantic friendships, for platonic group texts, for significant others, for prospective dates in the After Times, whenever those might happen. And they've all noticed a difference. They fall into two camps: those who want to thirst trap more—a desire that mirrors mine—and those who feel it impossible to feel oneself. Nearly everyone's relationship to taking sexy photographs has changed.

I repeat the same refrain as I speak to them all: I have never been hot before, and I'm afraid I won't be anymore when quarantine is over. That this state of being is delicate, ephemeral. That I am not quarantined with any trans people, and my slow werewolf transformation from butch to twink will not be properly witnessed, encouraged, or remembered. Some of my friends think I want to hear that I have always been hot; some of them tell me so. But some know exactly what I'm saying—this slice of time feels especially impermanent, and I cannot tell if it's hormones or pandemic or both.

Of course, more Sontag. Of physical photographs, she says: "They age, plagued by the usual ills of paper objects; they disappear; they become valuable, and get bought and sold; they are reproduced." This statement isn't entirely true anymore. Only some photographs disappear, and even then, not really, not the digital ones. They do not become as valuable—there is an ocean of them now, each one a single molecule that makes up the visual internet. Reproduced ad infinitum until, rather than aging, they become impossible to kill.

Is that what I am doing—becoming ageless? In the absence of my meatspace body living in the minds of my people, am I preserving this slice of time to be accessed later? Am I imbuing my early-testosterone body with immortality, marking its existence? Since when did I want my body at all, let alone to make it last for human eternity?

"It feels like a protest against this idea that it's polite to not find yourself attractive," my friend A. Andrews says to me over Zoom when I ask them about thirst trapping. A. is a writer and a comic artist. They think about the arrival of bodies in digital space quite a lot, usually because they are drawing bodies into existence. A. falls into category two—less thirst trapping, more existential crises. But they talk to me about it anyway.

"It's considered rude or self-involved to think you're hot," A. says. "This idea that we have to kind of think of ourselves as objectively neutral or below is weird. Thirst traps are a protest against this notion that we should all feel kind of medium about ourselves."

I consider my adherence to a politeness written upon the hearts of girl-children, the overemphasis of humble-as-virtue. It is an insurance that anyone with any relationship to girlhood, regardless of gender or outcome, will feel squeamish taking up a reasonable amount of space. Will disparage their own body until they feel less than they are: stunning. Everyone is stunning and I really believe that; everyone, of course, except for me.

Fuck that. I would rather be the Halloween crowd, unshackle myself from the normals. Love myself just a little bit more.

5 26 20. Same subject, wildly different house—the viewer can tell because the door behind the person is open to a wall of bright orange, and there was nothing nearly as garish in the last few photos. The left arm reaches up; a suggestion of joy. The hand is cut off at the top by an ornate, curling frame—the entire body is centered in the reflection of an oval mirror. A shining scar is visible, featured even, and extends from armpit to armpit. The red boxers make a reappearance.

The subject's smile seems forced.

The subject's gender is indeterminate.

I am locked down with one cis person and then, suddenly, I am not. I move into an Airbnb by myself. I don't want to talk about the details. I send thirst traps to a friend. He sends them back. We comment on our respective testosterone-induced babeliness: the cut of our shoulders, the shapes of our faces, the mechanics of shaving our whisker-whispers.

Sontag fights Sontag while I am here, alone: "To photograph is to confer importance. There is probably no subject that cannot be beautified; moreover, there is no way to suppress the tendency inherent in all photographs to accord value to their subjects." This idea brawls with: "The photographer's ardor for a subject has no essential relation to its content or value, that which makes a subject classifiable. It is, above all, an affirmation of the subject's thereness; its rightness (the rightness of a look on a face, of the arrangement of a group of objects), which is the equivalent of the collector's standard of genuineness; it's quiddity—whatever qualities make it unique."

I look at photos of myself. I describe them to myself. By taking the photo, by taking the time, I am conferring value upon myself and my body-in-process; neither would I suggest that the content or value makes the subject classifiable. It is an ouroboros of meaning: I confer meaning upon myself, I affirm my thereness, my rightness; my desire to confer more meaning upon myself increases.

"I've never before felt the full intensity of collective skin hunger like this," says Grace Lavery when I text her and ask her about thirst traps during the pandemic. "It is an unusual experience."

I've never said this to her, but talking to Grace (all two or three times I have done) always makes me sweat; it's the proximity to her sheer power. She's one of the most intelligent writers and academics in my extended community, and it's a privilege to live in a world in which I can DM her about the theoretical framework under which my friends and I do or do not get naked for photos. She falls into camp one, like me: never enough thirst traps.

"I find it hard to trust people who don't post selfies," Grace says. "I straight-up *don't* trust those who whine about the narcissism of the youth and the click-hungry jackals of social media. The will to objectify one's narcissism and displace it onto a network of others, to refuse to preserve the face from scorn or fetish, is a drive to begin the work of communalizing the body, to refuse the logics of organicity."

Naturally, I must google *organicity*—I decide this statement means holding only loosely to existence as an individual organic being, choosing to pivot instead to interconnected cyborg, but I could be wrong, and I am too nervous to ask her. Is this, perhaps, what we are doing? Or really, something we have already been doing—making ourselves into a superorganism? Is this one way trans people expand our Pando-esque roots absent communing with each other physically?

At the Airbnb, I try not to kill any of the spiders that share my strange twenty-eight-day home. They are everywhere and sometimes I slip—I accidentally wash one down the drain while I'm showering. One bites me on the toe and I look up what to do if it's venomous. I give the couch to the spiders, and I think that's fine as long as I can use the rest of the apartment. I cannot kill spiders just because I find them monstrous.

I take a lot of photos. I don't post them anywhere. I don't send them to anyone. These ones? They're only for me.

"I think the taking up thirst traps is the building of a performance archive."

Ari Monts is the kind of friend who gives out homework. Not by requiring one to do tasks, but by mentioning so many ideas in one conversation that it necessitates further investigation. We are talking on Zoom. (We are only ever talking on Zoom now.) They pull a book out from behind their couch. It is *The Sentient Archive*, which they tell me is edited by "Linda Caruso Haviland and some guy named Bill." Ari falls into camp two—for them, thirst traps are about the lead-up to a physical encounter. It's too depressing to take them right now. But their scholarly work is all about performance, gender, and ritual; they are a perfect thirst trap discussant.

The Sentient Archive, they say, "talks about an archive of something that's living and how we are archiving performances that live in our body. There's something about being both the person behind the lens and in front of the lens in a thirst trap. It puts the subject in charge of the way that they're being viewed."

Ari continues to talk, and I stare at the screen and I think about Diane Arbus. I've been googling and I find a strange disconnect with Sontag's imagining of Arbus and what I actually see: participation by the subject, a soft acceptance of naked bodies that fall outside classification—black-and-white photos of shirtless queens with proto-thirst-trap facial expressions, disabled people smiling directly at the viewer or else mean-mugging rugged, all closed lips and smoldering eyes. Her photos betray a kindness. An understanding of power. A thirst, sometimes. And yet it is still someone looking into a life, being a tourist, a voyeur. There is something attractive about being the subject and the artist all at once, of being entirely in control of how I am seen, who sees me.

I gently bring my focus back; Ari is talking about what trans people are not afforded in public spaces—the chance to experiment with our performed identities. "In public," they say, "we're just seen as strange and monstrous because of being trans or because of being Black or brown or Indigenous."

I isolate with the spiders for three weeks instead of two, just to be safe. I do not go to the grocery store; I do not go for a walk. I go no farther than the Airbnb gate. There are chickens here and I talk to them every day. I celebrate my birthday alone; my friends send me a bottle of Scotch and it arrives directly to my window. Two of them get a Covid test. It is negative. Together they drive ten hours to get me, ten hours back. I now live in their guest room; I don't know for how long. The house is full of trans people, and I have not taken one single thirst trap since arriving, until today.

7 9 20. The date stands out this time, against a white wall, gray couch, yellow throw pillow. The subject's hair is wild, reaching for the heavens (I haven't seen a barber in months). The eyes are cast down, toward the camera (which I have propped once more against a glass of water), and the wall behind the subject is busy with framed art, mounted nature, an embroidery hoop surrounding the backward letters "q-u-e-e-r." (Everyone else is out camping. I do not go camping. I am watching the cat, watering the garden, and taking

thirst traps because I am once again the only trans person here and every day counts.)

The subject kneels on the couch, knees wide, the arm placed between them. The posture is tall, rocked back on the heels, and their shoulders fill out a T-shirt. The arms are thicker; the fabric stretches over a pectoral muscle (hell yeah, I have a fucking pectoral muscle!). In the right hand, fingers lightly grasp a Kindle (I am still reading Sontag). The skin on the face is alive with zits, crawling like ants around the jawline. The ghost of the mustache is gone (I shaved it off and I shave it off every other day).

The subject's gender is indeterminate—because it is constructed to be so, for myself and mine; an unclassifiable monster.

Cut Knuckles

Forsyth Harmon

We know her by her hands, which are fine and olive-complected with long, pastel-painted, almond-shaped fingernails. She uses them to remove the Play-Doh Cash Register toy set from its box: a parade of colorful plastic components that, when assembled, form a cartoonish grocery store checkout.

"Today I'm super excited to bring you this cash register," she begins, voice cheerful, words clipped. "We'll be shopping and scanning." She presents to us the red plastic blocks that form the play register, along with its miniature accessories: a blue basket, a gray scanner, a brown wallet. "Here's a banana cookie cutter. We also get milk, an apple, broccoli, and a carrot!"

Welcome to the world of toy-unboxing-and-play YouTube videos, the kind with which my four-year-old son has recently become obsessed. "I want a Play-Doh video," he squeals as he squirms beneath my arm on the couch. "I want one with the girl." Yes, we're very well acquainted with his favorite kid-friendly ASMR darling's melodious voice, her capable hands. The nature of the genre is such that we don't see her body beyond the forearms. We've never seen her face.

In this video, like most, after assembling the play set, she shapes a rainbow of Play-Doh into toylike approximations of kids-menu favorites. While my son is mesmerized by her ability to model the dough into a tiny slice of pizza, a cheeseburger, a chocolate bar, I'm watching for a flash of her knuckles, which she's mostly able to keep outside the frame.

"And here's an apple!" she announces, rotating her neon-pink-and-green creation for the camera, and then there they are: the small red cut marks on the first and third knuckles, which any bulimic could identify as those made by the teeth when finger-inducing vomiting.

The first time I saw these wounds, I hoped my suspicions were incorrect. I reasoned this vlogger might have grazed her hand on a door latch or a lemon zester. And would she really bare her bulimic tell for more than 2.5 million viewers to see? But as my son's obsession grew, and we watched her sculpt one cupcake after another, my fears were confirmed. I saw those same wounds again and again, appearing consistently across several videos and manicures: lavender, light blue, mint green, pale pink, and an impressive iridescent. I wondered about those long, pointy nails grazing the back of her throat.

I recall the summer I worked the cash register at my Long Island hometown grocery store. It was a job my mother had had as a teenager, too—and, at that age, I flailed between attempts to fit into and break from her mold with equal fury. She had always been a slender woman, and that summer, I was recovering from a case of chronic anorexia. I'd lost thirty pounds, and my psychiatrist threatened in-patient treatment if I didn't put on weight.

I found my way back to food via weed. Marijuana re-awakened a long-repressed hunger for Snickers bars and Nacho Cheese Doritos. But once the high waned, I felt the fat course through me, collecting at my armpits, above my knees. Being inside my own body was an unbearable experience. The remorse was too great, relieved only by purging the milk chocolate–coated orange remnants of the binge, leaving me with red eyes, swollen cheeks, and cut knuckles.

My world became very small that summer, contained not just to the fluorescent-lit space behind the conveyor belt at my grocery store register, but bound by alternate starving, bingeing, and purging. I thought about little apart from what I'd eaten, what I'd eat next, and how fat I felt. This is called bulimarexia, since symptoms of both bulimia and anorexia are present, with their common body dysmorphia. I was disgusted with this progression of my disease, having imagined anorexia as clean, neat, and controlled. Now, my mind was reeling, my body expanding, consuming and ejecting inappropriate volumes of food engineered to inspire craving, full of salt, sugar, fat, and a host of hard-to-pronounce additives.

That I spent all day staring at the checkout candy rack didn't help. A tight circuit formed between growing faint, grabbing and guzzling M&M's, shutting off my register light, then running to the employee bathroom to expel a rainbow. I scanned and bagged customers' items with yo-yoing desire and revulsion. I wanted to tear the lid from a tub of Betty Crocker vanilla icing even as I wondered how this customer

felt authorized to buy it. At the time, the irony of a bulima-
rexic working in a grocery store didn't occur to me.

Allen Ginsberg's 1955 poem "A Supermarket in California"
is a conflicted paean to the suburban grocery store, reflecting
on the simultaneous glittering potential and hollow disappointment of these modern outlets of industrialized abundance. The poem is addressed to Walt Whitman—who is,
like me, a native Long Islander—and his presence acts as a
kind of lighthouse for a (perhaps mythic) more natural, hu-
manized time.

   "In my hungry fatigue," Ginsberg says, "and shopping
for images, I went into the neon fruit supermarket, dream-
ing of your enumerations! / What peaches and what penum-
bras!" Already, in this first stanza, Ginsberg is shopping not
for food but fluorescent-lit images of it, not unlike our vlogger's Play-Doh fruits, bright under the ring light.

   Ginsberg follows Whitman "in and out of the brilliant
stacks of cans," imagining the latter asks: "Who killed the
pork chops? What price bananas?" These questions are
meant to remind us that Whitman would have known the
farmer who produced his food, unlike Ginsberg, wandering
around a warehouse in which products are divorced from
origins.

   As a checkout girl, I never once considered where the
foods I scanned and bagged came from, instead memorizing
their PLUs, or price look-up codes: four- or five-digit numbers
used to identify produce based on commodity, variety, and
size. Apple, Braeburn: 4103; Gala: 4133; McIntosh: 4152.

Ginsberg ends the poem with an image of the river Lethe, which runs through hell. Drinking from it makes us forget our time on earth, the banal sufferings of our daily lives. And for Ginsberg, this is what consumer capitalism does: it makes us forget what's natural, makes us forget ourselves.

As an anorexic, I forgot how to sense and address my own hunger. I was fixated on an image—specifically, Kate Moss in a string bikini—and was determined to do whatever was necessary to mirror it. I survived on aspartame-sweetened nonfat yogurt, the euphoria of starvation, and the anticipation of achieving the perfect physique. Initially, this felt good. I enjoyed the predictability, the control and achievement I felt as I weighed myself each morning. But as my addiction progressed, starvation no longer produced the same high it did early on. And even as I moved into recovery, having suppressed my appetite for so long, I'd lost my connection to it.

Years past the last time I self-induced vomiting, I continued to move between calorie restriction, overindulgence, and overexercise. Certain foods, like garbanzo beans, were deemed safe and consumed each and every day, while others, like peanut butter, were eschewed as dangerous and avoided until the desire became so overwhelming, I'd eat a whole jarful. In my midtwenties, I exercised no less than three hours a day. This is what addiction does: it makes us forget what's natural, makes us forget ourselves. In Classical Greek, the word *lethe* (λήθη) literally means "forgetfulness"—and "concealment." As addicts, we forget—and try to conceal from ourselves—what we need to live.

I have made slow, somewhat-unsteady progress in recovery. After a flare-up of calorie restriction following the birth of my son, I've worked to reconnect with my body and its needs—for his sake. I was thrilled when I learned his birth gender, as I knew it made him less likely to inherit my disordered eating—but I worry about his propensity for addiction in general.

In twelve-step recovery programs, there's a saying: "Don't go to the hardware store for milk." It's meant to remind us that, no matter how hard we might try, we're never going to get what we need—nutrition, love, community, purpose, peace—if we look for it from the wrong source. I think of this as my son and I watch these wounded hands shape food facsimiles from water, flour, salt, surfactant, and humectant.

"Here's corn, a cookie, a croissant, garlic, and a pepper!" the girl announces as she removes each item—food without nourishment—from its plastic mold. I look down at his little blond head against my chest. My hand rests on his forearm. Twenty years later, the white scars are still there on my first and third knuckles.

Surviving Karen Medicine

Destiny O. Birdsong

It was a blisteringly cold day in March 2015 when I, exhausted and bundled in mismatched flannel, trudged into the IBD clinic's waiting room. The most pronounced symptom of my newly diagnosed autoimmune disease was exhaustion, and even though I'd been prescribed an emergency steroid, I was still feeling threadbare and wrung out like an old washcloth.

I was also terrified. I'd heard of Crohn's disease before, and everything I knew about it seemed terrible: intense pain, countless surgeries, extended hospital stays. I lived 550 miles away from my closest potential caretaker, and I had no idea whether this disease would do to me what it had done to many other people.

My first appointment was a relay of visits to small rooms. First, I met with a psychiatrist, who was kind if not a little condescending, calling me Dr. Birdsong in what I can only suspect was an ill-calculated move to make me feel important. Next, I met with a resident, who looked at my hands and asked if I'd ever had psoriasis. I'd been sick for so many months that I was dehydrated, and my skin, leathery beneath a sheen of ash, showed it. And finally, before seeing the doctor with whom I was supposed to co-plan my care, I had one more hurdle to clear: meeting with a dietician to discuss my new eating plan.

Carlotta, a white woman with stern, schoolmarm features, walked in wearing a T-shirt for a 5K and a string of Mardi Gras beads that made me wistful for home. *Somewhere in Louisiana*, I mused, *people are happy*. The thought made me hopeful. What followed was one of the most demoralizing exchanges of my life.

Carlotta had overheard the psychiatrist call me into his office, so her first question was, "Are you *really* a doctor?" When I explained I had a PhD, she frowned, typing furiously into the computer and looking as if I'd told a bad joke. Immediately, she began describing the depth of her own training. "Almost as much as they get in medical school," she insisted. Her previous annoyance morphed into anger when we began discussing the plan. If possible, I wanted to honor a diet I'd developed during a religious fast, so when she suggested sports drinks and meal-supplement shakes, my heart sank.

"Are there alternatives I can drink instead?" I asked. "I try to stay away from artificial ingredients. I'm also very intolerant of soy."

"Listen," she huffed. "Do you *want* to end up in the hospital, hooked up to an IV with a doctor cutting out your insides? If not, then you need to listen and follow this plan."

I don't remember much else from that session, or even how I got through the meeting with Dr. O, another white woman who, with the resident looking on, cheerfully explained my new medication. I vaguely remember the pharmacist, who demonstrated how I would weekly inject it into my thigh. I barely remember making it back home on the icy streets, but I do remember the phone call with my mother the day after.

When I told my mother about my appointment, I burst into tears. I didn't want to be as sick as everyone was telling me I was, but I also didn't want to be at the mercy of people who refused to listen, who weaponized my prognosis when they were intimidated by my education or resentful of the decisions I still wanted to make about my body.

Crying was, of course, a reasonable reaction, but I'd never in my adult life cried in front of my mother, partially because my mom is a badass. She slept outside overnight so she could enroll me in the best elementary school in the city. Every year, she'd go into the woods to cut down our Christmas tree because she hated fake ones. One of my most frightening memories of her is when I was four, and I had a terrible time learning to tie my shoes. One morning, in a fit of frustration, I yelled, "I just can't do it!" My mom grabbed me by the collar and yanked me toward her, so close I could smell the toothpaste on her breath.

"Don't you *ever* tell me what you can't do. Never say 'I can't.' Always say, 'I can!'"

I learned to tie those bad boys by the end of the week, but, interestingly, not the way everyone tried to teach me. There'd be no bunny ears crossing over each other. My method is tie, create a loop, slip the lace under the loop, and tighten. On the day my mom and I broke protocol and cried together over the phone, she reminded me of the importance of keeping my faith. And I would, but I would also need that four-year-old's audacity to do a thing the way that made the most sense to me. And succeed.

But first, I'd need to learn to read examination rooms and the slights that happened in them. Spending extended time in a doctor's office was new to me at that first appointment, but what happened on subsequent days wasn't. Soon, word got around the clinic that I was combative. Nurses eyed me with suspicion and steered clear when they could. One day, a receptionist told me I should go out and get some sunshine. It might have been a playful response to my clear discomfort, but I have albinism; the remark was an act of emotional violence intended to remind me of my place and what I was.

I know when the "angry Black woman" trope has been pinned to me like a name tag for everyone to read. I also know enough stories about medical racism to know the results of doing this can be deadly.

More than a century and a half after James Marion Sims's horrific surgeries without anesthetics on enslaved Black women, studies show that white medical trainees still presume Black patients have a higher tolerance for pain than white ones. Black mothers and their newborns are more likely to die in childbirth than their white counterparts, sometimes at the hands of doctors who ignore clear signs of the mothers' medical distress. And Black women like me, who are knowledgeable about their bodies and strive to be proactive in their healthcare, are demonized by the very individuals charged with nursing us back to health.

When Dr. Susan Moore, an internist who was living with

sarcoidosis and had been hospitalized for Covid-19 in November 2020, questioned a physician about why he refused
to prescribe additional doses of remdesivir, an antiviral medicine she'd been approved for in previous days, he replied,
"You should just go home right now." He didn't feel comfortable prescribing her "more narcotics." After more bouts
with nurses and other hospital staff, marginally adequate
treatment followed, but Dr. Moore would still die from the
virus a few weeks later.

To have one's curiosity and pleas for agency pathologized
is a familiar feeling, but it is also a deadly game that white
healthcare professionals play with Black lives. It is, in fact,
its own game of tag: Someone gets offended enough to make
you "it," and suddenly everyone is running for the hills. Or
they're taunting you from a few feet away, withholding care
because they know they can get away with it. You're too slow
to catch them. Maybe because you're sick. And you might be
lucky enough not to die from this, but you will absolutely get
sicker.

In the summer of 2017, just before leaving home for a six-
week string of writing residencies, I noticed a small cluster
of blisters in my right palm. Over the next several months,
my skin would erupt. My hands would peel to the point of
bleeding. My finger- and toenails would separate from their
nail beds. I woke up one day and a fist-size patch of my hair
was gone. So much would fall out in the coming days that I
shaved my head. My feet looked like I'd been walking on hot
coals, and I often hobbled because they were painful to stand

on. It was an ironic twist to the nightmare I feared living after diagnosis. I wasn't suffering internally. All the suffering was happening on my skin.

And the sicker I got, the more dependent I became on white women healthcare professionals who promised they could fix things. In exchange, I became a fascinating case as long as I stayed in my place. Dr. O seemed particularly confident she could help with a one-two punch: prescribing a new monthly biologic infusion known to treat both bowel diseases and psoriasis. She reasoned that, since people with one autoimmune disease often have several, throwing a medication with several approved uses (and side effects) at the problem should do the trick. Unfortunately, it didn't.

"I think maybe this has something to do with my past medicines," I offered, remembering an important detail from the summer: For more than a year, I'd been on both a biologic and a supplemental medicine designed to force my body not to reject it. And it worked, but you're only supposed to take the supplement for a year at a time. Two weeks after I'd discontinued it, my blisters appeared. I mentioned the coincidence to Dr. O and suggested that perhaps one medication had been suppressing the symptoms of the other.

"I don't think so," she bristled, though her smile never wavered. "I've been prescribing this for years, and I've never had a patient react like this."

I was doubtful, but she continued. "You probably have psoriasis. But the new biologic you're taking will take care of that. Give it ninety days."

Can you imagine waiting out the symptoms I described for ninety days? But I had no choice. I waited. And things got worse. I came back to the office, and this time I was angry. But next to each examination room's computer is a keypad with a series of buttons, and one of them is for security. I needed to be firm, but I couldn't risk further trouble. I voiced my frustrations. Dr. O wheeled her chair away from her screen to sit in front of me, close enough that she could reach over to pat my itchy hand.

"I think you just need to come to terms with the fact that you have another autoimmune disease and get over it."

I seethed, but I kept my voice low.

"If it's true, like you said before, that you're not a dermatologist, then how the hell would you know that?"

She couldn't answer.

I left. I also stopped showing up for the infusions.

The self-preservation that kept me from cursing out Dr. O that day has kept me sheltering in place for most of the pandemic, and, like then, my diligence is due in large part to my fear.

I've read about the death of Shalondra Rollins, a thirty-eight-year-old Black Mississippi woman who was misdiagnosed with the flu by a doctor who, at the time, was sitting on the city's pandemic task force. I also know about Rana Zoe Mungin, an Afro-Latinx writer whose Covid-19 symptoms were initially dismissed as a panic attack. All three of us share so many subjectivities: Like me, they were Black working-class women. Shalondra was from the South and had preexisting health conditions. Rana Zoe was an early-career writer.

And like me, these were tenacious women who returned for second (and third) opinions after doctors and EMTs failed them. But they still died. And this is why I worry—about my now in this pandemic, which is affecting Black and brown communities at staggering rates compared to white ones, and about my later, when I am pregnant and older than traditional expecting mothers. I worry about surviving childbirth and about the health of my children. But as much as I worry, I've convinced myself that I can make it, because while it's true that the odds are against me, the odds aren't all there is.

Yes, I'm a Black woman with a chronic illness in a healthcare system that hasn't always taken care of me and mine, even when we're healthy. And it's true that no matter how many degrees I have, how many notes I've taken about my symptoms, or how willing I've been to do what my doctors told me to even when I've had doubts, I'm not safe. But I am determined. This isn't four-year-old me struggling with a pair of laces. I've long since grown out of telling people what I can't do.

When I finally got in to see an actual dermatologist, she introduced herself by telling me my reputation preceded me. "Dr. O messaged me about what happened during your last visit and how frustrated you are. I understand that, but it's important to remember we're here to help." Moments later, I heard her outside, joking with one of her residents about my case.

"What a conundrum. Too bad you won't be around long enough to help me figure this one out. Lucky you!" she laughed. I left the clinic wondering how many other people had heard her talk about my body like it was a Rubik's Cube. That night, I wrote her a letter asking, among other things, for an apology, which I received, along with a slew of prescriptions for useless medications, which lasted another six months.

But the dermatologist *would* get to the bottom of things. Eventually. My primary care provider—a bright-eyed resident who was perhaps not yet biased against my subjectivity or threatened by my questions—sent a letter asking the dermatologist to perform a skin biopsy, and the results were clear: I had, of all things, eczema. Of course, this was eczema on steroids, or rather, biologics, which amped it up to wreak havoc on my body. I had so many new questions, but I was so happy to finally have *one* answer, I didn't bother asking them.

I'd like to think my healing was the sole result of my tenacity, but it wasn't. It was a combination move, just like learning to tie my shoes. I found a loophole in white privilege, and I threaded my way through it by convincing another white woman to plead my case. And let me be clear: I'm the last person to hold up a white savior as the answer to any of my problems. But if I am to be honest about my vulnerability as a Black woman patient, I have to understand the absurd necessity of this strategy, one in which I had to present myself tearfully to a sympathetic ear in order to get a procedure that took less than ten minutes.

But this, I would argue, is the crux of the Black woman

experience: once you decide on survival, the tools you come to use can be unorthodox. In some instances, they are the master's tools, finessed and repurposed. In others, like the case of my primary care provider, the master herself *becomes* the tool. In a perfect world, I wouldn't sound like a user, but my healthcare hasn't been a fair fight since Dr. Sims opened a Black woman's body with a speculum. I was never given a choice to select the weapons. So I don't care what—or who— it takes to keep me well.

And I have been fortunate enough to be well. Chemotherapeutic medication drastically improved my skin, and it is now healthier than ever before. So am I—arguably healthier than I was before my autoimmune diagnosis, though I never returned to biologics. Nearly all of my Crohn's symptoms are controlled by what I don't eat, which also happens to keep my skin clear. I know this is not the case for everyone with my diseases. It was a gamble, but I held on to my agency and trusted my instincts, and I haven't been sick a day since.

But if 2020 showed us anything, it's that good healthcare professionals ensure our survival. At least the conscientious and compassionate ones do. But we need more healthcare workers of color—especially more Black doctors—who are more likely to empathize with Black patients than misperceive them as threats. It also wouldn't hurt if more of those Black doctors were women.

During my last follow-up with Dr. O, a young Black resident came to the room first to discuss my case. Her visit was supposed to be brief, but I found myself telling her everything that had happened to me since 2015. We chatted for so long that she was still there when Dr. O breezed in, marveling at my progress and my lack of symptoms. Then, because the resident was sitting at the computer, Dr. O took a seat next to mine.

"I have a patient now who is having your exact skin problems. He's also on a biologic, and I've been walking his dermatologist through his care." She proudly patted my shoulder. "It's such a shame what you went through, but at least your story is helping someone else!"

Dr. O went on about the patient's other complicating factors, but I tuned her out and looked over at the resident. The whole time we'd chatted alone in the room, I thought to myself, *I'm saying too much. She probably thinks I'm exaggerating.* But she knew what it was. We were two Black women in a space never designed for us, but there we were, thriving. It feels good to thrive.

It also feels good to be proven right. But it feels far better to be seen. We looked over at each other and smiled.

What I Did for the Chance to Have a Baby Someday

Karissa Chen

The first time I dreamt of you, I was in my midtwenties. In the dream, I labored for what felt like an eternity and a mere minute (time being fluid and paradoxical in dreams), and then you were pressed against my breast. I could see the tuft of dark hair plastered against your scalp; I could feel the down of your skin prickle against my cheek. Your warmth filled my greedy body with something unnameable and I drank it in, the weight of you all that I had not known I wanted.

When I woke from the dream, it was too soon. The absence of something ghostly ached in the crook of my arms. I spent the hours after in a muted haze, an emptiness I had trouble putting a name to, until I recognized it for what it was: I missed you. It wasn't the same as longing, exactly, because it felt deeper, sadder, more confusing, more like grief. I felt the absence of a family I had yet to create, as if you already existed somewhere but were not mine to have.

I've had many dreams like this since. Sometimes you are a toddler, a little girl who loves dresses and climbs into my lap, chattering about a life I know instinctively includes me. Sometimes you are a boy who grows rapidly before my eyes into a young man. Sometimes you have distinct features, so known to me in the minutes after I wake that I'm certain I could pick you out of a picture. Other times you are anonymous—only a powdery smell, a soft heaviness in my arms, a giggle, a cry. In every dream, I know I am your mother, meant to love and protect you. Each time I wake, I am filled with the same ache. I wonder, each time, if there's a word in the English language that means "to miss and mourn someone who doesn't exist."

I flew back to Taiwan the year I turned thirty-six, for a three-week trip I'd booked solely for the purpose of freezing my eggs. In the two weeks leading up to the first appointment, I'd been taking estradiol and norethindrone (normally given to alleviate symptoms of menopause) to help me regulate my cycle and prevent the formation of cysts—a cyst had been the reason I hadn't been able to start the process several months earlier. My period arrived right on schedule, two days ahead of my first appointment at the IVF clinic.

I woke up at six forty-five that morning, jetlagged, jittery, and under the weather. As I got dressed and headed toward the train station, I fretted—would a cold affect the efficacy of the procedure? Would I produce fewer eggs because my body was too busy fighting off a virus? I thought about taking a cocktail of vitamin C, zinc, and echinacea tablets—what I usually took when I felt myself coming down with a cold—but then worried they might somehow interact with whatever injections they were going to give me. I bought a bottle of orange juice instead.

At the clinic, I was first called to have my blood drawn to test me for my hormone levels. I dutifully gave the nurse my left arm, looking away as she filled two tubes with blood. Afterward, I was called into another room for an ultrasound. The technician swiveled the wand around inside of me, taking pictures, drawing Xs that I guessed were to mark my follicles, typing in comments I tried to decipher. As I was pulling my underwear back on in the small changing room, I heard whispers, and then the technician called me back. "We have to do an outside ultrasound," she said, pouring gel on my belly. She pressed a different wand to my skin and then marked something on the screen. *Myoma*, she typed. I didn't know what a myoma was, but it sounded like bad news.

For the next two hours, I sat in the waiting room, inwardly panicking. What if they'd found another cyst? What if I wouldn't be able to start this round after all? I had been counting each cycle that had gone by without egg retrieval, aware of the fact that the number of "good" eggs I had dwindled with each passing month.

When the doctor finally called me in, I was so nervous I thought I would puke. She was the doctor I had met with months earlier, a woman with kind eyes and a slight smile. She waited until I was seated and said, "Everything looks good for us to begin." I almost burst into tears.

The doctor explained our plan for the next fourteen days. She showed me a table, with days marked across the top and the names of various medications and tests marked from top to bottom. She marked off the hormones I would take for the next four days: one long-acting Elonva shot, nightly injections of Merional, and oral dosages of Duphaston to be taken twice daily. The first two would stimulate my ovaries to produce multiple eggs this cycle; the latter would suppress early ovulation. "We're going to give you more medications because you're over thirty-five," she said.

She wrote down the date and time of my next appointment and the two days she thought we were most likely to do the extraction. She told me to drink at least fifteen hundred milliliters of water every day and to eat plenty of protein, particularly red meat. She warned me not to exercise. "As your follicles grow, your ovaries will swell," she explained. "If you exercise while they're swollen, they could get twisted."

Outside, I was called to the cashier's desk and presented with the day's bill. It came to approximately $1,220 (USD). Of that amount, forty dollars was for the doctor consult, ultrasound, and bloodwork. The rest went toward the hormones. I picked up the medication—presented to me in a silver insulated bag with an ice pack—and was brought into a room with a low leather couch, warm lighting, and a television showing slides on the IVF process. A physician's assistant was waiting for me. "I'm going to teach you how to do the injections," she said, smiling.

This was the part I had been dreading. The idea of having to stick a needle in myself even once was awful enough—to have to do it every single day was something I wasn't sure I could actually do. Most people I knew who went through this process had a partner to administer the injections, but I was doing this alone. I had been curating a list of friends who lived nearby who might be willing to help. One of them was a nurse—maybe she wouldn't mind me coming over every single night so she could inject me?

The PA showed me how to prepare the Merional solution and draw it into a sterile needle. "Now we want to inject in the fat of your belly," she said, and she showed me where to pinch. *Thank God I don't have a flat stomach*, I thought. *Maybe more fat means less pain!* "It has to go in straight, not at an angle. Let me show you—take a deep breath." She picked up the Elonva needle and stuck it in. "Push the fluid in slowly and steadily." When the liquid was dispensed, she handed the prepared Merional solution over to me. "Now you try."

I held the needle between my fingers. It was so slight, its tip tiny and sharp. I pinched my belly fat and took a deep breath.

"Don't look away," the PA warned me. "You have to see where the needle is going."

I shoved the needle in. To my surprise, I didn't feel a thing. Elated, I pushed the fluid in, watching the hormone solution drain into me.

As I walked out of the clinic, silver bag filled with needles and more hormones in hand, I suddenly felt like Superwoman. I was proud of myself. I had already proven I was capable of more than I thought. It didn't matter that I had no partner to help me. It didn't matter that I was far from my family. I was taking control of my life. I could do this.

A few months earlier, I'd gone to visit a friend, a single father with two young children. Every morning, we were woken

before 6:00 a.m. by his almost-two-year-old son. I helped
my friend shuttle his seven-year-old daughter from school
to after-school activities. I tried to feed his toddler toast. I
played hundreds of games of rock paper scissors. I hugged the
kids and held them and cuddled them and talked them down
from tantrums and held dance parties and played games and
more games and more games even when I no longer wanted
to play any more games. I was there for just three days, and I
was exhausted. I was in awe of my friend's resilience.

"Are you sure you want kids?" he asked me at one point,
our eyes locking over the heads of his fussy children.

The answer, I knew, was yes. It was yes more than ever.
Because all through my own exhaustion and the kids' occasional unruliness, even though I was aware of how this
would be a thousand times more difficult if and when this
became my everyday reality, I never once thought, *I don't
want this*. Instead, what I thought was, *I am ready for this. I
am willing to do all of this*.

What I mean, of course, is I want you, and will do whatever it takes to love you.

Within a day of those first injections, the hormones kicked
in. My sense of excitement was replaced with a heavy exhaustion like I'd never felt before. Almost immediately, most
food became intolerable, despite my ravenous and unrelenting hunger. I tried to eat as much red meat as I could, remembering the doctor's orders, but more than a few bites of it
made me nauseous. The only thing I could stomach was hot
pot and, strangely enough, fried chicken.

Other symptoms began to appear. I was continuously angry—not in an irritated, passionate sort of way, but in a detached rage that sat in the background of my existence, one that left me with no tolerance for acquaintances' poorly timed political jokes and fueled my calm but cold response to a man who told me in a tweet that my hormonal symptoms would be a lot less miserable if I were actually pregnant.

I slept a lot. This was an unfamiliar fatigue, one that wasn't about sleep deprivation but merely about my body's total redirection of resources toward producing follicles. I felt like a heavy cloak was draped over every single one of my cells. The one time I tried to go to a friend's housewarming party, I had to leave after an hour. The symptoms of my cold mingled with the symptoms from the injections, making it hard for me to track what was causing what. By the third evening, I was already over it—over the injections, which were getting more painful to administer each day; over my exhaustion; over my growing unfamiliarity with my body.

On day five, I went back to the clinic. This time, I noticed that nearly everyone else waiting was with a partner, and loneliness began to wind through my veins. During my ultrasound, I watched the technician count only two blobby follicles in one of my ovaries. Twenty was the magic number for an 80 percent chance of one live birth. I had hoped for fifteen. Before starting this procedure, I'd told myself that if I retrieved anything below twelve, I would do another cycle.

While I waited to meet with the doctor after the ultrasound, a waterfall of regret poured through my head—*I wish I had done this sooner, I wish I had done acupuncture and taken Chinese medicine to help my fertility, I wish I had drunk protein shakes, I wish I had forced myself to eat more meat.* In what was becoming a routine, I sat in that bright, sunlit lobby and felt on the verge of tears.

When I met with the doctor, she told me that in fact they had counted nine to twelve follicles—I had been mistaken in what I thought I saw—but that they were maturing too slowly. "Drink more water," she reminded me. "Eat more protein." She prescribed new meds, changing the dosage and type (including a click pen that the PA had to coach me to use, lest I overdose)—another $520—and sent me home.

The next day, feeling like I'd been run over by a truck, I intermittently napped through an entire morning and afternoon and forgot to take my morning dose of Duphaston. By the time I remembered, it was late afternoon. A few hours later, I discovered blood in my underwear. Panicked, I called the clinic, which had just closed for the day. I left a desperate message, then texted Denise, my contact at the clinic. While I waited, I wondered if I was getting breakthrough bleeding, if I'd ovulated, if something bad was happening and this cycle was forfeit. A familiar tornado of self-blame whipped through me.

An hour later, Denise called. She told me the bleeding was probably due to the instability of my hormones due to the missed Duphaston, but that everything was probably okay. If the bleeding continued, she said, I should go to the clinic the next morning, a day ahead of my scheduled appointment. But if I experienced no more bleeding, it was probably no big deal.

I hung up the phone and started to sob. I didn't see any more blood.

———

I spend a lot of time trying to convince myself that I'll be a better mother now than I would have been when I was younger. I'm more mature, less insecure, more patient, more thoughtful. Although I may be more set in my ways, more used to my own life, more "selfish" in some respects—I think a lot about the ways you will drastically alter my life and the freedom I have—I'm also completely sure that motherhood will be a choice I'll make because it's something I *want*, not something society expects of me.

But I also worry about the ways being an older mother might work against the both of us. I have less energy and stamina than I used to have to chase after you. By the time you're a teenager, I'll be going through menopause, and I can only imagine what colliding hormonal beings will be like. I also worry about your future, about what having an older parent will mean for you. Will you have to worry about taking care of me when your adult life is just getting started? Will I leave you too soon to see you get married, to hold the children you might have, to be there for you for as long I'd like to be? I know there's no point in thinking about this, because I can't change what has happened and I can't control what will be. But I worry for you—for us—anyway. And isn't that, too, a part of what motherhood is about?

Over the next week, my life consisted only of sleep, clinic visits, hot pot, injections, crying, more sleep. I was always hungry but had no interest in food. I was constantly battling headaches from the Merional and had to force down water even when I felt I could not drink any more. My boobs hurt. I was bloated. I could feel my swollen ovaries banging around painfully inside of me when I walked, so I walked slowly, my hand pressing down to stop them from moving.

The visits to the clinic became harder. My arm was covered with purple blotches from increasingly painful blood draws as they searched for new veins. Simple instructions— the addition of injections (up to four in one evening at one point); the directive for me to remove my nail polish before the surgery (for purposes of monitoring the anesthesia)— made me want to cry: the former because I just couldn't tolerate any more needles, and the latter because I was reminded there was a surgery at the end of all of this and it would require more needles. My loneliness and grief over freezing my eggs as opposed to trying for immediate conception was compounded with each clinic visit, surrounded by women flanked by their partners. Most of all, my mood was fragile, revolving around news on whether or not my follicle count had gone up, whether or not they seemed like they were maturing at a high-enough rate.

I had completely underestimated how taxing the process would be. When I realized it had been less than two weeks since I began injections, I was stunned. It felt like a lifetime. Before I started the process, I had considered doing another round if I didn't get the number of eggs I wanted, but now, in the midst of it, I couldn't bear the thought of suffering through all this again. Mentally, I was fraying at the edges. Despite loved ones who sent me messages of support and checked in, despite how grateful I was to have this option at all, I felt so isolated—emotionally, I felt I was walking this path alone.

I no longer had the energy to be angry about anything. I was tired, I was lonely, I was sad in ways I didn't know how to explain. I no longer felt like Superwoman. I didn't even feel like myself.

Listen: I'm not complaining.

Or maybe I am complaining, just a little bit. I know that actual pregnancy and motherhood are hundreds of times harder than those two little weeks. And I want to repeat that I was and am grateful to have even been able to do it. But it was still hard, physically and emotionally, and I kept wishing so many things had unfolded differently, in a way that didn't end up with me doing this thing that was so hard and tiring and lonely.

I never want to be the kind of mother who guilt-trips their child for their existence. That is to say, if someday I am blessed enough to know you, blessed enough to watch you grow from a sweet infant into a sullen teenager, I never want to point to this time and say, *Look how much I suffered to have you.* These were my choices. This is what I wanted. What I wanted was—is—*you*.

What I hope you know is that even when I was miserable and exhausted, even as I thought, *I can't possibly ever do this again; I don't think I can bear it*, I also always thought, *But I would do this again, I would spend all my money, I would inject myself with all these shots, if only it means I can have a baby.*

I want you to know how much I wanted you.

————

On the tenth day, my last clinic visit before retrieval, I was sitting in the reception area, waiting for my final ultrasound, when two couples came in, each carrying chubby babies. One of the babies had a headband with a bow wrapped around her head, like she was a pink gift; the other baby was in a white jacket covered in dinosaurs. Both babies looked to be about seven or eight months old, and they squirmed in their mothers' arms. The fathers were holding big flower bouquets. They went up to the receptionist and spoke to them briefly. A few minutes later, my doctor and a doctor I had never seen before appeared. The couples went up to them, shaking their hands and then handing their babies over. The doctors bounced the babies, cooing in their faces, touching their fat cheeks, everyone laughing and smiling. A receptionist took pictures of them standing together: the parents, the doctors, and the babies. And then the parents exchanged the bouquets for their babies, safely ensconcing them, and left.

I wanted to weep with envy and joy. I felt, in that tableau, all the possibilities of what could be—and at the same time, all that I didn't have. *Look how happy they are, how wonderful it is. That could be me someday, bringing my baby to show the doctor.* But also: *Those couples did IVF together because they could. What if I never get to be them?*

Later, when I met with the doctor, the image of her carrying that baby still fresh in my mind, it occurred to me that *she* was Superwoman. She was a hero, a magician, a genie. She made wishes come true. As she explained everything I had to know leading up to the extraction—the final four shots I'd have to administer the next day to trigger ovulation, the process of the extraction itself—immense gratitude washed over me. Even though I had no idea if any of this would lead to a baby someday, she had guided me through it. I thanked her profusely, hoping to convey everything I felt.

The next evening, with two friends by my side, I injected myself with the four trigger shots at exactly the time my doctor had directed me. They were large shots, the most difficult and painful shots of all, filled with so much fluid that I had to take breaks in the middle of pushing them in while a friend massaged my back. When it was over, I almost collapsed in relief. I had gotten through these eleven days, and now the hardest part was over. In two more days, I'd go in for my egg retrieval.

Is it strange that I didn't dream of you the entire time I was going through this process? I had dreamt of you before I started; I would dream of you in the months afterward. But through all the hormone-induced naps I took, you never once made an appearance.

Maybe I was just too tired. Maybe I was too busy, mired in the details of the thing, too busy dealing with symptoms and making sure I did my injections when I needed to and trying to keep myself from collapsing. You were the point of this whole operation, and yet a concrete idea of you, of some future in which you were a real-life person, was something I consciously dwelled on so rarely during those weeks that perhaps it makes sense it wouldn't occur while I was sleeping. Or maybe it was just too much, living with these surges of hope and fear and grief during the day, and my subconscious spared me of stirring it any further at night.

After nearly two weeks of injections and symptoms, the retrieval, in comparison, was over so quickly it was almost anticlimactic. I went in with a friend in the early hours, before the clinic opened, for blood tests and ultrasounds. I filled out some forms and talked to a nurse and was made aware of the risks. I changed into a gown and went into the surgery room and lay on the table, putting my feet in stirrups. I made small talk with the anesthesiologist, a kind man who joked with me and clucked in disapproval at the bruises tracking my arms. He then poked me with an IV needle—which I had been dreading—but I barely felt it. The last thing I remember is a slight metallic taste and the anesthesiologist murmuring something to me.

I awoke, groggy, to the nurses telling me to rest. I lay with my eyes closed for several minutes and then called the nurses. In my hazy state, it felt particularly urgent for me to know all of my doctors' names (including the anesthesiologist). "I want to thank them," I slurred to the nurse. I wouldn't be able to remember the names later. My mouth felt numb, and I wanted to pee, but the nurses insisted I "sober up" for a bit longer. After half an hour or so, they removed gauze from my nether regions—which I didn't even realize was there and could barely feel. After another twenty minutes, they finally let me leave the bed and change into my clothes. They called my friend to wait with me in a different room.

A PA came in and told me they had extracted seventeen

eggs, only two of which were fully mature. A remaining ten were semi-mature, and five were immature. They'd stimulate those to try to coax them into maturing. By the next day, they said, I'd know my final count for freezing. My friend looked at me, worried that I was disappointed, but I was too foggy for the implications of her words to sink in—all I cared about was that it was over and successful and I could go home and sleep.

The PA went over some other details: what to expect (pain, a heavier-than-normal period this month), how to care for myself (prescription painkillers, antibiotics, two thousand milliliters of water a day, non-oily and non-spicy foods), the signs of ovarian hyperstimulation syndrome (low urine output, fever, a swollen and painful abdomen, rapid weight gain), and when to come in for my follow-up (two days later). Then, with my friend's help, I went home.

As I lay on the couch, waiting for my friend to bring me some soup for lunch, my phone rang. It was the clinic. "We were able to stimulate the ten semi-mature ones," the woman on the line told me. "Your final count of eggs is twelve."

Twelve. The minimum number I had told myself I wanted to get, the number that was a line drawn in the sand. A lukewarm relief trickled through me. I thanked her and hung up the phone.

The next few days were rough. When the anesthesia had worn off, I discovered my insides hurt so much that a short walk to the bathroom had me panting and in tears; even painkillers only dulled the edges of the pain. I slept on my couch for three days before I started feeling normal again. But in those days, I also immediately felt a difference as the effects of the hormones receded. I was no longer so exhausted. My emotional state was brighter, less fragile.

At my final clinic visit, the doctor said that while it would take another week for my swollen ovaries to go back down to normal size, all tests indicated I was recovering normally. She green-lit me to get on a plane to leave the country.

All in all, the total cost of the process, including my first year of freezing, was $4,400, with about $2,190 going to medication/hormones, $1,800 for the procedure itself, and everything else toward physician fees, lab tests, and other associated fees. Though it was much less than what it would have cost in America, it was still a good deal of money for me. Maybe I'd need to do another round, but I told myself I'd think about that later, after I'd had time to recover from this one.

For now, I had twelve eggs. And twelve was enough: if not for certainty, then for my peace of mind.

Sometimes I think about the story I'd tell about how you came to be—if, indeed, you end up the product of one of those eggs currently frozen in Hsinchu. You'd probably hear the bits and pieces of all of this, everything I've already written about, from my symptoms to the blood in my underwear to my absurd request for the doctors' names as I woke from surgery.

But I imagine the story I'd most like to tell you is this one, about my final ultrasound. That day, I nervously watched the technician swivel the wand, doing her final count of follicles before I would go in for retrieval. In my right ovary, there were a cluster of jelly bean–shaped follicles, and the technician counted them one by one. She repositioned the wand, and suddenly a large spherical egg came into view, so perfectly round it looked like it belonged in a conception video. It eclipsed all the other eggs in its sheer symmetry and size.

Maybe it was the hormones at their peak, or maybe it was the lingering effects of having seen the IVF babies in the lobby. But in that moment, I felt a surge of pride and affection for that egg. My little overachiever. My little perfectionist, trying so hard to grow up, to get to *be*. *That's it,* I thought. *That's the egg that will be my baby.*

It was as if you were waving to me.

I still have dreams of you, but when I wake, I don't always have that feeling I have no name for. Sometimes I have the opposite feeling, a feeling I had when I woke in the days after my surgery, knowing it was over. It's more than the security of knowing that you are safely tucked away in a drawer somewhere, waiting for me to come back for you one day. It's also recognition. Because I had seen you on that screen, I had known you. You were tangible in that moment, real to me. You weren't a ghost or a figment of my dreams. You were right there in front of me.

The thing is, I don't know who you are, who you'll be. I don't know whose DNA will mingle with mine to create you or what you might look like. I don't know if you'll be the result of one of those eggs I froze or if you'll be conceived from an egg still sitting in my ovaries. I hold on to the belief that whomever you'll be, you'll get to *be*, because I have to keep believing that. And if it turns out the half of me that is you comes from one of those precious eggs, I know I'll always secretly believe that perfect, beautiful egg I glimpsed was the one that made it. Maybe it's silly how much comfort that idea gives me, but it does.

The Small Beauty of Funeral Sex

s. e. smith

For reasons I do not fully understand, every funeral home has a little basket of potpourri in the bathroom, placed there like a time warp straight to the 1980s. You know what I mean. The kind that looks like little pieces of bark, dyed in lurid colors and saturated in artificial scent, the kind that blasts you with the stench of cinnamon sticks and rotting honeysuckle vine left in a car on a hot day, making you question how badly you need to pee. Sometimes, to add insult to injury, there is a single drooping fake lily, stem gilded in dust, in a knobby white vase.

Milk glass, they call it.

It is the potpourri that spills to the floor when I push her back against the counter, one hand on her hip, rooting her to me. Her head is tilted back, and her eyes are dilated, bright with anticipation as the petal shreds crackle underfoot, releasing bursts of Spring-Fresh Scent. I rescue the teetering vase before it falls, too, and when she starts to laugh, I silence her with a hand against her lips, lightly, my thumb rolling over the salt on her cheeks. Her heaving breaths speak of hovering on the edge of emotions too great to be contained, not about me or the vase, and she struggles to find her ground.

"Do you want to . . ."

Her voice is rough with tears and talking, and I let her lead me out of the bathroom, weaving through the crowd of people who have gathered in the hall, lingering, unwilling to let go, to face the reality of leaving the body behind while the rest of us go on living. Her hand is hot in mine, and I will follow her anywhere.

There is a thing that happens with those adjacent to death that many people seem to be afraid to speak of, perhaps because it feels startling and shameful when it happens to them for the first time. Perhaps because no one speaks of it, they assume they are alone in this, perverse, broken. But those of us in the know are well aware that funerals—memorials, celebrations of life, transition ceremonies, Passages (always with a capital *P*)—are absolutely the best places for hooking up. Superior to weddings, better than hot rooftop parties in summer, certainly more than a long night at the end of the bar at a conference. (Remember when we did all those things? The very thought makes the skin sing.) Funeral horniness is real, even if no one will tell you, at least when it comes to white-people funerals, yes, even the ritzy ones, and yes, even the devoutly religious ones. Someone, somewhere in the cathedral has a hard-on during a funeral mass, I guarantee you, and bully for them, I say.

There is something about sex that feels like an unequivocal "fuck you" to death, taking something back from that which has taken something from you, making eros out of

Thanatos and keeping the Grim Reaper at bay. As someone who clocks a lot of funeral hours thanks to the disability community's excellence in death (grand prize at the fair thirty years running), what strikes me about funeral horniness is its immense equalizing power. It strikes across race, class, gender, faith, sexuality, across beliefs about death and dying, death culture; the twenty-three-year-old queer cousin with the eyebrow ring and rainbow hair just as much as the sixty-year-old older brother in the Savile Row suit. It happens at the weeklong party in the desert months after the funeral, in the corridor of the kitchen at Portuguese Hall (you know the one) during the gathering, years later, when you wake gasping, haunted by the smell of lavender soap. Whether it's your mother or your lover or someone else, if it gets you, it gets you, and you should not feel in the least guilty about it.

There are, assuredly, some sex and death psychological reasons for it. Confronted with your own mortality, you seek refuge in something primal and alive. Some people eat their way through funeral-baked meats and others fuck and others both, though likely not at the same time. Some people might want to make it about fertility, but that's garbage; it's about a visceral, vital contact with another human being, a sense of being in them and of them and part of them, and that doesn't have to be about the possibility of making more of you to die and start the cycle all over again.

It is a peculiarly specific kind of fucking that makes it unique, particularly when everyone involved was close to the deceased and is leaving some part of them behind in the grave or at the crematorium, slipping into the deeps or launching into the skies. You can search for that part of you forever and you'll never find it, but for a moment with someone else who has that same feeling of intense loss, you can pretend it isn't gone forever.

Maybe it's a furtive fumbling in the funeral home bathroom, biting your lip on the train home with your partner as you feel something crackling between you, or following someone home from the cemetery, swearing when you can't find parking without a meter and you don't have any quarters, weighing whether you're willing to run the risk of a parking ticket for a trip up a familiar set of stairs that feels oddly off-kilter, now that someone is gone. Maybe it's the small gathering that drifts back to your house, wanting more of each other, not yet willing to say farewell, where people slowly peel off until you are left sitting on the couch together with someone. Maybe it is someone you have orbited for years without knowing, maybe it is an old friend, maybe a stranger who got swept up in the migration. There is something there between you, coiled, patient. You will think that you really should vacuum up all the sand before it gets everywhere, and you will get up, wander into the kitchen, forget whatever it was you meant to do, and they will help you forget everything else.

There is a peculiar sense of concentration that forces the world to fall away, something ritualistic; it is perhaps simply closure, an endpoint to the intense emotion that drives and drives and drives with death, until the official ceremonies are done but you are still left gasping, teetering on a precipice of Nothing Else to Do, food in Tupperware and errant scarves reunited with owners, and the thought of sitting alone in silence with every nerve ending alive is unbearable.

Not everyone gets it, of course, because everybody is different. Every body is different. And bodies come wrapped in their own social and cultural expectations that push them to act, or not, on their feelings. Some people go along with their lives as they are, and others become repulsed by the very idea of sex; sometimes grief comes with trauma that wraps itself around sexuality, perhaps especially for those who lose a partner. "Sexual bereavement," they call it, a loss of a lengthy companionship complicated by a bewildering array of emotions, including a unique sense of loss.

I couldn't tell you when I first experienced that itching, pulling, longing sensation that later I identified as funeral horniness, but I do remember going to the funeral of a family friend in high school, generations milling in closeness at the house later, tables groaning with food as the sound of people playing musical instruments somewhere floated in. Someone lit a fire in the backyard, and it threw off sparks that arced into the growing darkness. The house smelled like old books and gun oil, and I felt like I was crawling out of my skin, unable to settle anywhere, evading well-meaning hugs and jowly faces arranged in expressions of sympathy, not understanding what this sensation was. I filched a beer from the fridge and sat out in the garden, away from the noise, by the fishpond, and tried to remember the last time I had sat there with our old friend, her gnarled fingers opening to release the cheap cat food she fed the fish. I wondered when they'd last been fed, and then someone sat down next to me and I decided it didn't matter very much anymore.

The funeral is for the living, a crowd of people who have this thing—a love for someone who was once alive and now is not—in common. The whole thing is profoundly unjust: we are supposed to live forever, or at least die in thrilling 1940s murder-mystery ways, slumped over our desks in locked rooms, not wheeled out of nursing homes or killed in pointless car accidents. The funeral is their moment to gather the parts of their loved one's life into a whole, one that is often messy and dramatic, saturated with tears and littered in tissues. It is likely the last time this specific group of people will ever get together, and this awareness sparks something troubled in us as we light candles or dig the grave or sit in awkward rows in an antiseptic funeral home while people bumble up and down from a lectern and insipid music plays overhead. It is not just the death of the deceased that has happened to us in this space, but the severing of our connections to one another. Some of these people, we know, we will never see again.

A friend writes of watching her mother buried over livestream, the camera slightly askew as the cemetery workers lower the casket. They never got to see the body, and it took days for the funeral home to wrest her from the custody of one of those long, chilly trailers that had popped up like mushrooms across New York City. There are painful pauses and silences. No one knows how to do this, to have a funeral that is not a funeral, because a funeral is fleshy parts crammed together and rustling skirts and awkward movements, dodging unwanted interactions and eating peculiar, earthy things at the after-party—sorry, the gathering. Small, family only. But these are the funerals we have now: clients banned from funeral homes, barred access to cemeteries and crematoria, bodies whisked away into the darkness, never to be seen again, arrangements made over the phone or through masks on the sidewalk, standing six feet apart, passersby averting their gazes from something that should be taking place in a nice quiet room somewhere *away*, with tasteful music and a box of tissues and an innocuous flower arrangement.

We do not get to prepare our dead anymore. We do not get to dig graves or watch as the cremation container proceeds into the retort. For those who value viewings, a stilted version, corpse propped up in the middle of a video feed, is all that is available. Even drive-by funerals have been nixed as we all hide at home from a virus that has killed over seven hundred thousand people in the United States alone as of September 2021, a tremendous number of funerals that proceed alongside the seventy-seven hundred or so other people who die in this country each day. Funeral rituals and traditions are being shredded. At times there is a strange, wondrous sense of incompletion, that perhaps someone is missing, not truly dead, in the face of all evidence to the contrary. Like children denied access to the funeral because it might scare us, we don't understand: How can she not be coming back anymore?

But that peculiar, tingling feeling, like someone running their fingers lightly across your arm, making the hairs stand up as your back arches—that feeling does not go away. It whispers at the edges of your consciousness when you get the phone call, tugs insistently as you ask about "arrangements," and claws at you in the night as you toss and turn in bed. When you sleep, you will dream of the dead, but when you wake, you will not remember what they said, only stand at the window watching the unseasonal rain, wondering where they are now. When the funeral horniness takes you, you are alone with it, sheltering, at home, at a moment when it is physical intimacy that kills.

But death, an ending, demands a beginning; sex, a beginning, demands an ending.

You will always risk the parking ticket.

The Year of Breath

Gabrielle Bellot

A feeling, I've learned, can live in your body for years, quiet and quiescent, like a sleeping volcano.

It isn't just a memory of the feeling that lingers; it's the thing itself, the sensation and all that surrounds it. We don't always know the feelings that will live in us; sometimes, they are brief and mundane, fleeting as frissons, while others you just somehow *know*, upon encountering them, you will never be able to forget. You may even imagine that you'll never be able to return to the life you had before this sensation, before you felt its wondrous or terrible weight.

But then, as always, life goes on, and the feeling seems to fade. You might think it has left you altogether, like the flecks of dreams you know you had but can't quite grasp, but sometimes that feeling is still there even when it seems it has vanished. It has become an invisible presence in us, a quiet, phantasmal passenger.

Instead of evanescing away, it lingers, lengthens, loops around your edges, grows hard and sharp like old coral. In a way, it is preparing for us to feel it again, only it will be sharper the next time we do. We don't know these old feelings are still there until something forces us, unexpectedly, against their edges again—and then, suddenly, we are amazed we ever thought they had left us.

I remember the feeling of Death's hand.

I am twenty-three feet under the surface of a lake in Pennsylvania, kneeling, blowing bubbles.

It is the summer of social distancing, yet under the surface of this lake, a group of scuba divers is arranged together on brown wooden platforms like a circle of praying monks; the platforms rise from the lake's bottom like great sunken rafts, the only sounds around us the surgical inhalation of air and the gurgling of bubbles, which float back up to the surface like blooms of curious jellyfish. The surface is warm, but down at the platforms, my ears, which poke above my goggles' strap, feel like ice.

We are doing exercises to complete our certification as scuba divers. Ten years earlier, I had been certified in Dominica, but I've become rusty, and so I'm here with my partner, who has never been certified, to refresh my memory. We have driven from Queens to Bethlehem, Pennsylvania, a journey unremarkable except that it is during a pandemic, and we have both already recovered from mild bouts of Covid-19. To scuba dive seems extraordinary now, yet when we reach the lake, there is a refreshing, almost cathartic sense of normalcy, or something like it, minus our masks and distancing on land.

For three days, we practice in the water, ladies of the lake, its reek clinging to our hair and dive boots. I fall behind every-one else, surprised at how much I've forgotten. *Diving is not like riding a bike*, my instructor keeps saying, and though I re-member some things well, the experience now intimidates me a bit. I have dreamt of diving with a hundred hammerhead sharks in the Galápagos, yet the sharkless cyan of this Pennsylvanian water makes me nervous the first time I see it, wondering what is down there now that I am almost a novice again.

And there are things in that murky realm of mysteries. Scuba dive deep enough, and you will find sunken vehicles that seem frozen in a moment: a firetruck encrusted with barnacles, a school bus dotted with gray-green bass and sil-very fish, even a vast helicopter. Down there, in the chill and silt of the lake, it is possible to forget for a few moments, under the mantra of your deep breaths, that there is a twin pandemic, one of a virus and the other of Black Death, not the bubonic plague this time but the systematic eradication of Black and brown bodies like my own by ravenously racist cops. You can even smile, letting the horrors of the outside world fade under the pull of the water.

How beautiful, too, it is to dive in the blue—the best of colors, I've always felt, for blue, to me, contains multitudes like no other: it is calm, balm, solitude, sky-lightness, the vastness of ocean deeps, the alienness of an ice crystal, the peculiar sadness of rainy city nights.

But I'm getting ahead of myself in this memory.

I almost skipped the part when I was sure I was going to die, when a hand held me so I couldn't swim to the sur-face. The part where, months later, I still worry I will spon-taneously stop breathing. Where, even now, I sometimes see *I'm going to die* flash across my mind when I hold my breath, when I kiss, when I push my face too deeply into a pillow. The part when Her blue-fingernailed hand touched my throat, and instead of air I got water.

I have to pause. I can't tell this story yet.

In the famous frame story of *One Thousand and One Nights*, a fanatical king, Shahryar, learns that his wife has slept with another man. Incensed, the monarch decides to punish not simply her, but all women. In one of the most extraordinary examples of toxic masculinity imaginable, he resolves to marry and sleep with a new virgin each night, then behead her the next morning so that she has no chance to be unfaithful to him. After killing a thousand and one women, he finds Scheherazade, who thinks up an ingenious plan to prolong her life: by telling him a story that ends on a cliff-hanger. The king, intrigued, refrains from executing her in order to hear the rest. The next night, she does the same. In this way, Scheherazade keeps herself alive for 1,001 nights, after which point the king decides to spare her life—for she is out of stories—and make her his queen.

I have always liked the idea of turning her name into a verb: *scheherazade*, meaning "to tell stories to survive." Perhaps we last after traumas by telling our stories when, finally, we can. It is a curious feeling, realizing that you are keeping yourself going by turning to other memories and stories first, because you cannot tell one story without first telling the others, and you can only survive if you tell them all.

———

Earlier this year, I watch a video of a white police officer in Minneapolis jam his knee into a Black man's neck, the man's face pressed against the pavement. The cop keeps the terrified man, whose name is George Floyd, there for minutes that feel like the eternity of a horror movie, because I know I am seeing a man's slow execution. *I can't breathe*, he says over and over, but the cop keeps the knee on his neck. *I want to dominate you*, the gesture says. *Do what I say, boy, and die slowly while I watch.*

It leads me to another video. On May 24, 2019, almost exactly a year before Floyd's death, two white police officers grab Breona Hill, a Black trans woman. They punch her savagely in the face, then press their knees into her neck, ribs, and torso. She, too, must be dominated, the men's violence suggests, for this is what so many men seem to believe of women's bodies, all the more so if a white man wants to feel that rush, that sharp-toothed grinning glee, in pressing down a Black body, his knee pushed against her neck like the Fates' shears against the thread of a life. That Breona is trans amplifies this—if too many men wish to control women's bodies, trans women like me are punished with violence, in turn, for not being the "right" kind of woman.

Eight weeks after George Floyd dies, a white policeman in the UK puts his knee into the neck of a Black man. Like Floyd, the restrained man yells that he cannot breathe; only when a crowd with cameras forms does the officer finally remove his leg. Remarkably, this knee-on-neck technique is not one taught by the area's police force, so it was a conscious decision by the officer, as if he had been inspired by Floyd's killer. "I was worried he was going to get executed," an onlooker told the BBC. "That's just how George Floyd got killed. If not for the crowds filming the police, they could have suffocated him or broken his neck." Would this man, too, have lost his breath if a crowd hadn't come?

2020, I've come to learn, is the year of breath. It is our cruel, funereal leitmotif. A respiratory and vascular virus, which has killed over 210,000 Americans, makes breathing harder for those it hits hardest, yet our president callously dismisses its danger; unarmed Black people are choked into homicidal submission by police officers in Britain and America.

As I write this, I become aware, again, of breathing. Normally, we don't feel ourselves breathe; it is one of our body's nonconscious functions, like the beating of our heart, that occurs without our conscious attention. Yet this year, I keep trying to feel my lungs expanding and contracting, just to make sure they still are. There is something soothing, like the indigo of a fading day, in that reminder.

I think I first felt it ten years ago, scuba diving thirty feet under the lapis lazuli surface of a patch of Caribbean Sea in Dominica. By this point, I had fallen in love with scuba diving, with being swaddled by the blue, with the crowds of corals colorful as crotons, even with the slow, constant breaths that reminded me, vaguely, of Darth Vader. Until then, I had never had anything go wrong on a dive.

Suddenly, I felt like I couldn't breathe. I tried to inhale through my regulator; nothing happened. I looked at the surface, a sun-dappled thing thirty feet away, and tried again.

Nothing. My dive buddy, who could have offered me his air, was a black shape far off in the blue—a mistake on both our parts, because you should always be near another diver, just to be safe.

I panicked. *I can die*, I remember thinking. It's a cardinal rule of scuba diving: *Don't hold your breath*. Another is to avoid rushing to the surface in a panic if something goes wrong. If you hold your breath and shoot to the surface, you can fatally injure your lungs; to ascend in an emergency, you need to continuously exhale. I braced myself, then kicked up to the surface, letting out a long *ahhhh* like some Amazon of the mermaids with the little breath I thought I had left.

At the surface, which now seemed choppy, I had someone check my gear. Bemused, they said everything looked fine. I felt strange, more flummoxed than flustered. Why couldn't I inhale in that moment? Had something malfunctioned, or had I inexplicably invented the issue in my mind? Would I even know the difference, really, if I couldn't breathe?

I decided to retry the dive, and this time, it was fine. I tried to forget that curious feeling, that fleeting frenzy of death-panic, when I had suddenly become aware I could stop breathing, and tried to focus, instead, on how remarkable it was that a human could ascend on a single breath.

A single breath may seem short at first, but it can be extended, I've learned, until that one inhalation can be held for amounts of time that boggle the mind, and you begin to realize, as Blake said of a grain of sand, that there is a universe in a single breath; and on that note, I am watching a

YouTube clip of William Winram, a record-setting Canadian free diver, the folks who cruise through reefs and wrecks for minutes at a time, all on a single, expansive breath without any breathing apparatuses; they mesmerize me, these thalassic thaumaturges, but Winram seems particularly extraordinary, for on a single breath this man clutches a platform and then hurtles down into the depths like a passenger on some infernal elevator hair lips cheeks flapping furiously all the way 145 meters down to the edge of the deep sea where it is always night and where the vast squids of legend wait and then he is hauled back up face pinched up like a caricature caught in a storm with little indication he is still alive but for the fact that he has not let go of the platform and then he begins to slowly swim back to the surface and breaches, sputtering but grinning, all on a single, unpunctuated, impossible-seeming breath, and that, to me, is as absurd as it is awe-inspiring, a human shot down to the realms of the sea we shouldn't be able to survive in; and yet here he is, back again, for breath, it turns out, is the vehicle that carries us, and it is, indeed, more durable than most actual cars, at least until we become aware that we have stopped breathing, and then it becomes an inexpressible marvel, like a blue glacier in the Caribbean, that we have ever breathed at all.

In Pennsylvania, I am trying to do a routine exercise I have done many times before. To dive, you inhale through your regulator, a mouthpiece attached to a tube that connects to your tank. Normally, you want to keep your regulator in your mouth, but if it gets knocked out for some reason, you need to be able to recover it underwater and put it back in. While the regulator is floating beside you, you exhale a stream of bubbles until the regulator is back in. You also take your regulator out to practice buddy breathing, where you rely on the secondary regulator that all divers have for emergencies because your own has malfunctioned or you're out of air. The exercise is notable because you can die if you make a serious mistake.

I'm already nervous this morning. The water feels too cold. The air in my throat is dry. I imagine tumbling underwater over the edge of the wooden platform. I've forgotten the love I had for diving; it has become something that intimidates me.

I fail to get the regulator back in. My exhale has been too rapid; I already feel out of air. I try to get it in again and fail. I swallow water and panic.

Suddenly, I realize where I am. I am over twenty feet down with no air coming in. My lizard brain takes over. *I might die*, I remember thinking, and then in a frenzy I go against every rule of diving and rush toward the surface, writhing, flailing, eyes wide like a rabid raccoon, for I have become nothing but an impulse to survive.

Something arrests my motion. I'm reaching for the surface but can't get there, can't go up at all. I'm clawing at the water like I want to rip it, reaching for the light above, the light that is at the end of this tunnel I cannot reach because I cannot go up, and I have no air but am still clawing, clawing, and then suddenly I can move again, and in a burst of energy I breach the surface. The sky feels too bright. I cough and taste blood. But I've made it. There is breath, there is breath.

My divemaster, who has surfaced beside me—it was his hand holding me down, I learn later, because he was trying to offer me his regulator rather than letting me rush upward, and in my feverish rush I had not even seen him—is calm-voiced, but I can sense his unease. What I did, after all, could kill me if I got water in my lungs. After getting me to shore and having a nurse check my vitals—my heartbeat is "very fast," she says—he sends me to the hospital with my partner to have my lungs X-rayed.

My body, fortunately, is okay. I swallowed rather than inhaled water, and I apparently escaped serious damage to my lungs by having exhaled before my ascent. I try to smile for the rest of the day, but I cannot get the feeling of believing I was going to die out of my mind. For a week, it keeps coming back to me. I imagine letting my regulator out of my mouth and then start shaking. I wonder if there is water in my lungs the doctors missed. One night, I cannot sleep because I keep being haunted by this ghost of the water: me, flailing, swallowing water, believing I could not make it to the surface.

For years, I've admired Neil Gaiman's personification of Death in his *Sandman* graphic novels: a kind, smiling Goth girl who can be terrifying in the rare moments she needs to be but is usually gentle and compassionate as she leads people to "the sunless lands" of lifelessness. She wears a signature ankh, the symbol of life, around her neck, and takes on human form one day a year to feel what it's like to be alive; she may be Death, but she has an endearing interest in trying to understand the living. Unlike the often-masculine images of the Grim Reaper, Gaiman's portrayal of Death is not some generic skeleton with a scythe; she feels, instead, like a true embodiment of the complexities of dying.

My own version of Death in my fiction, a girl with blue corkscrew curls who sometimes rides a pink Vespa, also smiles when she appears to others; she came to me in a daydream a decade ago, and I have always loved writing about her. Yet the week after the incident in the lake, I feel on edge to invoke her, or any personification of the same; all I see when I think of Death is my whirling arms, my manic fear. Blue, once my love, unsettles me, like the whiteness of Ahab's whale.

It is that *feeling*, that death-frenzy, that haunts me the most.

I realize, now, I felt it all those years ago in the Caribbean, when I thought I also might die, but it was muted. Now, the feeling is wild, vast, loud as the mind of an insomniac. I hate it, but it won't let me go.

After this, I think more often of images of white policemen suffocating bodies like my own. I think of people my age who thought they were invincible, suddenly hospitalized because the coronavirus gave them a stroke or worse. Once, I kiss my partner and feel, suddenly, like I cannot breathe and am returned, alarmingly, to the thrashing feeling of airlessness in the lake.

It is too much. I feel like a sinking thing. I have suffered from depression and suicidal ideation before; the twin pandemics and my near-death experience bring it back in bursts.

I often think and even hear in colors. America, for me, is usually a mélange, but in the immediate aftermath of the lake incident, America seems a sad, dissonant blue, the shade of a policeman's uniform, a blue even I recoil from.

Can you be betrayed by a color?

I imagine another story, where I am a witch. I imagine being faced with a cop who has decided I am his target, a brown girl to harass, harm, hurt, and I will transfigure him through the grimoire of my anger, yet were I Circe I would not even be able to turn him into a pig because he already too closely matches the part, and I realize that, at the end of the day, the witchcraft I want most to wield is the quiet magic of passing by unobserved, unfollowed, unhunted, because to be a trans girl of color in this asphyxiating America is to always know you may be in danger, no matter how mundane the setting, be it from cop or civilian, and though I abhor that all-encompassing uncertainty I must live under, this, above all, seems to be the story I cannot escape.

There is a curious grief in feeling you've lost a color—or perhaps not curious, really, because the colors that resonate deepest in us are almost like loved ones.

In the end, though, blue comes back to me. As depressed as I have been, I still want to love the color's Whitmanian multitudes again, want to dive through it once more. I am a thalassophile, a lover of the sea; I have dived through the sky's azure three times, walked on the ancient whiteblue of a glacier, and now I want to be swaddled, again, by the water's shades. Blue is too beautiful to keep me away, even as it has become braided to pain.

Two weeks after the incident, I return to the lake to redo my dives, so I can finally confront my fears, so I can dive again and feel the ultramarine peace it used to provide.

At first, on those platforms again, I cannot do the regulator exercise. My divemaster understands. He takes me to see one of the sunken vehicles, flecked with flickering fish, then to a shallower place to practice the exercise once more. His pedagogy has worked: I'm calmer, now, both by the joy of seeing the underwater monument and by being in a different spot from where the death-frenzy grabbed me. I complete the exercise multiple times, and do it again on my next dive, which takes us the deepest we've yet been to see another sunken beauty. It is freezing forty feet down, a far cry from the heat of July, but I'm smiling like someone in love.

Being down there, again, feels like a kind of simple, natural mysticism, a kind of meditation by being in the blue. It is that simple spell I've sought.

I've finally begun to reclaim diving and learned to respect my place in the water anew. I've learned, too, to calm myself in the blue. The death-frenzy is still in me, but it's quieter, and I accept it, like a shadow. It is a feeling I won't let myself forget because it has become a part of me; acknowledging it makes me a better, more cautious diver, and trying to overcome its grip has helped me appreciate the beauty of the blue even more, the beauty of figuring out how this story goes.

Before we surface, I think of the world beyond the lake. So often, I've lived in fear as a trans woman of color of being misgendered, ostracized, arrested, attacked. This entire year, moreover, is a sepulchral feeling I will not forget, where Death seems to be working overtime. It is a story none of us, least of all those of us who are Black and brown, can escape. This viral pandemic will end, to be sure, but the other pandemic, the one targeting nonwhite bodies, has no ending in sight.

But in the water, I feel free, for a bit. It is salvific. The water accepts us all. I smile before we ascend, grateful for such small moments of brief, sacred peace—and that is the new feeling I know I will remember, and cling to, out of the water.

Papi Chulo Philosophics

Marcos Gonsalez

Sidewalk strutting down barrio catwalks, like so many sum-
mers, in Loisaida and East Harlem and now in Washington
Heights, this short-short-wearing hustler that I am.

I give them body exposé and they love to hate me. I, freely
unfree, sashaying down concrete runways, their bold nega-
tion. Give them something to talk about: like the thigh-high
swag in my step, the chunks of my body bouncing to step, the
shoulders swaying in sharp angularity. This skin, darling, all
this skin. Who cares what they think? Not me, girl, though
I do occasionally have to worry of what they might do, how
they might respond to my strutting with a fist to the jaw, a
boot to the groin, a knife to th—

From across the street, "Oooooo, que papiii chuloooooo."

Who said that? There's a crowd of them, boys and men,
men still boys, boys not yet men. A passing car with windows rolled down, the neighborhood boys blasting beats on
their way to someone's mama's house.

Which one of them said it?

Keep strutting, don't stop, who knows what they might do. Don't look back, though you want to, though they wish you would, all of us hoping against hope the other will initiate our us, our being barrio boys, our momentary being.

The midday light against skinny musculature. Wide jawline converging to a chiseled point. Full set of teeth, the broadest smile. The torso and the hips and the groin a triangular continuity. Wanting to touch all his geometry.

What's his name? He told me somewhere in our initial messages, but I forgot. But can you forget what you really don't care to remember to begin with?

J, the name started with a J, so Jesus or José or Juan. One of those. I know what needs to be known of him: his body, the photographic parceling of chest, face, dick, legs, ass, that he sent me; tell me what that tongue can do, I ask him, and he responds in detail, poetic prose of the body; a video sent giving motion to the body in gravity, its rotations, its gyrations, its penetrations; my descriptions in text of what I will do to him, how I want to do it, how I need him to be when my body is on his, in his, indistinguishable from his.

Call me shallow, girl, but I like it how I like it.

He's here in the flesh, however, no longer a textual and visual erotic.

I have to reach out to touch him.

"You're so sexy," he says, still a few feet away, timid in the daylight darkness.

Who's this boy before me? This boy who poses as a man on the street. A big and bad drug dealer, the wideness of walk as if masculine swagger were embedded into the marrow of his bones, his cruel, masculine indifference.

"You, too." I put my body in a more inviting pose.

He stands there looking. What is he thinking? Man of so few words when in person but of so many through text message. I think he is thinking on this distance between us. The inches from his body to mine, the differences of our body proportions, my mass in contrast. He knows if he walks across the room and lands on the bed, it's all over for him. We will be, and there's no going back.

Their world happens on the corner of the block. Where my Jesus or José or Juan hangs out. The corner housed in scaffolding, scaffolding that will never go down because this neighborhood is not priority, because there is no fixing what never intended to be fixed in the first place.

The corner that houses a Dominican restaurant and a tenement building, where people struggle to make ends meet, struggling against the ever-increasing rents, struggling to remain in the neighborhood they fought to live in.

The corner where a subway stop is not too far, this stop that more and more every day sees the likes of nice white families going to and from work, their bags of downtown groceries from big corporate entities imported in, their over-eager hands ready and willing to call the police.

The corner of the block I pass by to get home to my apartment, to go to the bakery, to go to the park, to go and buy a pastelito or churro from the street vendor, to go down these streets for some fresh air on a long day, to walk down and feel nostalgic by the scents and smells and sights and tastes and touches of a family I left behind.

Their world is this corner of the block. As few as two of them, as many as fifteen. Some looking real young, seventeen or eighteen, and others looking much older, thirty-five or forty. They cluster, they congregate, they disperse: some sit on the metal bars of the scaffolding, others lean against the tanned bricks of the building, some bring out lawn chairs on fair-weather days, some even edge dangerously close to one another, shoulder to shoulder, mouth to mouth, man to man.

What do they talk about for all those hours? The boxing matches? Baby mama drama? Their abuelita who's sick in the hospital? It's an open secret of what they do there on the corner of the block. The cops don't bother them too much because the nice young white folks moving into the neighborhood need their pleasures. Just the occasional shakedown by the police, the being put against a wall and grabbed by their hands, the slamming to the curb's edge, held at gunpoint.

Not as bad as it used to be, my *vieja* neighbor reminds me, not as bad as it used to be.

This corner of the block, this end point where avenue meets street, where the busyness of Broadway begins and ends, is their world. Theirs for now.

Lounging in bed, wisps of smoke curling upward from between his clenched teeth, he's philosophizing. Using lots of hand gestures, double negatives, and rhetorical questions. He's giving thorough rationales on why white guys tend to like extreme kinks, well-thought-out hypotheses as to why we have not yet come in contact with beings from a different universe, and so many other thoughts on this or that subject.

He's more used to me now, so he's showing me the intellect so few think a man like him would have. He, nothing but a drug dealer, they think. He, nothing but a criminal, they want to believe.

After some time philosophizing, there's silence. Pigeons cooing on the fire escape, a woman speaking Caribbean Spanish in the next apartment, car horns in the distance, us together there on our sides of the bed.

Eventually, he breaks the silence by saying, "I have a girl . . ."

"Oh . . ."

"We're not too serious, though," he says, all papi chulo matter-of-fact.

She, whoever she is, doesn't know he likes his thick boys, boys in general, I suppose. She does not know him like I know him.

"I like fucking with dudes. But I won't ever love one, ya know? I can't ever be in love with a man . . ."

But who, chulo *lindo*, is asking you to love? He imagines queerness in relation to love, a romantically inclined one. To have to love, a commitment, to have to live out the white picket fence, the dogs, the children. But let us take love out of the equation. What is this between us? The text message erotics. The riding and the sucking and the eating out. The passing glance on the street. Does this have to be identified with a noun? Does this have to be named?

"I like you, I like this. What we have, how we have it."

It's rather cute, even poetic, how he tiptoes around

meaning, how he refuses meaning, to have to mean defini-
tively. He, this boy and this man, who has run these streets
for decades, this moment on 191st and then next on Dyck-
man, going and going in his day by day.

What does one make of a man who refuses to be cap-
tured by meaning? Him in the bed, lounging naked before
me for this moment, the features of his body darkening as
daylight recedes, the sharpening of the pelvic and torso lines,
the curve of the phallus a hard and then soft horizon, our not
needing naming, our just needing to be.

It could have been me. What a selfish thought. Selfishly re-
curring as it has done for so many years of my life. I could
have been a drug dealer, in a gang, in and out of the system,
like my cousins, my uncles, all those countless relatives who
have been in and out of prison.

But I didn't. I finished high school, learned to talk real
nice like a white boy, went to college away from my relatives,
and am now about to be a doctor of philosophy. I'm *it*, darling. What the ancestors prayed for.

Except a bit too queer, a bit too mentally unwell.

What the ancestors could never have imagined.

I'm so glad you did things right, my mother likes to remind me when we hear of a new incarceration, a new "ille-
gal" trade picked up by one of my cousins.

When she does this pedestaling, she puts me against my
cousins who sell drugs to get by, my undocumented father
who has worked the farms across the Americas since he was

six, her very self. All the criminals we have been through the centuries, all the lives lost to made-up criminality.

She puts me against them, and I try to explain this to her. These linkages between racialization and incarceration and generational poverty and criminality, but to do that is to flaunt the white-boy English I learned in school. To use my very expensive education, my thousands upon thousands of dollars of debt, against her, against my father, against my cousins, against those like me.

"You think you're so smart, don't you, because you went to school?" she says to me, out of anger, out of all the opportunities she did not have.

I don't know how to explain myself. The things I have read about, my own experience of the world in relation to the ideas I have learned. I am an anomaly. A college-educated MexiRican, queer as all hell, living with my boyfriend, using words they don't know, wanting to be a writer, an artist.

I am not meant to be because those like me, like them, are not meant to be such things, to be a writer, to be a thinker, to imagine other worlds besides this one, just not meant to be but instead meant to be dead, or dying, or somewhere in between, or something not at all.

Walking out of the subway ahead of me is someone like me: a flare to the walk, an attitude in the step; the tight pants, the spunky coat; the queerness in exuberance, atmospheric.

Nearing the corner of the block, where they are, one of the group members at the farthest edge looks at the approaching exuberance. I know that look. I have felt it. The stare, *that* stare. Where the eye has seen in its line of vision an aberrance, a deviation from the spatial regularity, an interest piqued with hostility.

This exuberance of a body nears the one on the edge, and, unexpectedly, against the narrative I thought would unfold, they clasp hands.

"Yoooo, wassup? Long time no see."

"I know, right? How you been, chulo?"

Cordial. Longtime friends? No hostility in sight. Out of place yet in place, not belonging though belonging, this person like me goes from body to body, hand to hand, chest to chest. Each enthusiastically saying hi, how you been, where you going?

How do they know one another? Did they share a childhood? Riding bikes near this corner of the block, kicking empty cans against the parked cars, shouting through tenement alleyways. Each has taken a path no one wanted for them.

Them, these street corner occupiers, peddling euphoria in dime bags. My fellow exuberance, strutting down barrio streets, pants a little too tight, feminine swagger in the walk, the posture, the look of the eyes. Who are we if not kin through our deviations? Street hustler and femme queen, macho and *maricóncito*, variations on a chulo aesthetic.

Little old me, still walking, wallpaper in stride, getting ready to pass them by—what of it?

Flowers and stuffed animals against the tenement wall near the corner of the block. In the center of this mass of plant and cushion is a picture. It's of a man. Well, a boy who has been a man for not too long. He's standing upright, slouched a little, to the side. Do-rag on his head, a sly smirk on his face, hoodie and sweatpants. *R.I.P.* in large, black, cursive-like typeface rests at the bottom of the picture.

When did he lose his life? For how long did he live, if he ever lived? Someone says it happened over a drug deal. Another says it was over a girl. All agree: it was a drive-by shooting. He was on the sidewalk, hanging out, philosophizing on the most importantly inconsequential matters.

After knowing this bit of information, I swear I heard the gunshots while in my apartment. That sonic breaking, that obliteration of air. I didn't know that at that moment skin and tissue and organ was being punctured, a body extinguishing. I thought it was merely a truck door banging shut, something falling from the sixth floor and crashing upon impact.

But it was, and it is, and it will be again, whether here in Washington Heights, or in the Bronx, or in Queens, or at the border between the United States and Mexico, Mexico and Guatemala, or in a little campo in the Dominican Republic or Honduras or Puerto Rico or El Salvador. Somewhere, someplace else, a gunshot is going off, and a life never lived is dying and is already dead.

He looks a little alike to my Jesus or José or Juan, my drug dealer papi chulo. They share that look in their eyes and smirking lips. As if they know the secrets to the universe, as if they and they alone can know anything at all. Will my Jesus or José or Juan be here next? Will his lean musculature be reduced to a flattened pictorial plane? Will he die before he has ever lived?

My family did such a memorial for my brother when he died. His picture surrounded by flowers, a teddy bear, a cross, a Puerto Rican flag. He, too, wearing a do-rag, sweatpants, and a hoodie on his large body filling up the frames of the picture. Not gunned down like this nameless sidewalk hustler, but destroyed by a drunk driver. Not a bullet that entered the body, but the body compacted into half its size. A different kind of violence. The memorial is cared for by my family for a little bit of time, but the living keep living, and, like those that live, lay claim to being alive, their attention goes elsewhere, they find new interests, they move on, they forget.

And, one day—what feels like a Monday, or I want to recall it being a Monday—the flowers and the stuffed animals and the picture are gone. The days and weeks passing it by, slowing my speeding brain down, all over. Just like that. As if it were not enough time, as if he were barely there, as if I, a stranger to this dead man, nobody to this sidewalk ghost, did not mourn enough. As if we were never an encounter between the living and the dying.

He's there on the corner of the block. Jesus or José or Juan, whichever name he gave me, doesn't matter because I to him am just a pseudonym, too, just the loaded adjectives through text and the orgasmic glossolalia, the lounging on the couch or the fucking on the bed, these unreal things.

Does he think of my form when he's with his boys there on the corner of the block? This femme and fat body as something fantastical, vivid, and alive as he goes about his day through city streets, this sheer barrio ordinariness?

That night, Jesus or José or Juan, whatever name he is in real life, if there is even a real life for men like him, texts me. *I saw you*, he says. *Oh, nice*, I say, disinterested.

Then, in his style, his adjectival excess, his up-front erotics, he writes of how he misses my body. The way my body moves. The way he does things to my body. The way my body is. His textual seduction, the thought of him, his sparse prosody, his syntactical penetration—I jerk off to it.

He asks me if I am free. He wants to see me in the flesh, in real life. I say I'm busy, though that's a lie. I'm just here in bed, in darkness, with phone in hand. I don't want to see him. I'm tired, I want my solitude. I want his words, I want his writing. There as unreal flesh, an erotic fabulation, a wild imagining, where I have him as I want him, at my pace, at my calling, at an emotional distance.

These glances on the street, the pictures and videos of dick and ass, the eyes and the smile in close proximity, the what we want to do to one another consolidated into the written form, our worded exchange. More real to me is his writing, more permanent than this papi chulo, this man who wanders the streets indefinitely, this boy who might be gone tomorrow, this disappearing act in the flesh.

So I place him within a structure of my devising. Walled in by language, limited by syntax, where he cannot get close to me, where he cannot entertain the idea of proximity to me, where we are nothing more than this intimate distance, these texts every now and then, little more and nothing less than this language.

This them and I. Them, hanging on the corner of the block, these pants-sagging Adonises. Them, in the bedroom, their silhouettes nude and opaque. I somewhere in between, the null and void body. We who are always on the horizon. Untouchable, though solid, the unreal proportions, reaching toward an elsewhere, an elsewhere not having to be like this one.

What are they? The child riding their bike through barrio streets shouting liberation. The teenager break-dancing on the subway, limber and wild. The boys and the men hanging out on the corner of the block philosophizing on the matters of the universe. They who were me and are me and might be me and never will be me. Him and me, they and us, our text messages proving yes we are, whatever this being us even is.

Little Pink Feet
Maggie Tokuda-Hall

I'm not a likely candidate for a baking hobby. I can't eat gluten. I'm married to a type 1 diabetic. In my culinary life, I have come to disregard recipes for being too bossy. So when I picked up baking, it didn't just feel sudden; it felt random. Stolen, maybe, from a better woman, a woman with no dishes in her sink.

First, it was a chocolate cake. It was pretty, but too simple. Then came the macarons. Hundreds of them. Pale pastel treats topped with edible gold leaf or glitter, beautiful and intricate. A worthy technical challenge to cut my teeth on. Too hard for most people, but not too hard for me.

They're temperamental. That's what every recipe says. They crack, collapse, are prone to fail. Search results are dense with guides for troubleshooting your macaronage. I loved making them immediately.

Later, I'd realize the timing of this new obsession was no coincidence.

The first time I made macarons was shortly after a miscarriage. The macarons failed. I'd folded the batter far too many times, added too much rosewater, too much dye. They tasted like soap. They emerged from the oven shriveled and flat. No "feet," as the ruffles at the bottom edge of the shells are called, a result gleaned from proper baking. I scraped the delicate pink remains into the trash. I was undaunted.

We started fertility treatment in the summer of 2018. Tests made it clear my husband and I would not get pregnant naturally. Ever. I wasn't surprised by the news. There were no obvious clues; it was just something I *knew*, the same way I knew I was in love, or that a recipe called for too much salt. What my mother calls "women's intuition."

I didn't go into treatment with any misgivings. The fertility center we chose boasted special care for women of color, glowing Yelp reviews, and a doctor educated at both Harvard *and* Yale. It did not occur to me to enter this arrangement with my antennae up—and even now, if that feels naïve, it doesn't feel foolish. We should be able to trust professionals with the care of our bodies.

"Pregnancy is going to be hard for you," the doctor told me. A signal that I was being too precious, too fussy. A gentle rebuke. I mistook it for candor.

It was the beginning of a process wrought with lies by omission, choices made on my behalf but not in my best interest. My chief concern that day, the day of our first consultation, was *all* the medication. It was a lot. But we plowed ahead anyway. Sure, this would be hard. All pregnancies are hard. That was okay, I told myself. I can handle hard.

I took a long and extreme list of medications leading up

to the surgery in which my eggs would be extracted. For the entire week leading into the procedure, I was in so much pain—like menstrual cramps, but more insistent, sharper—that my life was suddenly limited. No coffee, no sex, no alcohol, no exercise. No sudden movements. These were the rules. I was constantly nauseated, forever teetering on the edge of vomit.

"Is this normal?" I would ask.

"All bodies are different," the doctor would tell me.

The subtext was: something is wrong with yours.

Later, another doctor would name what happened to me: ovarian hyperstimulation syndrome. An injury caused by overmedication. My ovaries had been pushed into such artificial productivity that they could not bear the weight of their own fruit. My surgery date was bumped up because I was growing so many eggs. I was deeply uncomfortable, but I could handle that. I could handle that for a baby.

Macarons are essentially a French meringue with almond flour and powdered sugar folded into them. Their reputation is that they're difficult, but I'd argue they just require extra attention. Get to know your oven; learn if it runs hot. Fewer folds of your macaronage are better, but too few and they'll be misshapen. Don't bake on an especially humid day if you can help it.

Macarons are not hard, so much as they're particular.

No one has been more pleased by my new hobby than my friends. They reap the benefits of my obsession, eyes closed as they chew, as if they have to ward away all else in order

to fully reckon with such indulgence. This is the chief delight in baking macarons: the sharing. Pass the plate around,
bear witness to joy. All that hard work—piping, filling,
decorating—is worth it in an instant.

I felt it as soon as the medications wore off. Pain so acute,
it pushed a moan from my throat. I'd been sitting on our
couch when I realized that I needed to get to bed, I needed to
get into the bed that fucking instant, or I'd never get there;
the pain would only get worse, and I would be stuck, and
there would be no respite. My husband was out walking the
dog. I staggered down the short hallway alone, moaning and
weeping, my hand dragging along the wall for support, until
I finally reached the bed.

We called the doctor. "More meds," he said. I took them.

When I was seventeen, I had a spinal tap. I didn't cry.
When I was sixteen, a car accident left me in a neck brace
for three weeks, and when I cried it was from shock, not
pain. In my college softball career, when I took an unexpected line drive directly to my face, I didn't cry—I laughed,
which I'm told is a common reaction to the concussion I'd
just sustained.

So when I say that the pain only got worse, when I say it
is the only time I've wept solely from pain, when I say it was
the worst pain of my life, I mean it. It was ovarian torsion—
which is when the ovary twists, cutting off blood flow from
the body. I was put on an IV drip of painkillers again, just to
manage. I was bedridden for two full weeks.

"Is this normal?" my husband asked.

"Some women just handle pain differently," the nurse replied.

That subtext again—*it isn't hard for everyone; it is just hard for me.* The problem was not the treatment; the problem was that I was weak.

My resentment was as precise as any recipe.

Macarons require order. They create pleasure. They are delicate and lovely, like a baby's toes. I can take the care with them that was not taken with my body.

The months of attempts with that doctor left my body raw and aching. It felt as though I had been evicted from my own body and that it had been trashed in my absence.

That feeling of being violated in absentia wasn't new to me. It brought me back to years earlier, in my bed, the morning after being sexually assaulted. I'd woken up with the kind of pounding hangover one expects after drinking to the point of sickness. What I didn't expect was to see him. A trusted friend, but not a chosen sexual partner. He told me we'd hooked up, that he'd seen "everything I had to offer."

I went to the bathroom after he left and found drops of the thin red blood of injury on the tissue. My body had been trashed, and I hadn't even been there while it happened.

I wish I could say that I put a stop to the treatment I was receiving from that doctor, but it wasn't me who raised the flag. It was my husband. He demanded we get a second opinion.

Doctors are reluctant to critique one another. At first, she assumed we remembered things incorrectly. But my husband is a thorough notetaker. And slowly, over the course of the phone call, it became clear that all of this had been unnecessary. Because the fertility issues lie with my husband's body and not mine, medicating me at all had been a choice made to ease scheduling for the doctor's office. It did more to hinder our chances than improve them. But having tightly scheduled cycles allows for more patients. And more patients means more money.

It was terrible. And worst of all, it didn't need to be. My trust had been betrayed, again. All that suffering was for nothing.

Medical mistreatment around fertility is undoubtedly more common than we realize, just as sexual assault is more common than many believe. We trust doctors, just as we trust men—historically, the people with authority. We trust that it is worth it.

"I couldn't make a baby, so I made macarons" is too simple. "I was raped, so I made macarons" is also reduction to the point of absurdity.

But with no precious, tiny shoes to buy, no birth announcements to send, no baby bump to show, I post endless pictures of these confections, delicate and precise.

That I would be drawn to macarons and baking, with all its ladylike connotations, makes sense to me in a way. My body cannot seem to achieve its sole feminine purpose, but I can master this specifically femme art. It's a gentle hobby, interwoven with a dedication to aesthetic, to details that lend beauty. It is done with the express purpose of bringing others happiness, a gesture devoid of self, the ultimate maternal posture. Maybe I fancied that I was offering something precious to a child who was never born.

The best pain, we're told, is the pain that creates something beautiful. Pearls and cherry blossoms. Childbirth.

So what is there to do in the wake of pain that makes nothing? There was no result from my treatment, no baby with delicate toes and slowly blinking eyes. There is no bright side to rape. There is only me, and a recipe that can be endlessly iterated. Me, and the beauty I can control.

Counting to Ten Without Numbers
Sarah McEachern

I'm bad at math. Important numbers like my zip code, my Social Security number, and my cell phone number fall in and then out of my mind. I have a learning disability called dyscalculia, which makes numbers slippery for me and never truly knowable. I explain this a lot as "number dyslexia," except dyslexia is the difficulty of connecting a sound to a symbol (like a letter). Dyscalculia, to be specific, is the inability to connect values and meanings to symbols (like a number).

When I look at the number three, it's just a squiggly line at first, until I remember that it's supposed to mean the *amount* of three. Most people don't hear the number; they hear instead the value the number represents. It's in this act of translation where I get stuck.

I started giving numbers personalities when I was tasked with learning the multiplication table in third grade. After struggling with subtraction and addition, multiplication felt next to impossible, since its fluency relied almost entirely on remembering the multiplication factors of each number. I had trouble just recalling the numbers themselves, so I began to shape them into fully fledged people to get a better grasp.

One, naturally, emerged first. He's pretty much a non-person for a number with a personality, because coming in contact with One in a multiplication problem will not alter another number. One's boring. He makes a sandwich before bed, and then eats the sandwich at work the next day. One eats an apple every day to keep the doctor away. One enjoys armchair detective novels. And puzzles.

When I lived in Paris as an exchange student, I spoke French everywhere: at dinner with my host mom, in every restaurant, at the grocery store, the library, the pharmacy, in every class. I sank into a world of not knowing the meaning behind words. But as I became speedier at French, I still lagged behind when it came to connecting numbers to their meaning—the same as in English.

French numbers are particularly hard to learn. Eighty is literally translated into "four-twenty" while ninety is "four-twenties-ten." Ninety-nine is the worst: "four-twenty-nineteen." Numbers are already a challenge when learning French, along with gendered words and all the different articles. Very soon, though, it became clear that I wasn't learning French numbers, while I was becoming more fluent with pronouns, adverbs, nouns, and adjectives.

When I turned twenty-one, my host mother had bought birthday candles for a twentieth birthday, because I had told her the wrong number when she asked the week before. As

I blew out my candles, I knew something wasn't right about numbers in any language. I knew something was abnormally off in my brain.

Two is kind, peaceful, and reliable. When Two is in the room, everyone suddenly gets along. If you swore in front of Two, you'd slap your hand right over your mouth, although Two would only smile and make no comment. Two has read every Shakespeare play. Two always sorts his recycling. All numbers that interact with Two come out the other side with a 2, 4, 6, 8, or 0 on the end. Two is predictable like that.

I paid more than $500 to confirm my problems with math were caused by a learning disability. My insurance covered testing for some learning disabilities like dyslexia, but not dyscalculia, which has much less social awareness even though the two occur proportionally. Some estimate that nearly 20 percent of the population are dyscalculics.

I expected my parents to pay for the testing since our agreement was they would cover any medical expenses while I was a student. Asking for the money made me feel like the diagnosis was a luxury.

My parents had to cut corners to come up with the money, and they wanted to know why it was suddenly now, in my last year of college, that I needed a formal diagnosis, when I was already sure I knew what was happening. What would an expensive piece of paper signed by a doctor change?

I wanted confirmation of what was going on, to know for sure if my brain was flawed. But voicing this aloud, even to my parents, was too difficult. I was acknowledging that something was wrong with me. It felt like failure.

I didn't want to talk about it anymore, so I fronted the money with the expectation that I would be the only one paying for it. Since I had paid my tuition bill the week before, it emptied my bank account, leaving me with thirty dollars to my name.

I was tested alone. My friends and my boyfriend didn't remember that I was being tested, and I was annoyed at not receiving supportive text messages, as if I had expected everyone to set reminders months in advance. When the neurologist asked me if I felt supported by my friends and family, I lied and said yes.

In the end, my parents did pay for the test a few months later. They had realized how badly I needed it confirmed after I had gone ahead and paid for it myself. I emailed them my test scores and my neurologist's assessment of my math difficulties. I don't think they knew how bad my problems with math were until they saw it spelled out.

Three doesn't shave her armpits, has attended many political protests, and once punched someone in the face in a bar. Although she has good intentions and righteous reasons, Three stirs up a lot of angst among the numbers. Everyone has been cross with Three, but Three is the life of the party and is always worth asking to come by. Three's factors are very hard to remember.

———

The psychologist interviewed me about my history with math in addition to my general life and education, and then I performed forty-three tests as well as a general IQ test. I recited several numbers in a row backward, remembered sets of numbers, arranged blocks to make shapes, and completed arithmetic problems, including the dreaded long division.

I knew that I was getting all the math wrong, therefore confirming that I had a disability. I had fought with my parents about paying $500 to take a math test, and I was failing spectacularly.

All of my test scores were far above average, putting me into the "superior" bracket, which was a step below the highest range, "very superior." Except, of course, in math, where I scored in the lowest percentile: "borderline."

Because of my math scores, I averaged a normal score across the board, even though most of the IQ tests proved I had above-average intelligence. The hardest part of my eight-page assessment was the following line: "The disparity between her ability and information processing suggested she was prone to be inefficient at demonstrating her full potential."

My real capacity was pulled down from where it could have been by a defect in my brain. It's likely that my high scores in other areas allowed me to cope with my math deficiencies, hiding them from detection through most of my education.

Four is an anxiety-ridden perfectionist. Two respects and is often amused by Four, but not in love with her. Four believes they are halves of the same whole. And they are, because

Four's factors are always so close to Two's. They really are soulmates, even with the age difference between them. Two is waiting for Four to mature more, to have more factors under her belt.

When I went to college just outside of New York, I would ride the train into the city twice a week for an internship at a literary agency. Some Tuesday in chilly October, I was up late the night before, and I got to the station just as the train was pulling onto the platform.

I was in a rush to buy the ticket and entered the wrong PIN for my debit card. I tried twice more and realized that I had entirely forgotten the number. My card locked. A school-mate bought me a round-trip ticket, and we agreed I'd pay her back later. I had five dollars to buy lunch. It was enough for a slice of pizza and a can of root beer on Fifth Avenue.

After my internship, I called the bank. They told me there was nothing they could do after a card was locked and it would remain that way for another twelve hours. I explained that I had accidentally locked it myself because of my dyscalculia. The woman on the phone said she'd never heard of it. Her suggestion was to use a register and get cash back after buying something.

I tried this and my card was again declined at the drugstore. I immediately started crying and explained that I just needed a subway swipe. The cashier took pity on me and gave me his MetroCard. A week later, I brought him a MetroCard with ten dollars loaded on it and a thank-you note, which I left with his manager.

When I got back to my dorm room, I collapsed on my bed and sobbed. I was starving after only a piece of pizza to eat at lunch. I had been left destitute in New York City, had to rely on strangers because I couldn't remember numbers.

My day had been ruined because my brain functioned abnormally or was missing a section or was simply a bad brain. And there was nothing that could be done about it, nothing to resolve it, no one to blame. I simply had a brain that could do some things and not others.

Five is so full of himself. At any single moment, several numbers are irritated with Five. He wears a suit everywhere but is always late. Like most of the numbers, Five is obsessed with himself and moves through life with the need to stamp himself everywhere, to leave his mark. Half the time, his factors end in 5—his life's work. He's obsessive in his need to have things be all about him, reflections of himself. As annoying as he is, you know what you're going to get with Five and you can't complain.

My mother can rattle off the phone number, birthdate, and Social Security number for everyone in our family. She's good at math. More specifically, she's superhuman at what has always felt like an impossibility to me. I don't know if she knows what it's like to constantly forget numbers, to have to give them personalities just to solve a multiplication problem.

As a child, I believed my mother's skill at math was a sign that I wasn't bad at math simply because I was a girl. Even though I knew this, the possibility that my math troubles all had to do with my gender always felt present. No one seemed to question a little girl struggling at math. Girls were supposed to like pink and purple, while boys liked blue and green. Girls were good at singing and art, but boys preferred to build things. Boys were good at math, and girls weren't.

I was a girl who liked writing and reading, and no one seemed to think it was strange that, at eleven years old, I couldn't remember the phone number or zip code of the house I'd lived in my whole life. Because dyscalculia is less well-known, no one in my family was on the lookout or knew the signs. I only discovered the disability existed when I googled "bad at remembering numbers" in my twenties.

As a child, I was horrified at the possibility that something was very wrong with my brain, that I was not as smart as people told me I was. To blame my gender was to relieve me of faults. If the problems were because I was a girl, then my brain wasn't imperfect after all.

Six is cool. He uses a walking cane, and he has a mustache. Six has a pug named Aurora who sits in the sidecar of his motorcycle. Six is in many ways what Five aspires to be but cannot become, to which Six has responded with a lifelong campaign of rivalry. He's always disrupting Five's work. When Five ends a factor in a perfect 0, Six just hops along and suddenly transforms it so that the factor ends in Six's name. He loves that this gets under Five's skin. Secretly, it's all an attempt to attract Four.

———

I'm so good at compensating for my number troubles that, if you watch me closely, you might not realize how many little tricks I'm using.

The calculator app is always on my recently used page. I never carry cash and always pay in card to avoid the embarrassing hazard of giving the cashier way too much or too little money. I log every time I spend money in an app, which then recalculates and redistributes my paycheck amount over the rest of the month, so I don't overspend. I used to calculate my timesheet in the bathroom to avoid doing it at my desk, so no one at work could know how difficult it was for me.

If I take too long to calculate the tip, the person I'm eating with might realize I'm bad at math. But if I go too fast, I could make the wrong estimate and leave a tip too small. This anxiety builds the second my food is set down in front of me.

Seven is into herself. But don't be mistaken, she isn't self-obsessed like Five, or interested in morals or love like the other numbers. Seven is just an introvert. Seven speaks five languages, oil paints, and can solve a Rubik's Cube in ten minutes flat. Seven is so unpredictable that you can't guess any of her factors. All you can do is remember them—and even then there is no trick, no rhyme or reason. Seven is mysterious and no one knows her true hair color.

The older I got, the more I relied on the numbers. Their personalities only got bigger, maturing and evolving with me.

When I started having sex, all of them likewise escalated their little love affairs. The traits they had when I was eight years old evolved with me, into how I see them now.

Like everyone who lives in the world, I use math every day, which means I have to call on my numbers constantly. They're always with me, my odd assortment of personalities. As frustrating as it is, they feel like friends.

Like a few other numbers, Eight is in love with Four. His factors are inconsistent but can line up with Two's factors in an attempt to attract Four. Eight is a little overweight and loves the occasional donut. Eight also is sweet, thoughtful, and devoted, and Four does feel herself drawn to him because Eight feels like a real partner, as opposed to the perfect Two or the slippery Six.

Sometimes I imagine there is a whole world I'm missing out on. Math whizzing past me, predicting the weather, computer code lighting up my cell phone, algorithms that push my data to the top. All of it is impenetrable to me, something that I cannot see or touch or interact with. Because of difficulties with math and numbers, some dyscalculics shoplift to avoid making change at the till, max out their credit cards by accident, or use the same PINs for everything—making them perfect targets for hackers and identity fraud. Dyscalculia may cause its sufferers to perpetually arrive late, misaddress their mail, do their taxes wrong, or write the wrong number in frosting on their kid's birthday cake.

In the most extreme cases, some can't hold jobs, can't manage money, and need to rely on others for help on a daily basis. For some dyscalculics, the following occupations may be impossibilities: mathematician, physicist, scientist, chemist, doctor, nurse, teacher.

I'm not sure if I write because I like it or if my inclination toward writing is due to dyscalculia eliminating other possibilities.

Nine is a genius. Like Five, she's obsessed with having her name on all of her factors, but she's more clever. All of her multiplication factors spell out her name when the numbers in the answer are added together. Nine may be a mathematical genius, but she's also a poet. She went to college to study film and changed her major three times before settling on medieval literature. Nine has dabbled in Kabbalah and polyamory with Three.

When I do want to tell someone about my dyscalculia, I have to start at the beginning. It can never be so simple as saying, *I have dyscalculia*, and someone nodding and getting it. It's an unknown, and describing it can be harder than compensating for it.

Other times, though, I don't need to explain, like with my friend E, who also has a bad-at-numbers brain like me. When we have dinner together, figuring out the tip takes both phone calculators and several attempts. We take as long as we need to decide how much to leave for the tip. E is the only person I don't feel anxious eating out with. We're like Two and Four when it comes to putting our heads together and figuring out the tip.

Ten is the ideal. The aspiration. The perfection. The crowning moment of a number's life is to come in contact with Ten. Ten is the king, the president, the god of numbers. Ten makes possible what all the numbers want—to move from single-digit to double-digit and yet retain their integrity. Ten remains truly unattainable, something untouchable. Ten and One are lovers.

In Praise of Fast Girls Who Just Want to Dance

Aricka Foreman

The year I learned my body would betray me, Aaliyah's self-titled album dropped. Her melodies and sweet Minnie Riperton–like whispers wafted in and through my car as the wind whipped my hair around my face. I felt a kinship, or perhaps a desire to be like her: soft homegirl, more honey than vinegar. Be the girl who sang songs about love and want, though I didn't know the depth of my well. Those girls moved past leering old men outside the fish house unbothered—the way they rolled toothpicks from one up-turned edge of their mouths to the other while tracing the map of your body. Aaliyah exemplified the girl in me who had to speak sweetly. "We Need a Resolution" was my an-themic just-in-case song after watching the men in my family do what men do: "You fell asleep on the couch / I thought we was going out / I wanna know / were your fingers broke?" I was young, in love, and secretly engaged. (Or at least I thought. My grandmother would confess later she assumed we'd run off and eloped.)

The summer after my senior year of high school, I'd been driving around in my grandmother's hand-me-down, Smurf-hued, two-door Ford Tempo. The speedometer only went to eighty-seven, but its automatic seat belts and manual windows and AC all worked. The car was mine. I'd kept a GPA over 3.5, worked a part-time job, and used both as excuses to break from beneath my mother's strict rule. She was more terrified than anything: What could happen to my body, at any time, in any place?

On a particularly balmy night, I dressed to dance: a cream Girbaud tank top I'd cut and frayed along the sides of my ribs, paired with Girbaud jeans of the same color and slick all-white Pumas. I had long cornrow braids; the hot-watered curled ends grazed back and forth across the top of my behind when I walked. At five feet and 110 pounds soaking wet, I was ready to move.

We didn't stand in lines then, though we clocked the marketing behind it: Keep young women single file in front of your establishment and, inevitably, the men will come. We didn't know the words *patriarchal* or *power* or *transaction* in the names of our bodies. And we didn't care because the girls I rolled to the club with were fabulous and had illustrious names: Princess, Vanity, Aisha, Amaris. I loved the lilt of their various etymologies, how they hung on the tongue, sweet and thick like ALAGA Syrup. The ways we cackled and spoke back and forth at the speed of light, our excitement caught in the ethereal web of possibility. No matter that our mothers were afraid the world would think us fast and wanted us to keep our heads in the books and off boys, like we couldn't do both. We were free and naïve enough to believe we could navigate the terrain of men's hunger and their hands unscathed.

In Detroit, we would forgo "teen clubs" for The River Rock. Blue neon signs and chatter spilling from its numerous floors, popping with alcohol and problematic dynamics, situated just a block away from the burgeoning early development along the Detroit River. It boasted the best of the worlds we wanted into: DJs spun house and techno, hip-hop, neo soul, and Black radio hits. Vanity's godbrother was a DJ for the local radio station and did a set at The River Rock on Saturday nights. He could get us in for free. From my car, we charged to the front of the line, gave our names, and made our way upstairs to the bodies sweltering against one another.

We spent the next few hours mimicking men: Some of us were there to get numbers, scout out prospects for whatever we thought we needed. Men were a bonus if they were kind and worth a minute or two. But I was infatuated with the music, the abandon of lending my body to sound and the vibration of the amp's bass. We laughed loud and gave cool shoulders. We threw down slight invitations and watched them get lapped up like water.

The night began like every other. Walking up the stairs, to the dance floor, from the dance floor, walking to the outdoor deck, men on every side, men in endless gauntlets. Outside, the sweat from the last four to seven songs steamed off my arms and the back of my neck. I watched the lights along the river dance like stars from the Canada side along the water's dark surface. I watched the cars below, circling in search of free parking. A tall man in jeans and a polo shirt grabbed my arm slightly. I turned and slowly backed myself against the banister of the deck. Gave direct eye contact, or at least tried, as he traced the curves of my cleavage, trying to gauge if I had enough ass to bother. Bullet points fell from his mouth. "Sup, li'l ma." "How you doin'?" "I'm trying to get to know you." "What's your name?" "You got kids?" The bullets came fast and automatic and I became monosyllabic and lied.

"Nikki. No."

An alias, sometimes, is a crack in the doorway. But the last question rang odd, and I couldn't help but ask why. "Because your titties so big." Vanity and Princess headed inside, and without answering him, I followed after them.

He grabbed my arm again. "Wassup?"

I snatched my arm away and tried to exit gracefully, while behind me he yelled, "Fuck you, then, nappy-headed bitch," across the deck, across the parking lot. The men laughed. The women in acquiescence laughed. His insult landed somewhere like a rock in that narrow channel between two countries.

Another seed was planted in the crop of my shame. I thought it was my fault. I should've disengaged sooner. I shouldn't have left so abruptly. I should've given him a fake number. I'm smarter than this. I should've broken away as soon as he approached. I shouldn't have let it get that far.

Years prior, my grandfather died from a condition that caused several strokes until, eventually, his brain and his body gave up. Before the strokes came, he'd wake up in the middle of the night, muttering to himself, and he'd take off running down the block in full force like a haint. I was told fragments of his trauma: how, for instance, his uncle used to lock him up in that Yazoo, Mississippi, attic with snakes and rats. My grandmother said it was because he was the darkest of his siblings. Then she'd lament how he'd come home after school, once he migrated to Chicago, and find a different pair of men's shoes at the door, a signal his mama had company.

This was before my mother convinced my grandmother to put him in a nursing home. Those years were strange and strained and silent. We didn't and don't talk about the time I woke up in the middle of the night to find my grandfather hunched over his four-legged cane, slowly pulling the sheet from my body. I called out for my grandmother. Within a matter of minutes, she entered the room, yanked him up by his collar, threw him into the hall, then dragged him into their bedroom.

I could hear the ting of his aluminum cane as she cracked it over his back again and again. I learned his violence was an old one between each blow. How he'd beat her, lock her in their bedroom *like a child*. I sat still for a time, cataloging the specifics until the door slammed and he wept. And then my mother yelled more lessons for me to take in. How my grandmother found him on top of her when she was younger than me. How afterward, the women all tried to convince my mother that what she knew was true wasn't true. He was her father. Her mother's husband. He took care of them. He wasn't that kind of man.

We get language all wrong. We slip into metaphors, tumble and trip over allusions, in search for what we mean when we say *hurt* and *stop*. What some say is *toxic* or *power* or *desire* is something else, something twisted and relentless. Every instance of my body's betrayal that came after that night at The River Rock, I quantified. It could have been worse. I've heard worse: from my mother, from her mother, from cousins and friends and classmates. I hear it almost daily, everywhere. It's all bad. The worst.

The neighborhood boys outside, playing their music, leaning against Hank's indigo Regal, had me standing in the bathroom mirror, primping, flat-ironing my edges until they laid flat and complicit. Fuck the rims and rap hanging off the edge of the street, I was lonely. I was alone with my grandfather in a house with doors that had locks.

I'd heard his cane creaking down the hall. I'd heard the steady, slow grind of metal announcing his direction. It slowed down, paused, and I caught him in my periphery, standing in the short corridor from the bathroom into the main hallway. He slowly creaked again until he was in the doorway. *What you don't give attention to must eventually dissipate*, or some such was said. I sprayed the Luster's aerosol until a cloud rose between us. His arm reached out and tried to stroke my hair. I backed away. I don't remember if I asked him if he needed to get into the bathroom, but my hands hurriedly packed up my tools: a wide-toothed comb, some hair fasteners, and a short-bristled brush.

He said, "Naw." Told me how pretty I was. Tried to reach again. I collected everything into the bag, threw it in the cabinet under the sink, and tried to rush past him. He caught the edge of me, what was blooming. And I convinced myself he didn't mean it. He was sick. Wasn't in his right mind. He couldn't move too good. It was an accident. He was my grandfather. My mother's father. My grandmother's husband. He had taken care of me when my father didn't.

I went into the kitchen and looked for something to eat, though I wasn't hungry. I tried to identify which Country Crock tub had which leftovers before I heard the creaking start again. It couldn't have been what I thought—until he came reaching, reaching. Luckily his body had failed, was failing. Luckily there was a table between us. I ran to my room and called my mother, told her to come home. I could only patch together excerpts of details, but she knew the small anchor in my throat, recognized that same old song. I waited with my younger brother on the porch for her to come. I don't know if he remembers any of it, or if he understood what was happening. I never wanted to admit how unsafe I felt inside my own body. I was too busy doing what I'd been told for years: "Be sweet now." Like honey.

My grandmother came home first, then my mother. Then, the yelling and rehashing and packing and unpacking. That night, we all just went to sleep. Nothing else happened after that fight. Eventually, he was moved from the house, although the air was thick between my mother and my grandmother, no matter the season. And still, no one talked to me about what happened, so I learned then how to become a woman: move on.

My grandmother beating her husband was something my cousins and I would joke about while I plugged the *Contra* code into the controller after holiday dinners. How Mema, as small as she was, put in that work. I laughed, too, until tears came. None of them would ever know the word *hysteria*.

I started wearing my cousins' baggy shirts and cuffing my jeans. Just like them.

I marched back into the club, where my friends would ask nothing. Or maybe they did and I don't remember. Or maybe there was an unspoken thing beneath our glances that we knew in the bone, in the marrow of ourselves. There's a moment on the dance floor when one slow track melds into another: Kindred the Family Soul's "Far Away" transitions into the delicate beginning of Aaliyah's "It's Whatever." And I'm digging the heels of my sneakers into the ground until my waist winds into its own rhythm, since this is what I came here for. To feel myself inside my body, without the aid of anyone else's to call back to. This soft bend pulls my hands—bound together at the wrists—up into the low light, where no man enters. Until I say so. And I don't.

Weathering Wyoming
Jenny Tinghui Zhang

Four weeks before I moved to Wyoming, I stood in front of my open refrigerator in Austin, the yellow light illuminating my shins. I had already eaten everything immediately edible in there—five slices of sharp cheddar cheese and ten slices of deli meat, two avocados, leftover fried chicken (cold), the remaining half jars of almond butter and Bonne Maman strawberry jam, and chalky rice mixed with salsa.

I was still hungry.

It wasn't a real hunger. It was a void, a blackness that needed all the food in the world to occupy my body and fill whatever emptiness had dug itself in.

When you have an eating disorder, you forget what food was before being just "good" or "bad," what it felt like to eat with joy and warmth. You forget who you were when you didn't have one at all. My eating disorder had a lot of different names, but it came down to the same pattern: I would starve myself and, when my body couldn't stand it any longer, binge until I could feel the food in my eyes.

Up until this past year, my eating disorder was my life. I

obsessively planned my days around my meals and canceled plans if I was going on a binge, because the aftermath was me lying on my side, belly full and aching, as salt, fat, and sugar made deposits in all the swollen corners of my body. The next day, I would purge by starving myself or overexercising to make up for the binge. A few days later, depleted, hungry, and desperate, I would start the binge-purge cycle all over again.

When I moved to Wyoming for graduate school, my eating disorder moved with me. I didn't ask it to. In fact, I begged it not to. *Stay behind in Austin where you belong,* I told it. *I'm trying to start over. Stay in the heat, with the tech start-ups and the awful, congested traffic. Stay behind and let me live.* But of course, that's not how eating disorders work. At some point, you just learn to accept that this will be the way things are for the rest of your life. And you learn to live with it.

I chose Wyoming because I wanted a place where I could write undisturbed. I had built, in my mind, an image of Wyoming as a beautiful, idyllic place, a carbon-copy landscape of *Brokeback Mountain*, where cowboys looked like Heath Ledger and sometimes fell in love with one another. (The irony, I would learn, is that *Brokeback Mountain* is set in Wyoming but was filmed in Canada.) I wanted rolling plains and astounding mountains. I wanted clouds as big as the sky. Most of all, I wanted to find beauty.

I was laughably wrong, of course. Humans weren't meant to live in Wyoming. It is too cold, too windy, too dry. Laramie, the town where I live, enjoys two months of glorious summer before dropping directly into winter. "Fall" is a week in September—two weeks if you're lucky. There is no turning of the leaves, no waft of all things pumpkin spice. There is simply a moment where the weather hovers at acceptable before devolving into a bone-chilling winter that stays until May. (May 24, to be exact, which was the last day it snowed last year.) The cold here is invincible. It penetrates layers and lodges into bones.

Once you think you're getting used to the cold, there's the altitude. At seventy-two hundred feet, Laramie is considered relatively high altitude. High altitude lowers your appetite and makes you sleepy and dehydrated. You can never breathe quite enough because you're always two breaths behind. Then, once you think you've mastered the cold and the altitude, there's the wind. The Wyoming wind is one that can shut down interstate highways and overturn eighteen-wheelers. It gets particularly bad in Laramie—the town's latitude, coupled with weather from the Pacific, makes it one of the windiest cities in the state, if not the country. Last summer, winds reached ninety miles per hour, enough to blow trains off the tracks.

I moved to Laramie during a splendid, balmy August. By September, I was fully committed to braving a Wyoming winter; I learned to arm myself with a scarf and hat before stepping outside. I added eight steps to my skincare routine to fight against the dry wind. I even layered. By all means, I was well on my way to becoming a Wyomingite.

Throughout all of this, my eating disorder waited. It was patient; it watched me move into my apartment, sat nearby as I made new friends and acquaintances, tolerated my nervous giddiness of being someplace new. Then, a few weeks after school started, I felt that old hunger set in, that urge to binge and stopper the growing void of missing home, being stressed from school, adjusting to a new place, missing my loved ones.

One night in late October, I binged on an entire large pizza and two pints of ice cream, all while making a devout promise to not eat again the next day. *I'll go on a hike*, I vowed as I shoved spoonful after spoonful of salted caramel ice cream into my mouth. My mouth was numb, and my nose was running. *I'll go on a five-hour hike, and I won't eat at all to make up for this.*

A binge state is very much like a fugue state. You don't really notice what you're eating or how it tastes. All you know is that it, whatever it is, must go into your body, because something inside is wrong and needs to be filled. All you know is that you can't stop, and maybe you don't want to.

The next day, true to my word, I went for a hike at Happy Jack, a recreation area that doubles as a mountain bike trail in the summer and a cross-country skiing trail in the winter. Laramie had a few warmer days that week, and the snow was mostly manageable. I trudged along in my hiking boots, sinking into the snow with every step and welcoming the cold slush that bit my ankles. I deserved this discomfort, I thought, for my transgression the previous night.

Halfway through the hike, I realized that I had been going in circles. Everything was obscured by snow, so it was hard to differentiate between old landscape and new. I had no idea where I was. My phone battery had dropped to 13 percent in the three hours I had been walking, even though it was at 100 percent when I started. Technology, much like humanity, was no match for the brutality of Wyoming winter.

I walked ahead, then doubled back, my pant legs drenched, my socks iceboxes. I walked around and around again, watching the sky darkening and closing over me. Did the Little Match Girl die because she was cold or because she was hungry? Or was it both?

The pang of true hunger was setting in now, too. It was a hunger I had grown familiar with in my years of binging and purging. Like my body was screaming at me for forgiveness, like it was drowning and thrashing for a lifeline. I had grown very good at ignoring it, much in the way a cruel stepmother might tell her child, *Go to bed and don't even think about dinner.* I expected this.

But there was something new that I had not come to expect: the feeling that for the first time, my life was on the line. There, in the relentless landscape of Wyoming, wind and cold rattling my bones, I found myself lost, soaked, hungry, alone, and terrified. I had spent the past five years killing and resurrecting my body all within a twenty-four-hour period by choice, ignorant of the consequences. Now, death was a very real possibility, and it was not my choice at all.

Once upon a time, I used to judge how skinny I was becoming by how much my ring slipped around on my finger. It meant that I was doing something right, that I was working toward a glorious unbecoming. That day, when my ring loosened and slipped to the edge of my knuckle, I did not feel triumphant. I was shrinking in every way, caving into myself. I was finally unbecoming, but for the first time, it felt like dying instead of being alive.

When I finally found my way out of the woods two hours

later, it was dark, and my phone was dead. I sat in my car blasting the heater and feeling the cold degloving from my hands. All I wanted, in that moment, was a big bowl of phở.

I came to Wyoming to find beauty. Instead, Wyoming kicked my ass and taught me what it really meant to take care of myself. The things I could get away with in Austin—the constant food deprivation, the extreme binges and subsequent punishments, skipping meals for days at a time, working out, running, running, always running—I couldn't get away with here. This land, its climate, the atmosphere—it's unforgiving and ruthless. If you don't take care of yourself, you could very well die.

Wyoming is a place that humbles you, reminds you of just how mortal and insignificant you are. That night, I chose to eat. I ate again the next day, and the day after that. It felt like some sort of apology to my body.

The more regularly and frequently I let myself eat to comfortable fullness, the more I realized that food never had to be "good" or "bad." To force a morality on each bite, calorie, and gram was to turn food into something to be feared.

Instead, I slowly realized that food is allowed to simply be food: something that sustains, nourishes, and powers. I heard it in advertisements all the time: "Food is fuel." Until I really put my body on the line in Wyoming, I didn't understand what that meant.

Now, I do. Fuel, as in something to make sure every component of my body works the way it's supposed to. Fuel, as in what my cells are gasping for. Fuel, as in the thing that is keeping me alive. I stopped seeing my body as something to be changed (and food as a thing to manipulate that change).

Instead, my body was something that needed taking care of, because it was the only thing taking care of me.

Can nature change you? Yes. Nature reminded me how stupid and dangerous it was to think I was somehow immune to the consequences of the natural world. To starve yourself, in Wyoming, is to let yourself die. To not take care of yourself here is to give nature an open invitation to destroy you. My eating disorder came to Wyoming with me, but it could no longer possess me the way it had before Wyoming. Because I learned that I wouldn't be able to survive with it in Wyoming—nor anywhere else, for that matter.

In the spring, on a rare day when the snow had all but melted and the sun was actually high in the sky, I took my mountain bike out for a ride at Happy Jack. After an entire winter of avoiding cardio, I was winded after the first ten minutes. I dismounted and started pushing my bike uphill, every step the hardest thing in the world.

I don't believe you can ever really, truly heal from an eating disorder. Like I said, when you have an eating disorder, you have to find a way to live with it. My ED will be with me for the rest of my life, but I now realize that I can control how I let it exist. In Wyoming, and now in other parts of the world— when I go back to visit my grandparents in China, when I go back to visit my boyfriend in Austin, when I go back to visit my parents in Houston—my eating disorder is just a whisper. The practice is the same, whether it's with my relatives forcing plates of dumplings in front of me, or my friends wanting to go out to eat, or my parents wanting to express their love for me through food: I practice gratitude, not fear. Gratitude for the food, for my body, for making it this far.

My eating disorder cannot own me like before, because I know something now: I know how to take care of myself. And that's by letting myself eat. *You can exist*, I tell my eating disorder. *But only barely. And on my terms, not yours.*

The morning of my bike ride, I ate three scrambled eggs with spinach and a heaping amount of cheese, and two slices of toast with peanut butter. I was content and fueled. I packed two energy bars in my backpack, one for when I reached the top of the climb, the other if I got hungry on the way down.

I reached the top of the climb panting, barely able keep my eyes open. My body was under me, rooted firmly to the ground. I could hear my heart pumping blood to my muscles, could feel the insistent pulse in my neck. I felt strong—not just physically, but in my existence, in my tenure as a living, breathing being.

It was in this moment that I was grateful. For my body, this miraculous thing that sustained me, that tried so hard, that was always on my side. How strong it had been, how loyal, even when I did not want it. Even when I tried to destroy it.

I used to think that eating and showing hunger were signs of weakness. They are not. They're tremendous signs of strength—the strength to know yourself, to take care of yourself, to listen to yourself.

This body was mine, and it had been trying to speak to me all this time. Finally, finally, in the open plains of Wyoming, against the howl of the wind, I was ready to listen.

Attack of the Six-Foot Woman
Hannah Walhout

Recently, in the depths of months of quarantining, I was scrolling through the Warner Archive's database of films when I happened upon the 1958 cult classic *Attack of the 50 Foot Woman*. It felt like a wink from the universe.

Not long before, I'd had a conversation with a friend who lived across the country, who, like me, is a woman close to six feet in height. At some point our catch-up call turned, as it had many times before, to our shared experiences of tallness. We reminisced about the years when we had lived in the same city and how walking down the street together seemed to always amount to something near a spectacle. Being a tall woman means living with a running commentary from those around you—put two of them together, and the show is on. *What did people think of us, two blond giants towering over the sidewalk?* I sighed, and then laughed, imagining some five-foot-eight guy cowering in fear as we passed.

The opening moments of *Attack of the 50 Foot Woman* follow Nancy Fowler Archer, played in all her melodramatic glory by B-movie standby Allison Hayes, as she drives down

Route 66 through the California night. Suddenly, as the camera winds through the sagebrush and sandstone, a large, shining, spherical spaceship appears out of nowhere in the middle of the road. (Or, at least, that's the idea; the special effects leave something to be desired.) Nancy veers out of the way and totals her car. Somehow, she is able to escape from the scene—but not before the pilot of the mysterious ship emerges, a huge mottled hand coming into frame to grasp for the plum-size diamond around her neck.

The next evening, Nancy insists on returning to the desert, this time with her husband, Harry (William Hudson). Despite being waved away by the town's smirking police chief, she is certain that the previous night's events represented an encounter with an extraterrestrial being. She knows what happened to her, and she needs to be believed. This night plays out in roughly the same fashion as the first: ship descends, car swerves, alien emerges. But this time, Nancy isn't so lucky. She is snatched by the mottled hand of the giant man—who, for reasons unknown, is dressed like a medieval dungeon master—and, incredibly, Harry eagerly hops back into the car to go tell his side piece, Honey (Yvette Vickers), that his wife is finally out of the picture.

That is, until an unconscious Nancy is returned home by her kidnapper, placed gingerly on top of her pool house. She is taken inside to rest and be attended to by her physician, Dr. Cushing (Roy Gordon). But now, something in Nancy is changing. Unbeknownst to those around her, she has been exposed to that 1950s sci-fi bogeyman: radiation. Within a matter of hours, Nancy's compact, slender frame will expand upward and outward with vigor, transforming a troubled woman into the film's titular freak. Radiation, as we know, does strange and terrible things to the body.

I first learned that I was tall from a photograph. I don't think I quite knew it at the time the photo was taken—that morning I had simply dressed up, like everyone else in the fifth grade, for the class picture. I wore a navy-blue turtleneck with bright-blue cargo capris and, around my neck, the spoils of summer: a necklace from Girl Scout camp on which each pony bead and charm represented another year under my belt or another skill learned. I was proud.

When the copies of the class picture arrived at our house, I opened the envelope at our kitchen table and eagerly examined the outcome. Excited, as always, to see how my outfit had registered on camera, I scanned past the short kids sitting crisscross applesauce in the front row, the delicate littlest girls and the pipsqueaky boys. I noticed kids in prints of trains and butterflies next to kids wearing short skirts and brand-name sneakers. I saw our stern but caring teacher, Mrs. T. And then my eyes were drawn to a giant color block of blue in the center of the back row, a blond head rising above everyone around me. I felt exposed, my stomach sinking. Was that me?

At the risk of sounding dramatic, it may have been then that I developed self-consciousness—or, rather, a consciousness of my self. (If most people's existential crises stem from an awareness of their own mortality, maybe my first came from a sudden awareness of my own now-unusual body.) I hadn't been the tall girl in years past; now, I would be forever. Years later, this feeling would fleetingly resurface when I watched the 2019 Netflix high school comedy *Tall Girl*, which explores the experience of being just that—the stereotypes, the romantic complications, the insecurities of shorter men. "Having back-row-center placement in all of your class photos," Jodi, the six-foot-one main character, says, "isn't exactly a self-esteem booster."

That night, I lay in bed unable to fall asleep. My lower half was racked with growing pains—a sure sign, I thought, that my body was in the process of transmogrifying. The pain felt like tiny cranks in some sort of creaking bone-stretching contraption, slowly lengthening my shins upward and widening my hips outward. My growing body seemed achy and abuzz all at once, and I felt it wasn't quite mine. It is horrifying to realize that your body is doing something entirely independent of your brain.

Eventually, my mother, a doctor, came to sit with me, carefully swaddling my shins in tight Ace bandages to help with the dull throbbing. As she placed hot water bottles on each of my legs and pulled the blanket over me, I asked her to tell me what growing pains are for. I might as well have been asking, *Why is this happening to me?*

She couldn't tell me, of course; human growth is a complicated process. All she could do was stroke my hair and tell me my body was going to change, and that sometimes it hurts.

In my teenage years, all my cautious estimates and educated guesses as to how tall I could become came and went. (It didn't help that my body was also growing outward, fat rising like a proofing sourdough and bubbling up in heretofore neglected areas.) My grandmothers were both in the area of five foot five—a height I have no memory of being, since it likely didn't last more than a few months. My mom and her sisters were around five foot eight. I zoomed past that at fourteen. Feeling like my body was out of control, I figured that my only remaining option would be to try to fudge the numbers when people asked how tall I was.

In class, I would slouch, trying to appear shorter. If I was included in a group photo, I set myself a bit behind everyone else, trying to use perspective to my advantage. Every time I went to the doctor, I would hunch as the assistant lowered the spindly metal measuring device onto my head, as though tricking the official record could change the course of history. I'm not the only one who did this; studies have shown that women who are tall in their adolescence and college years often engage in such sleights of hand.

I began learning what female tallness meant: stares from oblivious strangers, observations from well-meaning classmates, clothes that never fit, dances never attended. (I tended to avoid situations that called for strappy, sparkly high heels, which struck fear in my heart, though dates weren't exactly knocking down my door.) I had boy friends, but no boyfriends. In the height of the boot-cut era, when awkward hemlines ensued, I defiantly made cuffed jeans my signature look—all the while wishing I could pull off the designer denim everyone else seemed to have.

So many of the ways in which teenagers "fit in" felt impossible to me, whether or not they actually were. The effect of all this is the same, I suppose: to let you know that you are different, and to help you internalize the truth of adolescence that difference is, for the most part, bad.

Other than being beautiful and white, Nancy Fowler Archer is far from the American "feminine ideal" of the 1950s— even when she could be measured on a standard human scale. This is not the demure suburban housewife. She's extremely rich, for one thing. She owns a modernist mansion, where she keeps her philandering husband well taken care of by her pocketbook and her faithful butler, Jess (Ken Terrell). Her marriage is messy; she's left Harry on at least one occasion, unwilling to abide his cheating. She is also, it's implied, an alcoholic, one who has been sent to the sanitarium on more than one occasion for her "mental exhaustion," "overworked imagination," and "violent headaches." Over the years, her family physician observes that "her health seemed to rise and fall with the tide of her emotions."

Later that night, as Nancy continues to rest after her mysterious kidnapping, her husband and his mistress concoct a plan. Harry sneaks into Nancy's room, intent on injecting her with a lethal amount of sedative, which would leave him free to run off with Honey—a woman far less complicated and difficult than his wife. He tiptoes up the stairs and past the sleeping nurse. But he promptly drops his deathly syringe when he realizes that his wife is no longer quite his wife; she has transformed into something much greater. This time, it is not a mottled alien hand that bursts into the frame but Nancy's giant, manicured fingers.

In the United States, the average height for those assigned female at birth is five foot four. I have that beat by about eight inches; Nancy has it beat by nearly forty-five feet, her body taking up every corner of the room in a display reminiscent of *Alice in Wonderland*. Dr. Cushing rushes in to investigate. He pokes and prods at Nancy, ordering that she be given forty pints of plasma and a hefty dose of morphine with an "elephant syringe." Then he calls in a second opinion.

Both doctors are utterly stumped. *What to do with this giant woman?* they ask. *What to do, what to do.* "I don't know," they say, hoping to find a medical solution. "I just don't know. We will find our answer when we operate." "You feel there's hope?" one says. "With surgery," says the other. When Nancy inevitably awakens, calling out for a Harry who is now back at the bar with his redheaded lover, we see that the doctors have chained her up. Watching her in captivity, I wondered how different this was from her time at the sanitarium.

Around the time the movie came out, a synthetic estrogen treatment for "managing" the growth of very tall girls was growing in popularity. Initially developed by physicians in the mid-1940s, these weren't the first hormone injections aimed at treating women for things that didn't quite need to be treated; in the late nineteenth century, according to a 2006 paper in the *Archives of Pediatrics & Adolescent Medicine*, nurses and midwives would collect extracts from the ovaries of animals to help with amorphous conditions like "hysteria" and "debility."

Being tall had effectively been pathologized. These injections were not meant to treat conditions that cause tallness—hyperthyroidism, for example, or Marfan syndrome—or even conditions possibly brought on by extreme tallness, like atrial fibrillation. Instead, the treatment was specifically aimed at girls with "constitutional tall stature," the medical term used to describe those whose tallness simply *was*. And still, parents and doctors alike advocated for medical intervention. When the treatment was first developed, the medically acceptable threshold for eligibility was a projected adult height of five foot nine. Today, the procedure is rare—but still considered an option for adolescent girls who show signs of hitting six foot two. Of course, various hormone treatments exist today that can be lifesaving and life-affirming; these injections, however, were neither.

A 1962 review of the efficacy of the injections noted that the "problem of excessive height in otherwise normal girls is evident." But what exactly the problem was had not quite crystallized. Some of the parents' concerns now read as dated, as with the respondents in a 1965 survey who expressed that tall girls face challenges in breaking into a career as an airline hostess. But many seem to be evergreen. A 2007 investigation in the *Journal of Medical Ethics* observes that the symptoms being treated were often lumped into the category of "psychosocial problems," which could include "feeling different, being subject to hurtful comments, withdrawal from social activities, difficulties in finding appropriate clothes and difficulties in finding a partner." All, it bears mentioning, problems created by other people.

No data exists to indicate how many girls have been given

these injections over the past sixty-odd years, but they almost certainly number in the thousands. What we *do* know is that possible side effects included ovarian cysts, missed periods, excessive uterine bleeding, and increased risks of infertility. One Australian survey found that "while untreated women were almost unanimously glad they were not treated (99.1 percent), no matter how tall they became, 42.1 percent of the treated women expressed dissatisfaction with the decision that was made." And yet, I wonder, how many of us would still have done it, had we been presented the option?

"All human societies have a conception of the monstrous-feminine," wrote the feminist film theorist Barbara Creed, "of what it is about woman that is shocking, terrifying, horrific, abject." The *Medical Ethics* paper, citing both the existing literature and the author's own interviews, notes that "the experiences of a tall mother are often the main reason why treatment is sought for a tall girl."

Women and girls are so often told, in ways both obvious and insidious, that we are not supposed to take up too much space. My tall body has often felt like a violation of this tacit rule of smallness, both a disruption and a liability.

Because of a general notion that women should be smaller than men, my height almost always makes me stand out to strangers, who frequently feel the need to talk—audibly—about me, as if I am an oversize object. I have heard comments on my height from people on street corners as I stare at my phone, waiting for the walk sign to change. I have heard them in elevators, and I have heard them on escalators.

I have heard them, loudly, from a repairman on his way to fix a flickering light, while I was working my student job on the quiet floor of the college library. He walked past me carrying a very large ladder, then stopped in his tracks and said, "Wow, you're a tall one!" I gave him a grimace-smile, then turned back to the shelf I was restocking. He remained there, silently, for what felt like a minute.

I have heard these comments from prospective dates and successful dates and men in bars and stores and airplanes and national parks. For as long as I can remember, I have heard them from relatives, friends, friends' parents, teachers, and volleyball coaches trying to recruit me. The remarks usually have relatively little substance beyond informing me—or the speaker, or anyone in the general vicinity—that I am, in fact, tall. Each time, I wonder: *Do they really think I don't know?*

Studies about the experiences of tall women show that this is not unusual. Of all the things participants have reported—bullying, fetishization, lack of understanding from their shorter friends who *just don't get it*—a common thread seems to be that strangers feel free to use their bodies as conversation starters. It seems that something about a woman standing out above the rest is cause for further inquiry. I feel a particular kinship with a respondent in one study, conducted at the University of South Florida, who noted that comments on her height "made her aware of her body" for the first time. For her, it escalated "to the point where she considered herself a 'freak.'" For me, even the acute awareness was, for a time, its own kind of punishment.

This exhausting state of being perpetually noticed often

made me not want to be noticed at all. And sometimes, the noticing crossed a line into something else. Once, as I rode the metrobus home during my sophomore year of high school, an older man struck up a conversation with me. He asked me about my favorite subjects, whether I played sports, whether I liked my school. He asked my age. He asked me how tall I was. I was not as accustomed as I am now to ignoring men on public transportation who ask too many questions. And I didn't know, as I do now, that inquiries about bodily measurements rarely come from a place of innocent curiosity. Something in his face changed when he asked me where I lived. I went silent, pulled the wire for the next stop, and got off the bus, miles from home. "Five nine already," he said as I stepped out the door. "Damn."

I can't stay when, exactly, I stopped growing. I think if that were a possible thing to know, if there was some sort of countdown clock and I could identify the precise second where my body finally decided to give it a rest, I probably would have celebrated. A dark thought, though, still has the power to tug at me when I let it: *What if it never stops? What if I become so grotesquely long that I simply flop over and break in half?*

The concept of body horror was first posited by the cinema critic Philip Brophy in his 1983 paper "Horrality: The Textuality of the Contemporary Horror Film." The idea is fairly straightforward: this subgenre of horror hinges on the modification, mutation, or mutilation of the human corpus. (Isn't having a body horrifying enough?) "The contemporary

Horror film," Brophy writes, "tends to play not so much on the broad fear of Death, but more precisely on the fear of one's own body, of how one controls and relates to it." Such films are so effectively horrifying precisely because "the fictional body," that which is portrayed on-screen, "is as helpless as its viewing subject."

Attack of the 50 Foot Woman might be taken as an early example of the form: after all, the core conflict arises from stretching bones, bursting muscles, and limbs made unruly. (Brophy writes that such films "accentuat[e] the very presence of the body on the screen," which happens here in the most literal way.) The classic science fiction of the 1950s, so reliant on themes of infiltration, contamination, and bodily tricks like shape-shifting and size-switching, helped set the stage for the cinematic landscape Brophy came up in.

He would later describe 1983 as "the peak of a small 'golden period' of the contemporary horror film." Films that debuted in the early eighties include *Videodrome*, in which a man's body opens up to become a cassette player; *The Evil Dead*, in which bodies become fleshy killing machines controlled by demons; and *The Thing*, in which on-screen bodies, human and otherwise, are revealed to be not bodies at all, but rearranged forms of some mysterious parasitic organism. The common, disturbing thread: We do not have inherent control over our own bodies. In fact, human bodies are sometimes not what they appear and have endless potential for change.

This golden period also saw a flare-up of discussion over what makes a monster monstrous—what makes a horror film horrific. Many scholars agreed that it had something to do with difference. "The concept of a border is central to a construction of the monstrous in the horror film," Creed wrote in 1986. For her, the role of a monster is to cross one of those borders that already exist in our world: "between human and inhuman . . . normal and the supernatural, good and evil . . . the border which separates those who take up their proper gender roles from those who do not." The monster, in crossing it, reinforces that it should be uncrossable.

Body horror, then, reflects back our ingrained assumptions about what a body should be—and should be capable of. "That which crosses or threatens to cross the 'border' is abject," Creed writes. "Although the specific nature of the border changes from film to film, the function of the monstrous remains the same."

"At what point do you think being tall became a good thing?" asks my dad, after I tell him about my research into the hormone treatment and the panic that seems to have gripped 1950s parents of oversize girls. He is surprised that the hormone treatment ever happened; I am surprised that he is surprised. I am also surprised that he thinks tallness is always good, though he does make reassuring comments like this every so often, perhaps because he had a tall sister himself and knows what it can be like.

"You know," he says, "they say the taller of the candidates usually wins the presidential election." He's not wrong, necessarily. Scholars of human behavior note that tallness tends to correlate with social status. In the U.S., the average person will overreport their height—a phenomenon that has been described as "social desirability bias."

But further research confirms what I already knew: that there may be something of a "ceiling height" to all this, a limit to what is considered normal, after which the alleged advantages may give way to stigma. One study has suggested that women's satisfaction with their height is at its peak for those between five foot eight and five foot ten. Six feet, or fifty, is a different story. And stigma for women who break that particular glass ceiling is magnified for those who are tall but not white, not cis, not able-bodied, not thin.

Look to media and myth and you'll see that a woman who is too tall is something to be feared. She can keep up with the men, or even fall in line with them—like Brienne of Tarth in *Game of Thrones*, who can swing a battle-ax with ease and bite the ear off a man even larger than her (but whose inner, sensual life is mostly a mystery). Or maybe she titillates with her destructive power; see macrophilia, which usually manifests as a desire in men to be overpowered, or even eaten, by a very tall woman. *Playboy* reports that, between 2014 and 2015, Pornhub searches for "giantess" increased by 1,091 percent. It's all too easy, I have discovered, to find elaborate YouTube montages stringing together all of Allison Hayes's fifty-foot woman scenes, to be used for unknown—read, prurient—purposes.

Perhaps the most famous trope of the tall woman in the Western canon is the Amazon, a woman often described as being "unusually" tall and muscular—and one who threatens the power of the patriarchy itself. The origin of the word *Amazon* is not entirely clear, but the meaning couldn't be more so; etymological theories posit translations such as "husbandless," "virility-killing," and "without breast." (It was believed that the Amazons would cut off one breast, so as to more easily draw the strings of their bows.) These descendants of Ares—natives of a distant and dangerous land, either Libya or the Black Sea, depending on whom you ask— were a mythological thorn in the side of ancient Greeks, whose art enshrined defeats of Amazon warriors as a record of enlightenment prevailing over savagery.

The Amazons lived a life mostly uninterrupted by men outside the context of war. They were sometimes depicted wearing pants. They were, as the classicist Peter Walcot has noted, "as monstrous in their own fashion as the snake-limbed Giants or half-horse Centaurs and a race just as expressive of the forces which threaten to destroy civilized life." The tall woman, in other words, was a threat to the entire realm of man.

And for three thousand years, more or less, the idea of the Amazon has been used liberally as a misogynistic epithet for women who threaten to cross these unspoken borders. In the years following the French Revolution, for instance, a number of politically astute women saw that once-sacrosanct social hierarchies were becoming slippery as political power was redistributed, traditions smashed, and new titles, calendars, and religions created. Some women took advantage of the relative chaos to attempt to gain some political power. They sat in on meetings of the Jacobins, who had helped overthrow the old monarchy and who dominated French politics for several years afterward, finding ways to mingle with (male) members whose number they were not officially allowed to join. This was not entirely popular. One foreign observer, noticing a woman descending from the upper gallery to actually take a seat in the main hall, likened her to the mythical man-eater. "On inquiry, I was informed that the name of this amazon is Mademoiselle Theroigne. [She] has a smart martial air, which in a man would not be disagreeable." Just as the Amazons, she is, to this man at least, taking up an unnatural, almost savage amount of space.

I do not believe that a tall woman is a monstrous thing—in fact, quite the opposite. But I do believe that, when my friends set me up on a blind date, I should make sure the guy knows how tall I am; that I should wear big headphones on the train, just in case someone wants to tap on my shoulder and ask; that every time a stranger tells me, with mock terror, that I look "like I could kick his ass," something in him is actually terrified. I believe the studies in which tall women report an "inability to be feminine," defining "the ideal female body as being petite and dainty," and the studies that show that shorter and smaller women are perceived to be more expressive, more thoughtful, more nurturing. Softer, more sensual. Code, probably, for *more woman*, as much as that means anything at all.

I also believe their findings that the taller a woman is, the more she is perceived to be strong, assertive, ambitious, intelligent, affluent, professionally successful. I believe you already know what's wrong with strong, assertive, ambitious, intelligent, affluent, professionally successful women.

What is the function of the monstrous in *Attack of the 50 Foot Woman*? Where are the borders drawn? I see them in familiar places, delineating the same cognitive dissonances of my own life: between masculine and feminine, big and small, powerful and powerless, longed for and longing, taker and taken. Nancy smashes them all, and her transformation, visceral in the most literal way, is one my own body remembers.

At the end of the film, Nancy goes on a rampage. How could she not? She finally has all the power: to force her husband to stay faithful, to pick *him* up, to lock *him* up, to make demands. She awakens from her morphine coma, easily breaks her bindings, and lumbers away wrapped in a bedsheet. Townspeople look up at the massive woman, frozen in place as she stomps down the street. A pair of police officers try to track her down by following a trail of giant footprints. "She'll tear up the whole town until she finds Harry," says one to the other. "Yeah, and then she'll tear up Harry."

There are other plot points here and there: something about diamonds, which are used to power alien ships in one of those futuristic alternative-energy subplots that proliferated around this time. But this is most of all a story of a woman who is, and does, too much. Nancy shows us the lengths she might go to gain control of herself and her circumstances, and she gets what is coming to her. She is unmanageable, and so too her body becomes.

Eventually, arriving at the bar, Nancy squishes the mistress with a wooden beam and picks up a wriggling Harry like a worm in her hand. She holds him, as though to behold him. She knows, now, who she is in relation to her husband, what he's actually worth. Gunshot after gunshot rings out to no effect—how difficult this woman is to kill!—until the sheriff pulls out a rifle, blowing up a telephone pole and knocking her to the ground. She has fallen, her pulse gone.

Harry writhes in her dead hand, then goes limp, too. Says the doctor, "She finally got Harry all to herself."

For a few days after I watched the film, the background noise of my brain mostly concerned imagining alternative storylines for Nancy, who in so many ways deserved better. What if she had been allowed to ask for more, without punishment? What if a big body weren't a punishment at all? Why do the loud women always have to die? What if she had put her tiny husband down and walked back out into the desert, wandering through the cactus and into the moonlit mountains?

My idea of my own height only recently lined up with reality. I don't know what exactly helped me get there. It was probably, as with anything, a gradual accumulation of minor events and small recalibrations: a conversation here, a casual touch there, time spent, self-talk, moving toward acceptance of the things I cannot change. Even still, I remember exactly the first time I was able to utter the words "six feet." As I crossed the border and broke through the roof, I briefly felt that mix of fear and frenzy that comes when you know you're about to give yourself over to the unknown.

What if Nancy's very existence didn't have to be an attack? What if her world required less navigating and let her simply be? I think often about how much we lose when we try to make our bodies behave. There is some power, I think, in feeling unmanageable. In surveys of very tall women, most report feeling more confident as time goes on: as they spend another year, and another after that, being themselves. The stooping and slouching slowly ceases; the anger at the world abates. As one respondent in a 2011 Texas Woman's University study observed, "I had to grow into this body."

Of course, the work of growing into your body never ends—you must constantly remind yourself that it is yours, touch it, put it into motion, listen to its different parts. Lately, as the nights have become long and cold, I have been taking extra time to move and stretch. I close my eyes and flop in half. When I roll up to stand up straight, my body feels seven, eight, a thousand feet tall.

The Privilege of Having Soft Hands
Kaila Philo

"You have the hands of somebody who doesn't work," my father always joked. My hands were smooth, soft, and unsullied. The rest of my family's hands, if placed in succession, could create a spectrum of ruttiness with my father on the very end.

My parents' hands were the remnants of great struggle; my siblings' hands were wiry, thin, darkening when exposed to sunlight. Mine somehow remained untouched by the inheritance of labor, and sometimes, the darkest times, I'd pretend I had been born into gentility—the daughter of a renowned history professor and an adventurer, or maybe an opera singer and a documentary filmmaker—before being stolen in the night by these strangers.

My mother met my father as a cable man. I was seven and convinced he was the largest man I'd ever met, towering at a little over six feet with the hands of John Henry. They were considerably ashy and hard. My mother didn't seem to care—at least, not at the time. To her, they were Atlas's

hands, big enough to bear some of the burden of our house-
hold, and careful enough to catch it if it dropped.

Before Comcast, my father had a brief foray into the mil-
itary, stationed in Panama. I imagine he spent those days
with his hands in soap buckets or nestled in dirt, grabbing
at thorns and carrying his own weight across metal bars. In
reality, the only thing that remains from those days is a black
hunting knife reminiscent of a small sword. He returned to
America with a GI Bill earned by rugged hands learned in
the art of killing, and wouldn't use the document until years
later, when he and my mother acquired a house.

My mother eventually found comfort catering to gifted
hands. Today she's a surgical assistant at a children's hospital, learning how to help repair babies' hearts. Hers were
delicate but hard as a tortoise shell, cultivated as weapons to
shield us from predators. Her hands hardened alongside her
heart, and both became good for work, tough for mothering.
You can hold a child with sturdy hands, but they won't feel
soft against her skin.

My father eventually dropped out of school, finding that
there was more money in practice than theory. He seemed
to study everything and nothing at all, briefly majoring in
general studies before leaving indefinitely with the belief that
there would always be a need for strong hands; this became
his calling card. Cable guy, bodyguard, mailman, all depending most on the body, none taking much note about their
effect. His hands became tools to be worn out, so he paid less
attention to caring for them. He forgot to lotion so often that
the skin between his index fingers and thumbs turned ashen
and cracked. Though I moisturize as if it's a papal tradition,

I haven't gotten a manicure in months. This wasn't deliberate, not at first. I'd admire people's nails from afar, planning my next manicure in the back of my mind—*Next week I'm going to get lavender gels with glitter on the edges*—but that week passed and something else always took its slot.

Gradually, I found myself avoiding manicures altogether, as if, over time, I'd begun to link ornate nail designs with frivolity. At first I embarked on a Mission to Feminize: I chose a pink glittery Black Power fist as the cover photo for an on-campus activist group; I placed Glossier stickers on my laptop—a peace sign here, a rainbow there; I browsed Verso, *The Nation*, and Lauren Conrad's lifestyle blog; I injected a healthy dose of performative femininity into my daily praxis, but deep down I secretly yearned to be seen as a serious woman of serious means, sexually attractive but only through minimal visible effort, who keeps her nails haphazardly clipped because they're easier to type with, who's too busy to devote an hour to something as trivial as nail polish, too thoughtful to cover her hands in jewelry. Working girls can't keep pretty hands. We can't afford to.

Last summer I got my first full set of acrylic nails because a writer referenced laying her clean-cut manicure over *Slouching Towards Bethlehem* for an Instagram photo. Hers were a sleek lavender against neat, milky cuticles. This was the way of the literary woman, I thought, so I shelled out twenty dollars for an ombre of beige setting into cream tips. One afternoon I spread them across *The Sympathizer*, casually, under that miasmic kind of summer sunlight that coats everything it touches in a soft halo, and took my own literary woman's photo. One week later I found that I couldn't use the POS system at work with these kinds of nails; every time I brought my index finger down to the screen, the nail would hit it first, rendering it impossible to press the buttons necessary for ringing up a small coffee unless I bent my finger upward, allowing the skin to do its duty but pushing the nail against it, just enough to make it sore.

I didn't replace the acrylics when the time came to remove them, partly because of my mother: She took one glance at my nails—scraped and jagged, all moisture sucked clean from the beds by glue—and launched into a lecture. "You have to take care of your nails. You have such beautiful hands." She peered through the windshield, as if unable to look at me. "You have to take care of them. It's important." I nodded and said, "Okay, Mum." The usual, though I felt awash in shame that I couldn't understand.

You can't climb the economic ladder with a manicure; you need the steady hands to keep you steady.

My father got a package from Amazon: a rose-gold watch from some high-end company I didn't recognize. "I'm going to buy a few of these," he said, "y'know, for different out-fits." I told him I was happy he could treat himself. He said he was, too. Up until that point, the only jewelry he owned was his class ring and a wedding band from a past marriage. He hadn't gotten the former until ten years ago, fifteen years after the school had shut down.

Over time all of our hands have changed. I now wear less jewelry than before and, for a while, I'd brave wintry morn-ings without a tube of lotion on hand. As a result, my hands have roughened. My mother's hands, I imagine, have soft-ened at the same rate as her demeanor. She lives in Houston now and, while I saw her last summer, I can't recall the last time we touched.

My father's hands are covered in rings and watches, all placed against calloused skin. He bought a Lincoln last year: used, but sleek and creamy, the shade of butter pecan ice cream. The last car he owned was a black 1995 Geo Prizm with two broken doors that only cost $500 because he bought it from an old hoarder who never left the house. I began leaving little bottles of lotion in the cup holder, for both of us, because he still gripped the steering wheel with cracking hands, and I didn't want him to stain it with blood.

Teshima

Austin Gilkeson

The dark room was lined with mirrors and lit by the beating of my son's heart. He'd fallen asleep, so I held him in my arms as my wife, Ayako, and I stood quietly. We watched his heartbeat illuminate, in flashes, the single light bulb that hung suspended from the center of the ceiling, and listened to its rhythm pulse through the speakers. It was so loud even my deaf right ear could hear it.

Les Archives du Coeur, The Heart Archives, is an art installation created by artist Christian Boltanski. It sits in a small building on the shore of Teshima, an island in Japan's Inland Sea. The facility—which at first glance resembles a doctor's office, its clean white reception room staffed by friendly women in white lab coats—features rooms where you can record and upload your heartbeat to the archives, computer terminals where you can browse and listen to thousands of other heartbeats, and the long, dark room where the beat of a single human heart is turned into light and music.

We had first heard our son Liam's heartbeat nearly three years to the day before, in a small clinic in my wife's hometown of Ashiya, on the other side of the Inland Sea. On the sonogram screen that day, our son looked like little more than a black smudge, a Rorschach test for us to imagine into a future infant, toddler, child, teen, adult. But his heartbeat came through clearly in a sharp staccato: a steady beat nestled inside a rushing whoosh like the sound of the ocean in a conch shell held up to your ear.

I remember holding my breath as the sound of his heartbeat filled the room, exchanging smiles with Ayako, and feeling an intense surge of different emotions—mostly joy and anxiety. I recognize now that it was the first of many such moments: the first time I held him ("He's so beautiful, what if I drop him?"); his first words ("He said, 'Uh-oh!' Wait, why did he say 'Uh-oh'?"); his first steps ("He's walking! Now he's running away!"). His heartbeat was the rhythm we'd need to move to in this new and ever-surprising phase of life.

A year after we first heard our son's heartbeat in the clinic, I woke up one morning and heard silence on my right side. I write "heard" because the sudden absence of sound was as clear and startling as a siren. I didn't worry about it at first, assuming it was wax buildup or my ear stopping up from a recent flight. That had happened before. My hearing always came back.

But this time it didn't. Days later, I still couldn't hear out of my right ear. My son was six months old then, a chubby, happy baby full of giggles who had an adversarial relationship with sleep. I was scared: What if he called out in the night and I couldn't hear him? What if something happened to him and I was just sitting there, totally unaware?

At an audiologist's office, a friendly woman in a white lab coat led me into a dark, soundproof room with a two-way mirror and conducted a series of hearing tests. I pushed a button when I heard a beep. Voices spoke words into my ears—first right, then left—and I repeated them. Distracting noises (beeps, whooshes, static) were played over the voices, to test how well I could distinguish sounds. When the tests were over, I waited nervously, as if I were a college student waiting for my midterm grades. The results weren't good. My right ear had only heard 30 percent of the beeps and words: severe hearing loss. My left ear fared better, but at 70 percent it still had moderate hearing loss. Probably genetic, the audiologist said.

The ENT doctor decided to inject steroids straight into my inner ear, an attempt to jump-start the tiny hairs that form the basis of our sense of hearing. If the hairs are damaged, the doctor explained, they can't regrow; if they go, the sound goes with them, like a radio switching off.

Having a long needle stuck into your inner ear and then having the cavity flushed with steroids is precisely as unpleasant as it sounds. After a few months of injections and audiology tests, the doctor told me the steroids hadn't worked. I would have single-sided deafness for the rest of my life.

I'd never been to Teshima before our visit in the fall of 2016, but it felt familiar as soon as we stepped off the ferry. Ten years prior, I'd lived in a small town called Toyotama on the

Japanese island of Tsushima in the Korea Strait. Teshima's small farms and fishing villages felt like home to me. The two islands share something else: Teshima, like Toyotama, takes its name from the Shinto goddess Princess Toyotama, daughter of the dragon king of the sea.

In Japanese mythology, Toyotama marries a hunter deity named Yamasachihiko. After years of living in her coral palace at the bottom of the sea, with her sea turtle and jellyfish attendants, they move to the land. Toyotama becomes pregnant and warns her husband not to look at her as she gives birth to their son. He does anyway and sees her in her true form: in some versions, a shark; in others, a dragon. Betrayed, Toyotama returns to the sea.

Ayako found a tiny shrine to Toyotama tucked away in one of Teshima's villages, where we stopped and paid our respects. On Tsushima, where I'd once lived, Princess Toyotama and Yamasachihiko are venerated at Watazumi Shrine, an ancient waterside site with three torii gates leading to the shrine buildings (where the gods are embodied, typically, by a sacred mirror) and two more out in the sea, where they seem to float at high tide. I used to visit the shrine frequently on weekends; there weren't many other places to go in town, and the beautiful grounds provided a favorite spot to sit and read. I'd often find my students fishing there, or see families having picnics when the cherry trees were blooming. Once, I saw a crimson Nomura's jellyfish the size of a washing machine floating just offshore.

Sometimes I daydreamed about walking through the floating gates and into the water, down, down into the deep to find Toyotama's palace. I imagined standing there in the abyss among swaying seaweed, my lungs screaming for oxygen, my ears bursting from the pressure, trying to catch a glimpse of those coral walls and otherworldly lights.

When Liam was a toddler, his favorite *Sesame Street* bit was the one in which an increasingly frustrated Bert tries to tell Ernie he's got a banana in his ear, until Ernie finally shouts, "I'm sorry, you'll have to speak a little louder, Bert! I can't hear you! I've got a banana in my ear!" Whenever he got his hands on a banana, Liam held it up to his ear and giggled, and we acted out the skit until he yelled, "Banana ear!"

I feel like Ernie these days, only nobody can see I've got a banana in my right ear. People call to me, and I don't hear them until they're right next to me. Sometimes I don't even hear them then, and they have to tap me on the shoulder— which scares the hell out of me. I can't tell where individual sounds come from, either. You can find me in the lobby of my office building some mornings, pirouetting like a confused ballerina as I try to figure out which elevator has dinged open. Once, in the middle of the night, Ayako woke me and asked, "Did you hear that?" Like the world's most doomed horror-movie protagonist, I answered, "No?"

A few months ago, I unknowingly ignored a clerk at Trader Joe's trying to chat at the checkout. "Not a big talker, huh?" she said when she finally caught my attention. "Sorry," I replied, and shook my head. What I wanted to say was that I used to be a big talker; I loved going to parties and talking people's ears off. Now I'm more reticent. I dread random conversations, because my lines are always the same: "I'm sorry, could you say that again?" So often I just smile and nod my head and hope I haven't agreed with, or to, something terrible. It's disturbing to realize that we are such changeable beings, that a bit of faulty biological wiring here or there in our bodies can alter our behavior and even personality.

But life with hearing loss is also familiar, in the same way Teshima was familiar. Not understanding most of what people around me are saying, and not being able to fully express myself, is something I'd gotten used to in Toyotama. Then, too, I had to become adept at piecing together the meaning of a phrase from a few understood words, context, and body language.

I found communication easiest with my elementary school students, even though they understood little of my native English; their Japanese vocabulary was limited, too (though still far, far better than mine), and they conversed as much through playing as talking. One day during recess, as I was failing to explain something in my broken Japanese to a group of increasingly distracted students, a girl named Nanami snuck up behind me and lightly smacked me on the head, then ran laughing across the field. The frustration I'd felt trying to communicate popped like a bubble as I chased after her. Here was a language I understood. I couldn't talk to those students about much, but I could play tag with them, and that was its own kind of conversation.

Liam is six now, and so much of how he interacts with Ayako and me is through play—playing with his action fig-ures in the basement, freeze tag in the yard, or acting out wild scenarios, like the living room couch is a high cliff from which we must dive into a sea of ice cream. It can be a relief to communicate in ways beyond words. I sometimes have trouble understanding him because of my hearing loss, or because he's speaking a new tongue all his own. Like most kids his age, language is like a plaything for him. He rakes in new words in English and Japanese and then assembles stories, songs, and jokes the way he does Legos: excitedly and imaginatively, if sometimes haphazardly. The other day, I told him about krakens, the mythological sea monsters, and then this afternoon, as I wrote this, he came over and breathlessly told me about a new creature he'd dreamed up called the fire kraken that lives in a lava lake on a distant island. He spins out these tales at a dizzying speed, so fast his own mouth can barely keep up, let alone my poor left ear. I love and envy him for it.

I've adjusted to living with single-sided deafness over these past few years, but I still worry I won't hear something dangerous, or important, or adorable. And then there's the lingering fear that one morning I'll wake up and my other ear will have suddenly gone out, too, and I'll no longer be able to hear my son's voice—or his laughter, or his heartbeat, which fill me with electric joy every time I hear them.

When I was younger, I found the tale of Princess Toyotama cruel and arbitrary, how she must leave her husband and son behind on the dry shore, but I understand now the betrayal of bodies and the permanence of transformation. But that's not, it turns out, the end of the matter. A couple of years ago, my in-laws gave me a manga edition of the *Kojiki*, an ancient book of Japanese history and myths, including Toyotama's. Most of the story matched what I'd heard before, but in this version, Princess Toyotama and Yamasachihiko continue to correspond after she returns to the sea, sending each other love poems, still able to communicate across the vast and quiet deep. There is more than silence.

On the ferry back from Teshima, I chased Liam around the deck and then tried to help him settle down by looking out for whales and dolphins. Suddenly, he pointed to the water and said something to me. I couldn't hear him, so I leaned in close, my left ear right next to his face, and asked again what he saw.

"Big shark in the water, Dada!" he said.

I didn't see a shark, but I found myself imagining he had seen Princess Toyotama, circling her island and surveying her watery domain. Now, when I daydream about her palace at the bottom of the sea, I picture swimming down through swaying seaweed, my lungs screaming for oxygen and my ears bursting from the pressure, until I glimpse coral walls and otherworldly lights. Inside the palace is a white lobby like a doctor's office, staffed by friendly sea turtles that lead me into a dark room with sacred mirrors and a single light bulb, fat and luminescent as a jellyfish. For a moment, the darkness and silence are complete. And then the room is full with my son's heartbeat, bright and loud, a sharp staccato nestled inside the rushing whoosh of the ocean.

In Utero, in a Pandemic
Marisa Crane

You look like Bane, I say when you pull on your homemade mask. Mine has the Batman logo all over it.

Give me your city, you say in a gruff voice. I bump my masked mouth into your masked mouth and laugh. Everywhere, we search for tiny pockets in which to store our joy for when we need it.

The masked employees are waiting at the bottom of the parking garage stairs to check patients in. So many layers between all of us.

Do you have an appointment today? one employee asks me while the other checks you in.

Oh, no, I'm with her, I say, gesturing toward you.

Sorry, you'll have to wait outside or in your car.

I feel stupid. Obviously, I should have known.

It is a small, sad thing, the fact that I cannot attend your fifteen-week prenatal appointment. I want to see Wilder Fox relaxing in their spa environment. We part ways and I head home. *Tell me everything*, I say, feeling deflated but trying to keep things in perspective.

What I know about distance: my body aches when your two bodies are away from me.

On the drive home, I listen to "Don't Let Us Get Sick" by Warren Zevon on repeat. The first time I heard this song, I was watching *Californication*. Hank Moody, the heavy-drinking, messy-hearted protagonist, sits next to the love of his life, Karen, and as their daughter, Becca, sings, "Just make us be brave / and make us play nice / and let us be together tonight," a few proud tears fall down Hank's aging face.

Not everyone experiences chills or shivers when they listen to music. According to research, those who do experience chills are likely to experience more intense emotions in general.

My ex-girlfriend, J, asked me to move across the country with her, then backed out about ten hours before our flight. But before she backed out, before she did the most generous thing she could have done for me, we spent a lot of time with her family, including her five-year-old and three-year-old cousins. The older cousin was fierce and adventurous. The family seemed to prefer her. Or perhaps *prefer* isn't the right word, but they appeared to understand how to relate to her—she was easy, predictable.

The younger cousin was sensitive, hot to the touch. I was the only one who believed that what she needed was not to change who she was, but to savor who she was. I held her in the moments in which she couldn't understand herself. I still think of her whenever I burst into tears for no reason.

We always recognize our own kind.

I am dabbing my eyes with a tissue when you text me,

Do you want to FaceTime and see Wilder? As always, I quickly recover, embarrassed of the tiny disturbances that inspire monsoons within me. Over FaceTime, I hear Wilder's muffled yet unmistakable heartbeat. It sounds like when you speed through a tunnel with the window down, and your blood makes music in your ears while the wind rips at your cheeks.

The doctor, who is new to us, says hi and introduces herself, then talks us through the ultrasound. *Here's the head and the curved body,* she says.

Holy shit, is that the spine and ribs? you say, awestruck. They look like a real human being today. They even do a little flutter kick for us.

Look, arms and legs. Those are some beautiful thigh bones, the doctor says, tracing Wilder's leg with her finger.

Hopefully, Wilder got my thighs, you declare, laughing.

What I know about distance: I feel it everywhere, in my shoulders, in my pelvis, in the shivers of my feet.

In a Pavlovian response, I cry every time I hear "Don't Let Us Get Sick," whether I feel sad or not. It reminds me of watching *Californication* for the first time, years ago when I was lost and feeling very sorry for myself. I saw myself in Hank, although he was an old straight white man. I felt most seen when Hank was drinking too much, romanticizing Karen, and trying but failing to get her back for good. I've always queered heterosexual media without trying or even being conscious of it.

Perhaps *Californication* felt familiar to me because, before you, my relationships were troubled and tumultuous. Being gay made me feel as if I were predisposed to disaster. I had no examples of queer joy or happiness in my life. Knew no role models, no older queer people who had gotten it right, who'd found the Big Happy, credits roll, fade to black.

I went to gay bars and got sad with all the other sad gays. At night, I wrote out reasons I shouldn't die just yet; they never seemed like enough. Despite the series finale, we aren't certain that it ever works out for Hank and Karen, but it works out for you and me.

What you don't tell me until you come home, after I'd sent a flurry of anxiety texts—I'm scared, babe, I don't want you going into homes, so many people are dying, I don't want to lose you and Wilder, I don't want any of us to die, I can't stop crying, Odie just howled at the mailman, I received a package, what a whirlwind of emotions—is that the doctor told you they just had to intubate a woman who was fifteen weeks pregnant.

I don't want to hurt Wilder, you say, and it breaks me in even my strongest of places.

You provide in-home services to children with autism and other developmental disorders. Your job has been deemed a necessary service. I don't want to let you out of my sight, but I know I must. You wear a mask and gloves. Only prison is like prison. Only war is like war. I have always been adamant that some things are too cruel and unimaginable to be diluted to a metaphor. And yet, my terrified lizard brain imagines you showing up to a battlefield holding a pocketknife.

What I know about distance: every night I go to sleep wondering, *Is this the end of our lives and we don't even know it?*

Historically, I have always berated myself for my sensitivity, my intense emotions. For so long, I was used to being the person who overreacted to things. A dropped plate, a forgotten meeting, an argument with you. But finally my sensitivity feels normal, like an appropriate response to helplessness. To collective grief, both anticipatory and afterdeath grief.

There is a Warsan Shire poem I will never forget. The end goes like this: "I held an atlas in my lap / ran my fingers across the whole world / and whispered / where does it hurt? / it answered / everywhere / everywhere / everywhere."

I have no refills left on my Xanax; I call anyway; the doctor refills it without a word. I don't tell you how frequent my panic attacks have been lately because it would be like alerting you that the sky is out today. Plus, I don't want to stress you out any more than you already are. Do you think Wilder can feel your stress? Your pain? My mother used to say she could feel my pain from across the country. I never believed her. I didn't want to believe that my pain was a living, breathing, whinnying thing that, once born, would take off running toward home.

Time—no one feels it more than the dying and those surrounding the dying. With nearly over eighty-five thousand U.S. deaths, as I write this, we are all surrounding it, to varying extents. Every day, I open Twitter and read dozens more tweets about loved ones dying, and I sit with the ache, wondering how one can possibly mourn through a screen, grieve in isolation. I cannot imagine having to FaceTime you to say goodbye, I love you, I'll always love you.

Even as I sit here writing this essay, I wonder if I am spending my time in the wrong place. Could I be in bed reading and cuddling with you? Could I be tracing that vein in your hand that I adore and asking you which Mary Oliver poem you think Wilder wants to hear?

My pregnancy app says that Wilder is as big as a cootie catcher—or, as I knew it as a kid, a fortune-teller. If I was lucky enough, my teacher wouldn't catch me opening and closing it under my desk, *One, two, three, four, five, g-r-e-e-n, you will become the greatest basketball player of all time!* For fifteen years, basketball consumed my life, but I haven't thought of it too much in recent years, having pivoted to writing. Yet, now I've returned to basketball, my childhood comfort. We go for walks around the neighborhood, and I take my ball; I dribble between my legs, behind my back, pretend to break your ankles, make like people are not losing each other across the globe.

Do you have your mask? Your gloves? Your hand sanitizer? Your wipes? I say, before you leave the house. I am overcome by the desire to hug you tightly, for a long time, to hold you like I'll never get a chance to again, but I fight the urge. We kiss goodbye, and I remind you to be safe, as if you are walking alone at night. There is only so much you can do.

To think, when you were just three weeks pregnant, you came home from the CrossFit gym with a bloody shin, having scraped it doing box jumps.

You're pregnant! What were you doing box jumps for? I'd yelled, half-laughing at myself. I'd behaved as if you ought to be on bed rest for nine months straight. I'd thought you a fragile thing. *Handle with care*, I wanted to stamp on your forehead.

If six months, one year, two years ago you'd asked me if I was afraid of death, I would have said, *No, not really*, and then swallowed a baby aspirin, just in case of heart attack or stroke.

I know that I am more terrified of death than usual because I don't have any desire to watch new TV shows. I want my old favorites. Even the problematic *Californication*, which I fall back on time and time again when my brain feels too messy for words. In the best episode, my comfort episode, which is called "In Utero," we are given access to Hank and Karen's backstory; we get to see how they met ten years prior when they were both cheating on people.

Hank pours himself a large glass of whiskey after the third positive pregnancy test. They discuss their options. Neither of them wants to be a parent right now. They barely know each other. But they are bluffing; they know each other intimately despite having only just met. There's something there. They lie together in bed, her head in his lap. He strokes her hair; they look desperately in love. She plans to leave, abort the baby, and never talk to Hank again.

He writes her a grandiose letter in which he says, I met someone. It was an accident, I wasn't looking for it, it wasn't on the make. It was a perfect storm. She said one thing, I said another, and the next thing I knew, I wanted to spend the rest of my life in the middle of that conversation.

A beautiful, love-smeared montage follows. They walk around New York City together, arms around each other. They laugh and play, they kiss, they make eyes at each other. Hank rubs her pregnant belly and kisses it.

At fifteen weeks, you have just started to show. People have not stopped asking me, *Is she showing yet? Can you tell she's pregnant?*

Those are, of course, two different questions. I can tell you're pregnant because every time you lie down, your heartburn becomes unbearable. I can tell you're pregnant because you, for the first time since I've met you, aren't craving coffee at every turn. I can tell you're pregnant because I have turned primal in my providing for this family. I want to cook and cook even when the fridge is full of food I've already prepared. I am obsessed with making you Mediterranean salad, even if you don't want it. The Mediterranean diet is good for longevity, I am told.

On Saturday, it is sunny for the first time in a week. We decide to sit outside in lawn chairs and read. You change from a T-shirt to a tank top, and upon seeing your tiny bump, I am once again reminded you are pregnant. It's not that I ever forget, but the visual reminder sets off a few sparks in my brain: *She is pregnant! We are going to be parents!* I try to hold on to this piece of joy for what it is, and not for what tragic thing it could become.

A few days ago, a Louisiana newborn died after a coronavirus-positive mother had to give birth four months early. Her premature labor was likely due to oxygen deficiency resulting from the virus.

Another infected woman was asymptomatic until she went into labor. She spiked a fever, and as the doctors were stitching her up after a cesarean section, she began to hemorrhage and her breathing worsened. They quickly intubated her. Once she was stabilized, they tested her. She was positive for Covid-19.

For weeks, I've been trying to find the words to ask you if we should write up our living wills. Our friend, L, is an estate planning attorney. She tells us never has she had as much business as she does now.

I once read that I ought to write about what scares me, to tackle those fears head-on. So I wrote a novel in which a fictional version of you dies during childbirth and then a fictional version of me is left to raise the baby alone. In it, my protagonist says, *This isn't fair. We only just found each other.* Every morning, I wake up at six to revise it, and by nine, I am gutted.

What I know about distance: the space between my reality and my unreality is shrinking.

When my mother was pregnant with me, the doctor covered her mouth to hide her laughter during an ultrasound. *What is it?* my mother asked. *I've been a doctor for twenty-eight years, and I've never seen a baby this active,* the doctor said. It can be easy to mistake preoccupation for activity.

Long before I'd come out to my mother, she'd casually mentioned my future babies as if she could already see them, as if she'd dipped her hand into the future and plucked my little athletes out of a pile like one of those claw game machines. At the time, her words had felt like a threat.

I'd resented her assumption that I wanted kids. I'd resented a lot of things about her, including her ignorance about my sexuality, although had she assumed I was gay without asking me, I would have resented that, too.

My childhood was not a happy time, and although I've blocked a lot of it out, what's left over is an ongoing feeling of unease. I didn't want to become a parent because I thought that making a child meant creating more resentment. I'd wanted the line to stop with me. And then I met you. You know the story; you know how much I relish telling it. Like Hank and Karen, we were cheating on people. That part wasn't good. But upon first seeing you, there was a recognition, an instinct—*I should follow her.* I emailed you from a beach in Croatia: *What are your favorite baby names?* You emailed me: *I think at our wedding it will just be you and me and Lord Huron on repeat.* And it was settled.

For you and me, for so many queer and trans people, *family* is a complicated word. For this reason, I have always hated the antiquated idiom *blood is thicker than water.* What a harmful phrase. I want Wilder, in all their wild, animalistic freedom, to choose us because they want to, because there exists between us a bond far more lasting than blood.

In "In Utero," after the flashback, after the romance and hope, we are brought back to the present in which Hank and Karen are not together. Karen looks at Hank and says, "Fourteen years ago, *I love you* was more than enough. I mean, it was almost revolutionary. And now, I don't know, they're just words. I know you mean them but, Hank, I don't know what they mean to you." They talk about this while their daughter, Becca, is in the other room, knowing she has been lied to once again about the nature of their relationship. Their daughter who, at such a young age, has already become fed up with and disillusioned by her parents' countless mistakes and broken promises. Thinking about Becca makes me feel as if I've been pushed through a spiralizer.

I hope Wilder is happy, you say while fighting with a chair you're assembling in the kitchen. There is a weight to your words, a rough-to-the-touch texture, an understanding that both of us have had to fight, tooth and nail, to learn the habit of happiness. So much of my progress has been undone by the pandemic; my negative self-talk has creeped back in: *You don't deserve a happy ending; this will all go away soon.*

The day we found out you were pregnant, the world was different than it is now. We left the house in T-shirts and shorts and drove to our favorite bookstore, where we bought Wilder their first book. The cashier, a gay man, smiled and gave us a knowing look at checkout. I rode that look all the way home.

What I know about distance: This morning, I wake and slip my hand underneath your T-shirt, placing my hand on your warm belly, on Wilder. There is skin and muscle and fluid between us, but nothing else. When I say, *I love you,* you know exactly what I mean, that this, our love, our family, is a small, fierce revolution.

To Swim Is to Endure

Melissa Hung

Most days, this is what I need—a splash. Even on a cold day like today when I want to go home and get under the covers, I'm compelled to strip down, put on the thin skin of a swimsuit, and jump in.

The water is cold, so I have to keep moving. This is what water does for me. It clears my head. Banishes my worries to half sentences. I don't feel so sad. If I was angry when I got to the pool, I work it out as I crash down the lane, arms punching the surface of the water. I hit it and it does not hit back. The water absorbs me.

There was a time that I swam for fun, but now my body demands it. If I don't swim, the pain grows. If I'm in more pain, what will become of my life?

The headache came on suddenly. I woke up with it one day in August 2013. On the eighth day, I saw a nurse practitioner.

I've had the headache now for three years, six months, and counting. I wake up with it and go to sleep with it. The headache lives in my forehead, pulsating continuously, from one temple to the other. On good days, if I concentrate on something else, I might almost forget about it. On bad days, light and sound irritate me, and the constant awareness of the pain fatigues me. On terrible days, I stay in bed.

I don't have a history of headaches; no one in my family does. I've tried so many things: this kind of drug, that kind of drug, drug infusions administered through IVs, chiropractic care, acupuncture, cranial sacral massage, medical marijuana, amber-colored liquid from a Chinese medicine doctor ferried to me by an aunt from Taiwan, a gluten-free diet, a caffeine-free diet, an everything-free diet, meditation, electrical pulses that prickle against my forehead for twenty minutes a day, leaving my stressful job running an under-appreciated arts education program with ever-decreasing funds. I have figured out what makes the headache worse: lack of sleep or interrupted sleep, onions, some types of tomatoes, bass-heavy sounds, the rush of consternation when I find myself in a fight with my partner. But I have found little that makes it better.

Somehow swimming helps, gives me some semblance of control over a body that will not behave. I swim four to five days a week, for at least thirty minutes at a time. When I emerge from the pool, my breath returning to me, the water dripping from my body, relief settles in. My body feels looser. For a few hours after each swim, the pain in my head dials down a notch.

In the room I shared with my sister growing up, the leg brace hung on the doorknob of the closet door. It consisted of a white belt that circled the waist and metal rods that connected to the bottom of attached shoes. Mimicking bones, the rods had joints at the knees. The joints scratched against the white paint of the closet door, leaving gray marks. Sometimes I wrote faint words on the closet door with the joints.

As soon as I entered this world, my body did not behave. I was born with my feet turned inward and started my life in orthopedic shoes. During the first few years of grade school, I wore the leg brace at home, including while I slept. Today, the American Academy of Pediatrics says this treatment hasn't proven effective.

With my pigeon-toed feet and mediocre posture, my body and I have always had an uneasy relationship. I don't generally think of myself as clumsy, but sometimes I find bruises or cuts on my body and I don't remember how they got there. When I was fifteen, my shoulders—specifically my trapezii, located at each slope of the shoulders and down the upper back—began aching. My mother took me to a rheumatologist who was always accessorized with a colorful bow tie. He prescribed muscle relaxants, but they made me unbearably thirsty. He drew my blood, ran tests, and sent me to a physical therapist.

Eventually, Dr. Bow Tie was stumped with me. He declared me a "conundrum." He suggested that maybe I just had the shoulder muscles of a much larger person crammed into my petite frame, where they strained against their confines. My body, he said, was unexplainable.

I originally took up swimming to temper the shoulder aches but discovered it had other benefits as well. Though I'm not much more graceful in water than I am on land, swimming gives me the illusion of grace, makes me feel fluid in my movements. In an alternate reality of weightlessness, the water takes me—a teeth grinder, a lopsided walker, a smacker when I eat—and makes me elegant: all my limbs flutter, one side and then the other, a constellation of moving parts propelling me forward.

Henry David Thoreau famously wrote in his journal, "How vain it is to sit down to write when you have not stood up to live! Methinks that the moment my legs begin to move, my thoughts begin to flow . . ." Studies have shown that walking can boost creativity. If walking is a creative stimulant, for me swimming is a creative intoxicant. When I walk, even if I have no destination in particular, a part of my brain constantly scans my surroundings. In a pool, I go from one wall to another and back again. My mind stops scanning and can wander freely. I have done some of my best thinking in the pool: generating story ideas, writing haiku in my head, retrieving memories.

Sometimes I let a thought repeat until it becomes a kind of mantra. Once I was close to tears because I was on deadline for a newspaper feature story and I could not write. As I swam, I kept repeating to myself, "I can write this," a stroke to each word. For over twenty laps, I told myself this, until the words became a rhythm in sync with my limbs, until the thoughts became as automatic as my movements. Afterward, I went home and wrote the story.

Some days, I swim for an hour without stopping. That is the other thing about swimming: the endurance you build.

Swimming has enabled me to walk the hills of San Francisco without getting out of breath. It has also helped me to get out of bed, to write the story, to approach a life of constant pain with calm acceptance and a drive to do better.

I've swum in YMCAs all over the country, from the antique basement pool open for just a few hours a day in Somerville, Massachusetts, to the renovated Prospect Park location in Brooklyn gleaming in white-and-blue tile work. I've swum tiny figure eights in hotel pools. I swim wherever I am. In brutal Chicago winters, I trudge through the snow to the campus aquatics center. In downtown Houston, I take my lunch break at the indoor pool a few blocks away. When traveling, I always look ahead of time to find the nearest pool. I've swum the Kitsilano Pool in Vancouver, the largest outdoor saltwater pool in North America. At the time, it didn't have lanes; swimmers circled, and I marveled: *This is what it must feel like to swim like fish in a school.*

I remember that the room had no windows. The judge sat behind a raised wooden desk with a phone. The only thing I can remember about him now is that he was a white man. I sat before him at a small table, my handwritten notes in front of me. I had carefully chosen my outfit that day, one that I hoped would signal responsibility. I remember exactly what I wore: a lace top, a black pencil skirt with a floral digital print, and a cream blazer.

I had decided to leave my job, a job I cared about deeply, because it compounded my stress and made my headache worse. I lived off state disability for a while as I pondered what to do next. One day, the state denied further payments, writing that "the normal expectancy of this medical condition is three days." If only my headache had lasted a mere three days.

To appeal, I had to appear before the judge. And so, in the windowless room, the judge questioned me, and I made my case. My partner was the only other person in the room. Still, I shook with the nervousness of having to speak in a legal proceeding, and with the indignity of having to prove my medical condition.

For the first two years of my headache, I hoped that medicine would find its cause; then I would solve it and return to my headache-free life. Neurologists, though, still don't know why I woke up one day in throbbing pain that has yet to cease. The search for a medication that might help is a slow exercise in trial and error. It often takes six months to know if a drug has had any effect.

Sometimes I think of my headache as a star that is light-years away, pulsing in our earth's night sky. We are seeing a star that might no longer exist because its light took so long to travel to us. Somewhere in the future, I think, is a headache-free me. But I've had to come to terms with the possibility that my headache may never leave. After applying for a few full-time jobs, I realized that I needed a flexible schedule to tend to it, one that would accommodate the hours out of my day I spend swimming. The headache has also forced me to bow out of social events, made me fearful about attending concerts. It has complicated the already-complicated question about whether or not I should be a mother. And it has added another aspect to my identity, one that I am still reluctant to claim—that of a disabled person.

Does a never-ending headache make me disabled? Some days, I think the answer is yes. Yes, because the headache has become a central fact of my life. A constant source of pain. A thin layer of sadness, like the first dusting of a snowfall, blanketing every aspect of my life.

It's Friday evening, and I'm at another YMCA. The pool is packed with the after-work crowd and a youth swim team. I've spent my day in front of a computer, researching and writing. I work from home these days, in the corner of a room with a gray rug, a gray couch, and two simple desks that almost match: one for my partner, one for me. I'm attempting the freelance hustle as a journalist, though it means financial uncertainty.

I survey the lanes and pick one where the other swimmers are about my speed. I jump in, completely in, so my entire body is underwater. Then I push off from the wall. Every part of my body engages: legs straight, feet pointed, stomach tight, shoulders-arms-head swiveling. Water parted by my arms moves back into place behind me. What my body does, it does on its own.

Sometimes, when I'm swimming, I think about the sisters who fled Syria in a dinghy meant for six people but packed with twenty. When the motor failed twenty minutes into their journey and began sinking into the Aegean Sea, the sisters and two others who knew how to swim jumped out and swam for three and a half hours in open water, dragging the broken boat of refugees with them. They survived. At other times I think of my mother, who never learned to swim at all.

Left behind by her parents and raised by her grandmother, she grew up feisty and independent in so many ways, deeply fearful in others. She has never let go of her fear of water.

As I swim, I turn my head above the water and inhale. Muffled sound envelops me. I exhale in the water, and bubbles cascade around me. I may never be completely free of the fear of living the rest of my life in pain, but every day or two, I release it again into the water.

Swimming soothes me in a lullaby of repetition. Swimming is uncomplicated. It does not need machinery; every day, it is just me and the water, a space entirely my own. Even if the pool is full of people, there I am by myself, breaking the surface again and again.

The Climate of Gender

Callum Angus

A season is hard to move, but not impossible. History is replete with stories that tie the revolution of the seasons to mourning mothers and lovers. It was Demeter's tears that brought winter's frost, not her daughter Persephone's six-month absence; Ishtar's joy at being reunited with her husband Tammuz brought forth the blooms, kick-starting the cycle once more.

Much more recently, in his 1999 book *On the Natural History of Destruction*, W. G. Sebald writes about the second spring that visited Hamburg during what should have been autumn of 1943, when "many trees and bushes, especially chestnuts and lilacs, had a second flowering" following the firestorm by the allied forces attempting to subdue the Third Reich. Here, Sebald notes, horror has essentially caused a season to shift, so that what should have been autumn became an incongruous spring.

Of course, we don't need wars to cause seasons to happen out of sync; climate change is already slowly causing the same. New England has warmed by an average of three degrees since 1901, and that's enough to start to blur the seasons together. Sap running early rarely excites anyone whose income doesn't depend on it, especially when an approximation of the real thing sits on grocery store shelves. This has meant that maple trees in the region today begin to release their sap at least two weeks earlier than they did a century ago.

It was once thought impossible to scale up the bleeding of maple trees for bigger agricultural production, but, like most commodities in late capitalism, maple sap has also been bent to the whims of increasing profit margins and market shares. There are now operations in Vermont with enough tubing to stretch all the way to San Francisco and back again, employing evaporation technologies that can produce fifty-five gallons of maple syrup in less than two minutes. The biggest global producers of maple syrup, however, are found in Quebec—members of an exclusive cabal called the Quebec Maple Syrup Producers guild, or PPAQ—yielding hundreds of thousands of barrels in a season, some of which end up in a strategic reserve, an OPEC-like cartel that in 2019 stored almost one hundred million gallons of syrup.

A reserve is necessary, PPAQ says, because syrup production can vary wildly from year to year and region to region, depending on small swings in weather. The optimal conditions under which maple sap flows best and maple seedlings germinate is a precise roller coaster of freezing and thawing: days in the forties and nights in the twenties or below. With climate change bringing an increase in severe weather, though, temperatures have become more unpredictable. PPAQ cautions that although the amount of syrup in reserve sounds high, it can be depleted rapidly, such as in 2016, when they found themselves completely cleaned out after several years of low production.

Upon noticing that one tree in their data set had produced a considerable amount of sap despite missing most of its crown—the leafy top of the tree—researchers set up an experiment in which they lopped the tops from a stand of maple saplings, which were then tapped. The saplings produced a healthy amount of sap, despite missing half of their aboveground mass. Leafless trunks proved to be sufficient when the end goal is production with maximum efficiency.

Meanwhile, I wonder if some trees have problems with the slow siphoning of sap, if the *tap tap tap* on their tin buckets reminds them that they are a conduit for sweetness in this world, unasked.

How to tell a story about climate? By necessity, it is an average drawn over a long period of time. It's not a fixed point. There is no inciting incident.

In this way, a story about climate is a lot like a story about gender.

So many of us watch the weather of our own bodies, ready to sound the alarm in case things get out of control. We keep detailed logs and journals of our atmospheres each day.

When I was younger, I was like an anthropologist observing my own body. I'd look at my chest and wonder if the top surgery scars fell too low, if my nipples stretched too far vertically. I was always under observation—by family, by doctors—but most of all, by myself. I filled journals comparing myself to others, always collecting data for an experiment of one. I watched the seasons march across my body, the shelf of my breasts calving in the surgeon's office, the sprouting of male privilege and a five-o'clock shadow after just a few weeks on testosterone.

For me, this was the appeal of transitioning. The ability to track and measure and watch for hair growth and octave drops in voice and the redistribution of fat from hips to stomach, the way people started to ignore me in public, how men spoke to me differently. Eventually the changes slowed down and there was less to track; I moved away from studying the physical details and shifted, over time, to focus on the climate of my self.

Time ages a body and changes its shape like a frost heave buckles asphalt, expanding in the cold and then leaving it to crumble and collapse in the thaw. Only age is linear, and there is no going back, whereas I can move around inside of gender, forward and back, kicking off against its walls like a small aboveground pool, returning to recognizable terrain when things get too uncomfortable or unsafe.

The story arcs I learned in school about rising and falling action hold little relevance here: the action is up and down, hot and cold as mercury in the thermometers we no longer use.

Bud break refers to the moment when the sap stops running and the tiny scrunched-up packets of green and red maple leaves burst out of their pistils, but it sounds like a bad euphemism for losing one's virginity. Many aspects of

sap production have, historically, been described in feminine terms. Perhaps it's because of the way it depends on
the mercurial shifts between freeze and thaw, night and day,
winter and spring, the unpredictable fluctuations providing
the engine behind the gravity-defying flow—and in science,
most things not clearly understood are described with a
feminine bent, like the way that the sea—"unpredictable,"
"seductive"—was so often written about as if it were female
in natural history accounts of previous centuries.

If I'm telling stories about seasons and gender and change,
then I should reach for a tool to pry apart bark and skin and
get at the tantalizing meaning just below the surface. The
spile and the speculum are similar in shape and appearance,
metal tubes that taper at one end to allow for ease of inser-
tion: With a delicate touch, the spile is tapped into the rough
bark of the sugar maple to allow sap to flow out, while the
speculum is inserted by the ob-gyn to stretch apart the vaginal canal and allow the swabbing of the cervix during a Pap
smear. Plastic versions of both are now modern and more
popular than their metallic predecessors, albeit for different
reasons (not as cold; cheaper).

I have difficulty believing that tapping a tree does not
hurt, in part because the speculum, and, really, vaginal penetration of any kind, has always been a multiplied hurt for me:
one, it just plain hurts; and then it hurts to hold a hurt like
that so close to the center of me; and it hurts a third time, as a
trans person, to have this pain reallocated in doctors' offices
and web forums to cis women. When I started transitioning, I would sit in the fertility clinic—the only place where
hormone replacement therapy could be prescribed to me at

the time—among the many pregnant or hopefully pregnant people, feeling extremely out of place, feeling poorly understood, like that "feminine" sea.

Now, after close to ten years on testosterone, my body has become a recalcitrant trunk; dried and atrophied tissues refuse to allow the speculum through; and anything that attempts to force its way in results in the most exquisite pain imaginable. This is unfortunate, partly because I already experience frequent, painful cramping, a common but poorly understood experience shared by many trans men on testosterone, which some doctors say is related to increased uterine musculature pulling on surrounding organs. The recommended solution by my physician is a hysterectomy. This is not a measure I'm against on the grounds of preserved fertility; I don't fear losing the ability to have children, and I don't mind adding more scars to my body—although these days they can go in through three tiny incisions around your belly button, leaving you lighter one uterus with almost no scarring at all.

Rather, I worry that whatever shriveled feeling my ovaries have left to impart will be lost to me. I've been a man for a long time, but it's always been the layering that's been the important part, not pinpointing the time when I became a man—at birth, with the first hormone injection, or the last time I had a period. The feminine has always been a part of my personal climate, and while I don't subscribe to essentialist notions of gender residing in specific body parts, removing this part of me had never been part of my plan.

This isn't about sap and flow and blood and menstruation as inherently feminine things to escape, but the fact, instead, that we all have a territory to which we dream of returning, trees and people both. And as our climate shifts, changing our homes and the seasons we grew up with, we'll need to find new ways of living with and telling stories about how things used to be and change in the land.

Within the next century, and likely long before then, the Northeast will almost certainly cease to be the prime climate for maple sugar production. Already, scientists and maple producers are seeing signs of limb mortality and bark grown too tough to let the sap squeak by, like a kitchen sponge dried up on the sink. Debates rage at the University of Vermont's Maple Research Center as to whether or not bud break will move earlier and earlier due to climate change, or if it's merely dependent on the length of daylight and therefore untouchable.

There is so much hand-wringing about bud break and syrup reserves for lean years, and yet so few people, by comparison, seem to be concerned about something much more important, to me: the stories slowly being lost about one tree's unique ability to thrive and create sweetness during a disappearing season of transition.

In college, I knew someone somehow related to the painter Grandma Moses; this is perhaps unsurprising, given that, in a Genghis Khan–like scenario, 75 percent or more of New Englanders carry some Grandma Moses in their blood, symbolically. Her folksy interpretations of New England agricultural scenes have gone through variable periods of popular and critical appreciation since her work was discovered in a drugstore by a New York art dealer in 1938. It's hard to imagine a time when thrift stores existed without her detailed two-dimensional planes of figure skaters and farmers and sleighs full of children.

Sugaring Off is Grandma Moses's rendition of what it was like when an entire community came together in late winter to boil sap. The painting is dominated by the brilliant white of the snow and the pallor of the sky. Children run every which way, careful to avoid a large cauldron of sap bubbling over and orange and red fire. Delicate, lacy maples bare of leaves punctuate the scene. There is no hint of the war that was raging just outside the frame when it was painted in 1943—the orange and pointy flames lap at the bottom of the cauldron, scorched black, while Sebald's firestorm rages off-screen.

The image is sweet, in the generic sense of the word; it also depicts the concentration of sweetness in the boiling sap, therefore doubly deserving of the descriptor *saccharine*. *Saccharine*, a pejorative meaning *overly sentimental*, derives from the same linguistic root as *sugar*, the Sanskrit word *sarkara*, meaning *gravel* or *grit*. It is a decidedly textured descriptor of sweetness.

Sometimes, when I'm home alone, I will sip it straight from the jar. The syrup coats my mouth and throat, and for a short while after even air tastes sweeter. Will maples miss the land? Will they miss the feeling of slowly being drained, or will they celebrate, as I did, when I stopped the flow?

———

The maples where I live now are broad-leaved, foliage often reaching the diameter of a dinner plate, and their trunks grow gnarly with age and moss. They support rope swings and many smaller creatures. I don't know the details of their relationship with the sugar maple, though if it exists it is likely distant and diluted, as they are unsweetened and untapped; what their future holds is unclear, their uselessness placing them beyond concern.

My future in the Northeast is as uncertain as the maples'. The forces that may push us out—rising temperatures, warmth and hate caused by ten billion combustions every day in the hearts of greedy men (for they have mostly been men)—are already here. Maybe this is about bodies and trees once planted in the land and now forced to move, despite their rooted histories. Or maybe it's about finding ways to mourn the loss of green glossy maple leaves in summer, sweetness on pancakes, and other ways of being in the world. I'm trying to find another way of remaining legible and physical, while holding mourning and joy in equal measures.

At its heart, a season is a story told to predict the movement of a year, when to plant and harvest crops, when to hibernate and when to move on. Now, in the throes of climate change, the story of seasons is being revised: scorching days in March, wintry blizzards in May, stronger and more frequent storms at any time of year. The story is changing, fracturing.

We face the challenge of telling a new story: the story of a larger season, one more confusing and less straightforward, with significant changes that are already affecting everyone around the globe, a new season of suffering and adaptation and altered ranges and resilience, which, if we listen closely, can tell us something new about ourselves. I write about climate change and transition in the same breath because they are the two dominant forces that have shaped my life in almost every way. I think of them as part of the same process. Each—gender, climate—has historically required a knowledge of what came before in order to define their characteristics, whether that was biological sex or weather patterns.

But these a priori categories can no longer be relied upon, thanks to changing social and environmental climates. Some groups have seized upon this moment of transformation to forecast an inescapable future of doom: the Deep Adaptation movement, for instance, urges humanity to prepare for the coming precarity and inevitable global catastrophe as climate becomes more unpredictable and resources scarce, deliberately misrepresenting the science behind climate change in the most negative light possible. Meanwhile, in the present, new anti-trans laws are floated daily in the United States, and conservative talking heads muse loudly and dangerously about the "loss" of women to a transgender "craze," our existence itself a fearful new climate to these lawmakers. Such fearmongering would have us believe that the breaking down of old categories spells disaster for the human race, rather than a chance at rewriting past wrongs.

I'm not here to draw any conclusions about the future myself. Instead, I am simply looking at the maple and wondering where it will grow next, how its meaning might change were its physiological rhythms no longer so uniquely adapted to the spring season, and thus no longer so easily exploited. I am simply looking at myself and how much change I've had to adapt to in order to still be here, how change has become a part of who I think I am; I'm looking at other trans people, too, seeing how we've continually shaped and reinvented ourselves, and I can't see anything but hope in that.

Trees and people live in transition now, perhaps permanently, and I do not think this is all bad. Such a shift in climatic thinking requires accepting loss sometimes, and remembering where we've been, what we've done wrong, and a willingness to find new things beautiful. It requires recognizing the beauty in new definitions of gender, allowing the expansiveness and creativity of trans people to revise what we thought was known about gender in the past. It requires adaptation to new seasonal rhythms, yes, but adaptation with an awareness that this is not the first time whole societies have been forced to adapt to change they didn't want, and a willingness to listen to those communities with much more respect than we have in the past.

It may not seem like it, but the stories we tell now will one day become the foundations of new myths, the Ishtars and Demeters and firestorms of the past made new once again in narrative. Perhaps future civilizations will tell stories in which wildly oscillating weather patterns at the turn of the twenty-first century were the result of great planetwide suffering. Or they might inherit a legend that tells how great change sparked great cooperation in nourishing the land and each other because, as is often the case with transition, the possibility for new stories opened up.

Mapping My Body with Sewing Patterns

Haley E. D. Houseman

My early memories involve pins and needles and the rattling sound of a sewing machine on the dining room table, watching my mother. She would alter my clothes, sew my family pajamas for Christmas and elaborate costumes for high school drama productions and Halloween. In between making doll clothes and reupholstering living room sets, she spent weekends recovering chairs for friends and family. My mother drafted a pattern and sewed my senior prom dress, finishing it moments before I popped it on to take pictures. In pictures from her childhood, she and her seven siblings are in matching plaid outfits they made themselves, like the von Trapps on summer vacation.

I remember constantly being frustrated once I was freed from a grade-school uniform at fifteen. My body was suddenly so difficult to fit into this new kind of clothing, all low-rise bell bottoms and baby tees, even though I fell firmly in so-called straight sizes. In high school, even as my mother told me that my body was perfect and my own and that I should never feel pressured to change it, we fretted together about our weight gains. Constantly tugging my necklines up, she feared I would expose something intimate or sexual or monstrous or beautiful to the world. What if they knew? What if they saw my shape? When eventually I gained hips in proportion, my waist slimming out, giving me an hour-glass shape, I attracted unwanted attention when clothed too closely in body-conscious fabrics. My flesh was perpetually trying to escape my clothing at every turn, and I tried desperately to contain it in the kind of fast-fashion mall clothing that I saw everywhere.

When I discovered vintage clothing, I remade how I clothed my body. Often handmade or altered, always fitting like a glove, never slipping or spilling illicit flesh, the modest cuts of the 1940s and '50s were a revelation. I discovered high waists and non-stretch cotton and linen, nipped-in shapes, and low hemlines. Suddenly I was presentable, even conventionally beautiful. Nothing about my body had changed. It was the cut of the clothes, sewn from patterns that had been drafted with a different kind of body in mind. I was liberated even as I felt jolted into the past. My modesty was considered becoming, despite constraining my style. But clothing that fit without struggle was such a relief, I wore those clothes for years, through stints in fashion magazines, law firms, tech and publishing companies. I wore those cuts like a suit of armor that rendered me visible in an acceptable way.

The world is a strange place for women who love their bodies. We are taught from a young age that there are acceptable ways to use it, to display it, to dress it. We are taught to shrink. The bodies that are small and smooth and unobtrusive are the most desirable ones. The definition of desirable bodies is perpetually shifting and narrowing, an unwinnable contest no matter which body you walk around in.

When I think about my hips, I think about what it feels like to have someone else's hands rest on them, how my legs have carried me all over the world. The shape of my body is an inheritance from the women in my family, otherwise invisible in the freckled fair skin and red hair and green-blue eyes I inherited from my father. My thoughts about my body consider how it moves through time and space, rather than the space it takes up.

It's been a long time since I could be made to feel bad about this body, which I consider a lovely vessel for my mind and not the other way around. There is no separation of church and state here, just a tangle of nerves and skin and bone that holds my books and eyes that read and a brain to hold a mind that contains all of that. Bodies are wild; mine has carried me across continents and gotten me lost in cities. It is joy and warmth and scent and sweat, and I refuse to be ashamed of it. I just want to clothe it in what it deserves, all the joy and celebration and thoughtless ease of its normal nakedness.

Later, when my beloved body changed again, not because of age or hormones, but because of a more nebulous nexus of stress and loneliness and medication and chronic illness, it left me larger, though no less beautiful. My clothes didn't fit, but I didn't blame my body for that. Instead I blamed the fashionable cut of clothing shaped for a particular body type or types. I headed out to shop for vintage items but found myself too large. I tried to buy clothing new and found I now lay in the murky territory between straight- and plus-size fashion, always too big for patterns graded up from a two, always too small for patterns graded down from a sixteen. Nothing fit right; everything had to be altered.

More comfortable in body and confident in my sense of style, I want clothes I can dream up, pulled from my imagination, not clothes culled from the past. And I won't wait for some distant future, where it makes economic sense for brands to grade their clothing patterns to the middle of the road or somehow intuit my exact and perfect shape. There's no one quite like me anyway, and I have an inheritance that goes beyond my hands to what they can do. I have the tools and the skills. I can draft the patterns myself. I create my future. I'll sew the garments myself.

This is how you make a garment from scratch as an amateur in 2017:

First, you lose hours on Pinterest looking for the perfect pair of trousers or the ideal summer sundress. You follow the links in frustration, everything overdone or too expensive or made in synthetics or in a limited size range or in a mystery factory overseas. You despair, and then you remember you have a heavy-duty Singer machine and have been sewing for ten years.

Second, in a fit of resolve and a lost Sunday afternoon, you haul the enormous rolls of pattern-drafting paper from under your bed in a tiny Brooklyn bedroom. After tracing likely garments you already own, measuring and making tweaks and messing up at least twice, you cut the pattern. It is now 1:00 a.m. and you have work in the morning.

The third step is to forget your pattern, or rather, let it lurk guiltily on the edge of your consciousness while the rest of your life sweeps you up in a never-ending stream of to-dos. This step will last several weeks to several months.

Finally, you hit the fourth step—another free Sunday evening in which you cut and piece fabric in a fever dream of joyful accomplishment. You sew darts in opposing directions and lose an hour pulling stitches while watching Netflix. It is now, again, somehow 1:00 a.m. and you must go to bed without hemming this new item of clothing.

Step five is to hang the garment on the back of your door to glower at you as another two weeks rush past you. Feel a mix of pride and shame every time you see it. Try not to look at the undone hem.

Step six usually happens when you are procrastinating on something important. Seize the moment and hem your dress. Wear it immediately the next day with total disregard to the appropriateness to occasion and weather. Revel in the compliments, answered with: "Thank you, I made it myself."

This desire to take up the needle is in my birth and blood. Born just outside the Industrial Revolution–fueled textile manufacturing belt of Northern Massachusetts, my childhood landscape was dotted with converted (and dormant) textile mills and the U.S.'s original garment factories. My mother's family traces lines of textile tradesmen all through our working-class Sicilian heritage. My grandfather and great-grandmother worked on Singer sewing machines and created commercial upholstery. Another great-grandfather

was a tailor, and it was common to be handy with a needle. My mother learned to sew from her mother, a practical
mother of eight and a teacher, though my mother and her
enterprising older sister learned garment work in home eco-
nomics and applied it to making swimsuits and prom dresses
that would otherwise be out of their reach.

It's not just my heritage. Our grandparents and great-
grandparents made their own clothes or bought them in a
store and had them altered. Maybe they weren't good with
a needle, and so took fabric or a pattern or a beloved item
to a tailor and asked them to create the world anew in fabric. Prior to the late nineteenth century, clothing was handmade as a rule. There were the fashionable and the rich, who
commissioned designs, and the home-sewn clothes made by
parents and aunts or middle-class tailors. It was assumed
clothing was sewn, or at least altered, to fit your precise and
unruly body. The idea that you could walk into a store and
walk out with a perfectly fitted garment, no alterations, was
not a part of the equation. Clothes were expensive, precious,
and customized in hem and cut.

With the rise of the industrial production of clothing
through factories, clothing became mass-produced, sewn in
standard sizes and sold at fixed prices. When we talk about
modern clothing production, it's easy to lose the hand in the
process, but clothing is still handmade. Though it's cut in
lots and sewn by the piece, often at high speed and volume,
every step requires the human hand. A person drafts, a person fits the test model, a person sews every seam and stitches
every button. For the sake of efficiency, a "standard" set of
body measurements is chosen brand by brand. But your jeans

passed through many skilled hands that could not possibly imagine the landscape of your particular body with the familiarity you can.

Sewing your own clothes gives you a crack at a particular kind of bodily autonomy that seems only available for the wildly wealthy: custom designed to your distinct taste and a pattern cut for your anatomy, every bump and curve, taking in seams where the fabric pools or buckles. When my mother sewed my clothing, I took this process for granted, only remembering the occasional stick of the pin and the feeling it was my body's fault that my legs were too short for my jeans, that my wrap neckline needed extra fabric tacked to the bodice to cover my chest properly. Surely no one else felt like their clothing pinched and pulled and warped on their frame. Who else's mother added straps, took off inches, fixed a broken zipper instead of buying a new garment? The uniqueness of my clothing always made me squirm, even if no one knew I was wearing something homemade or customized. Now a one-of-a-kind garment makes me shine.

As I've gotten older, I have grown to admire the simple lines of a hand-stitched dress. Walking into the Brooklyn Museum's recent exhibit of Georgia O'Keeffe's handmade clothing alongside her artwork, I had a new appreciation for the art of the craft of sewing, but also the independence from stores and brands and runways. This famous, wildly talented woman focused on functionality within her own style, crafting detailed tops, wrap dresses, jeans, tunics, smart suits, skirts, and trousers. With small touches of ornamentation, hers was her own particular austere glamour. Her wardrobe oozed the determined minimalism and self-sufficiency of

Georgia O'Keeffe; her particular tastes only refined as she aged. The artist almost always made her simple clothing herself or had it made for her, freeing her body from the styles of the time, asserting her independence. How she clothed herself shaped how she was perceived, and she had total control over this image, down to every stitch. It wasn't just about fit, or about affordability. It was about style, freedom, and joy in being adorned with specificity, far outside of the dressing room.

Submerging myself in the gallery filled with O'Keeffe's gorgeously, meticulously simple clothes lent gravitas to my yearning for my own wardrobe autonomy. My body's changing shape and size had refined my taste, but I had no visual vocabulary for homemade that did not look homespun, where simplicity translated to elegance rather than a lack of skill or imagination. My desire for ankle-length cotton voile dresses became an achievable victory, rather than an expression of my limits as a seamstress or the outline of my hips. The clothing I produce may be simple, but it belongs to me and my body in a way nothing else can.

Women in the Fracklands

Toni Jensen

I.

On Magpie Road, the colors are in riot. Sharp blue sky over green and yellow tall grass that rises and falls like water in the North Dakota wind. Magpie Road holds no magpies, only robins and crows. A group of magpies is called a tiding, a gulp, a murder, a charm. When the men in the pickup make their first pass, there on the road, you are photographing the grass against sky, an ordinary bird blurring over a lone rock formation.

You do not photograph the men, but if you had, you might have titled it *Father and Son Go Hunting*. They wear camouflage, and their mouths move in animation or argument. They have their windows down, as you have left those in your own car down the road. It is warm for fall. It is grouse season and maybe partridge but not yet waterfowl. Despite how partridge are in the lexicon vis-à-vis pear trees and holiday singing, the birds actually make their homes on the ground. You know which birds are in season because you are from a rural place like this one, a place where guns and men and shooting seasons are part of the knowledge considered common.

Magpie Road lies in the middle of the 1,028,051 acres that make up the Little Missouri National Grassland in western North Dakota. Magpie Road lies about two hundred miles north and west of the Standing Rock Reservation, where thousands of Indigenous people and their allies have come together to protect the water, where sheriffs' men and pipeline men and national guardsmen have been donning their riot gear, where those men still wait, where they still hold tight to their riot gear.

If a man wears his riot gear during prayer, will the sacred forsake him? If a man wears his riot gear to the holiday meal, how will he eat? If a man enters the bedroom in his riot gear, how will he make love to his wife? If a man wears his riot gear to tuck in his children, what will they dream?

Magpie Road is part of the Bakken, a shale formation lying deep under the birds, the men in the truck, you, this road. The shale has been forming over centuries through pressure, through layers of sediment becoming silt. The silt becomes clay, which becomes shale. All of this is because of water. The Bakken is known as a marine shale—meaning, once, here, instead of endless grass, there lay endless water.

There, just off Magpie Road, robins sit on branches or peck the ground. A group of robins is called a riot. This seems wrong at every level except the taxonomic. Robins are ordinary, everyday, general-public sorts of birds. They seem the least likely of all birds to riot.

When the men in the truck make their second pass, there on the road, the partridge sit their nests, and the robins

are not in formation. They are singular. No one riots but
the colors. The truck revs and slows and revs and slows beside you. You have taken your last photograph of the grass,
have moved yourself back to your car. The truck pulls itself
close to your car, revving parallel.

You are keeping your face still, starting the car. You have
mislabeled your imaginary photograph. These men, they are
not father and son. At close range, you can see there is not
enough distance in age. One does sport camouflage, but the
other a button-down shirt, complete with pipeline logo over
the breast pocket. They are not bird hunters. The one in the
button-down motions to you out the window with his handgun, and he smiles and says things that are incongruous with
his smiling face.

II.

The night before, in a nearby fracklands town, you stand,
with your camera, in your hotel room doorway. You left
Standing Rock for the Bakken, and the woodsmoke from
the water protector camps still clings to your hair. You perform your fracklands travel protocol, photographing the
room—the bedspread and desk, the bathroom. In your year
and a half of research for your novel, of driving and talking
to women in the fracklands, you have performed this ritual,
this protocol, dozens of times. You upload the photos onto a
website that helps find women who are trafficked, who have
gone missing.

The influx of men, of workers' bodies, into frackland
towns brings an overflow of crime. In the Bakken at the
height of the oil and gas boom, violent crime, for example,

increased by 125 percent. North Dakota Attorney General Wayne Stenehjem called this increase in violent crime "disturbing" and cited aggravated assaults, rapes, and human trafficking as "chief concerns."

In each place, each frackland, off each road, you wait until checkout to upload the photos of the rooms. In the year and a half of driving and talking and driving and talking, if you've learned nothing else, you've learned to wait. Because it is very, very difficult to sleep in a hotel room once you learn a woman's gone missing from it.

III.

In the Marcellus Shale in Pennsylvania, a floorhand shuts the door to his hotel room, puts his body between the door and a woman holding fresh towels. A floorhand is responsible for the overall maintenance of a rig. The woman says to you that he says to her, "I just want some company." He says it over and over, into her ear, her hair, while he holds her down. She says it to you, your ear, your hair. She hates that word now, she says, *company*. A floorhand is responsible for the overall maintenance of a rig. A floorhand is responsible. But who is responsible for and to this woman, her safety, her body, her memory? Who is responsible to and for the language, the words that will not take their leave?

In a hotel in Texas, in the Wolfcamp Shale, you wake to the music of the trucks arriving and departing. This hotel is shiny tile and chrome bathrooms. It is a parking lot overfilled with trucks, with men from the fields who have an arrangement with management. An arrangement can mean flowers in a vase. An arrangement can mean these men pay for nothing, not even a room. In the morning, the parking lot is all trash can. Beer bottles and used condoms and needles, the nighttime overflow.

In a hotel in Texas, in the Permian Basin, you report to the front desk re: the roughneck in the room above. You dial zero while he hits his wife/girlfriend/girl he has just bought. You dial zero while he throws her and picks her up and starts again. Or at least, one floor down, this is the soundtrack. Upon his departure, the man uses his fist on every door down your hall. The sound is loud but also is like knocking, like *hello*, like *Anybody home?* You wonder if he went first to the floor above but think not. Sound, like so many things, operates mostly through a downward trajectory.

At a hotel where South Dakota and Wyoming meet, you are sure you have driven out of the Bakken, past its edge, far enough. That highway that night belongs to the deer, and all forty or fifty of them stay roadside as you pass. You arrive at the hotel on caffeine and luck. The parking lot reveals the calculus of your mistake—truck after truck after truck, and a hotel clerk outside transacting with a young roughneck. Their posture suggests a shared cigarette or kiss or grope—something safetied through vice or romance or lust. You'd take it. But here the posture is all commerce, is about the positioning of the body close so money can change hands. You are in a place that's all commerce, where bodies are commerce only.

When two more roughnecks stagger into your sight line, the hotel clerk and her partner are heading inside. She meets your eyes like a dare. The staggering man is drunk, the other holding up the first while he zips his fly. This terminology, *fly*, comes from England, where it first referred to the flap on a tent—as in, *Tie down your tent fly against the high winds.*

As in, *Don't step on the partridge nest as you tie down your fly.* As in, *Stake down your tent fly against the winter snow, against the rubber bullets, against the sight of the riot gear.*

The men sway across the lot, drunk-loud, and one says to the other, "Hey, look at that," and you are the only that there. When the other replies, "No. I like the one in my room just fine," you are sorry and grateful for the one in an unequal measure.

You cannot risk more roadside deer, and so despite all your wishes, you stay the night. A group of deer is called a herd; a group of roe deer, a bevy. There is a bevy of roe deer in the Red Forest near Chernobyl. The Bakken is not Chernobyl because this is America. The Bakken is not Chernobyl because the Bakken is not the site of an accident. The Bakken is not Chernobyl because the Bakken is no accident.

IV.

On Magpie Road, the ditch is shallow but full of tall grass. With one hand, the button-down man steers his truck closer to your car, and with the other, he waves the handgun. He continues talking, talking, talking. The waving gesture is casual, like the fist knocking down the hotel hallway—*Hello, anyone home, hello?*

Once on a gravel road, your father taught you to drive your way out of a worse ditch. When the truck reverses, then swerves forward, as if to block you in, you take the ditch to the right, and when the truck slams to a stop and begins to reverse at a slant, taking the whole road, you cross the road to the far ditch, which is shallow, is like a small road made of grass, a road made for you, and you drive like that, on the green and yellow grass until the truck has made its turn, is behind you. By then you can see the highway, and the truck is beside you on the dirt road, and the truck turns right, sharp across your path. So you brake then veer left. You veer out, onto the highway, fast, in the opposite direction.

Left is the direction to Williston. So you drive to Williston, and no one follows.

At a big-box store in Williston, a lot sign advertises overnight parking for RVs. You have heard about this, how girls are traded here. You had been heading here to see it, and now you're seeing it. Mostly, you're not seeing. You are in Williston for thirty-eight minutes, and you don't leave your car.

You spend those thirty-eight minutes driving around the question of violence, of proximity and approximation. How many close calls constitute a violence? How much brush can a body take before it becomes a violence, before it makes violence, or before it is remade—before it becomes something other than the body it was once, before it becomes a past-tense body?

V.

   Q&A

Why were you there on the road?

   Because Indigenous women are almost three times more likely than other women to be harassed, to be raped, to be sexually assaulted, to be called a *that there*.

Because when the governor of North Dakota made an order to block entrance into the camps at Standing Rock and then rescinded it, he said the order was intended toward "public safety."

Because in his letter to the Standing Rock tribal chairman, the commander of the Army Corps of Engineers said he was "genuinely concerned for the safety and well-being of both the members of your tribe and the general public located at these encampments."

Because these statistics about trafficking, about assault, are knowledge considered common, but only if your body is not considered a general-public body.

Because you're a Métis woman.

Because you and they and we misunderstand the danger at Standing Rock, the danger of this pipeline going in there or elsewhere or everywhere. Because you and they and we misunderstand the nature of danger altogether.

Because each person in Flint, Michigan, for the foreseeable future, is rationed four cases of bottled water per week. Because you can see this future upriver or down. Because everywhere is upriver or down.

Because your first memory of water is of your father working to drown your mother. Because you are four or five, and you need to use the bathroom, but instead, find yourself backing out the bathroom doorway and down the hall where you sit on the rust-colored shag. Because you wait for your father to quit trying to drown your mother. It seems crucial in the moment not to wet your pants. It seems crucial to hold the pieces of yourself together. If you make a mess on the carpet, if your father doesn't kill your mother, then she will have to clean the carpet. It seems crucial not to cause any trouble. So you sit. You wait. You hold yourself together.

Because all roads used to lead back to that house, and it is a measure of time and hard work that they no longer do. Because all roads lead to the body and through it. Because too many of us have these stories and these roads. Because you carry theirs and they carry yours, and in this way, there is a measure of balance. Because you are still very good at holding yourself together. Because these times make necessary the causing of trouble, the naming of it.

Because to the north and west of Magpie Road, in the Cypress Hills of southern Saskatchewan, in 1873, when traders and wolf hunters killed more than twenty Assiniboine, mostly women and children in their homes, the Métis hid in those hills and lived. Because they lived, they carried the news. Because they lived, you carry the news. Because the massacre took place along the banks of a creek that is a tributary that feeds into the greater Missouri River.

Because these times and those times and all times are connected through land and bodies and water.

What were you wearing, there on the road?

Not riot gear.

Why didn't you call the police?

See the water cannon on the bridge at Standing Rock. Listen to the sheriff's department men call it a "water hose" like this makes the act better. See also: Birmingham, Alabama. See the dog cages constructed outside the Morton County Sheriff's Department to hold "overflow." See the overflow— the water protectors, Dakota and Lakota women and men in cages. See it all overflow. See the journalists arrested for trespass and worse. See the confiscated notebooks, the cameras they will never get back. See the woman struck by a tear gas canister. See how she will no longer be able to see through her right eye. See the children whose grandmothers and grandfathers are hospitalized with hypothermia. See the elder who has a heart attack. See how science newly quantifies what some of us have long known—how historical and cultural trauma is lived in our bodies, is passed down, generation to generation, how it lives in the body. See the fires that elders light to keep warm. See the water extinguish those fires. See the children seeing it.

Why were you by yourself?

On a road like this, you are never alone. There is grass, there is sky, there is wind. See also: the answer on historical and cultural trauma. See also: Cypress Hills. See also: the everyday robins who are in formation now. See also: their ordinary, general-public bodies in riot.

What did you do after?

You drove north and west and sat in rooms with friends, old and new. You hiked and ate good meals and talked about art. You wrote things down. You began the work of stitching yourself back together. You did this on repeat until the parts hung together in some approximation of self. In Livingston, Montana, you made use of the car wash. You left the tall grass there.

Further questions should be directed toward: Proceed to the Route. Upon arrival, pick up loose, roadside threads. Use them to stitch shut the asking mouths.

VI.

At Standing Rock, the days pass in rhythm. You sort box upon box of donation blankets and clothes. You walk a group of children from one camp to another so they can attend school.

The night before the first walk, it has rained hard and the dirt of the road has shifted to mud. The dirt or mud road runs alongside a field, which sits alongside the Cannonball River, which sits alongside and empties itself into the Missouri.

Over the field, a hawk rides a thermal, practicing efficiency. There on the road, in the mud, three Herefords block progress. The cow snorts to her calves, which are large enough to be ambulatory, young enough for the cow still to proffer protection. She places her body between you, the threat, and her calves. She stamps her hooves into the mud, and they stick in a way you imagine unsatisfactory.

In that letter to the Standing Rock tribal chairman, the Army Corps commander wrote that the people must disperse from camp "due to the concern for public safety" and because "this land is leased to private persons for grazing and/or haying purposes."

A cow holds public hooves whether stuck in mud or otherwise. A cow is not a concern to public safety. But what of these children? Are they considered public or private? If they don't graze or hay, if they cannot be leased, what is their value, here on this road, in this, our America?

That day, there on the road, once the mother cow allows safe passage, you walk on. After school but before the return walk, the children and you gather with hundreds to listen to the tribal chairman speak of peace, to sit with elders to pray, to talk of peace.

On this day, it is still fall. Winter will arrive with the Army Corps' words—no drilling under Lake Oahe, no pipeline under Lake Oahe. The oil company will counter, calling the pipeline "vital," saying they "fully expect to complete construction of the pipeline without any additional rerouting in and around Lake Oahe." The weather will counter with a blizzard. After the words and before the blizzard, there will be a celebration. A gathering of larks is called an exaltation. Even if it wasn't so, you like to think of them there, like to think of their song, there with the people in the snow, there, alongside the river.

Back in the fall, you walk the children home from school, there on the road. You cross the highway, the bridge, upon your return. This bridge lies due south of the Backwater Bridge of the water cannons or hoses. But this bridge, this day, holds a better view. The canoes have arrived from the Northwest tribes, the Salish tribes. They gather below the bridge on the water and cars slow alongside you to honk and wave. Through their windows, people offer real smiles.

That night, under the stars, firelit, the women from the Salish tribes dance and sing. Though you've been to a hundred powwows, easily, you've never seen this dance, never heard this song. You stand with your own arms resting on the shoulders of the schoolchildren, and the dancers, these women, move their arms in motions that do more than mimic water, that conjure it. Their voices are calm and strong, and they move through the gathering like quiet, like water, like something that will hold, something you can keep, even if only for this moment.

Connecting the Dots

Bassey Ikpi

It's the summer of 1988 and I am twelve years old. My mother and I were visiting Nigeria for the first time since we left when I was four. Of course, I didn't recognize anything or anybody. Especially the many uncles and aunties who surrounded me, urging me to remember them, reminding me of sweets and songs. Many of them attempted to engage with me in the language I packed away and forgot to bring back with me. "Wolidiyan?" they'd ask, first gently and then with increasing urgency. "Wolidiyan?" My face would remain unmoved, my blank eyes darting around for my mother or anyone who would help me understand what was being bellowed at me. I knew the response was there. The word itself was buried underneath the English I'd wrapped around myself like a comfort.

"WOLIDIYAN? HOW ARE YOU? Aha! MMABASSEY! Heeeeeeey!"

Their disgusted faces looked like crumpled origami. The parting blow, "Ame-ri-ca! Na wa!" was spat from their mouths with bitterness. They walked away, and the response, "Ayeah, I'm fine," came too late to satisfy anyone.

My favorite auntie saw the shame shadowing my face and

pulled me away from the angry, disappointed looks. "They think that if you forget the language, you have forgotten them," she explained, rocking me against her chest. "But you have not forgotten, have you, Nyono? You may not remember, but you haven't forgotten."

I wasn't sure what she meant, but I nodded anyway.

I stayed away from the rest of the party, choosing to hide behind the compound on a makeshift bench hidden by trees. I'd hear my names being called and draw my hard twelve-year-old knees closer to my face, resting my soft cheek upon them, willing myself to disappear or transport across the ocean back to what was familiar—back to the language I didn't need to force myself to remember.

It wasn't long before someone found me beneath the tree. I felt the bench sink under the new body. I braced myself, waiting for the next new way I could disappoint.

In soft, hesitant English, he said, "I'm your father's third brother's eldest son. I am your brother Otu."

Third brother could mean *uncle*, and there was no word for *cousin* in Yakurr. No term for "distant relative." It was only colonization that introduced the English words to separate these relationships. I noted that he pronounced *brother* as "brodda," so in my head, he became Uncle Brodda.

"People want to see you," Uncle Brodda said, his voice barely a whisper beside me. "Your father is a great man."

I nodded into my knees and watched the wind and moon play with leaves. I waited for the rest.

When he didn't continue, I finally looked up and found him watching me. His eyes were kind. I could see my father's side of the family in them. Part of his face was dark like the color of the sky after the sun disappears to make room for the moon. But patches of his skin were like the moon itself—pale, with a half-crescent shape around his eyes and cheeks, as if God had forgotten to color in this abstract painting of a face. I must have stared a bit too long, something he seemed used to.

"The English doctors call it vitiligo. Some of our people have it."

I wanted to ask him, *Does it feel like you're melting? When you wake up, do you find bits of yourself coating your pillow?* But instead, I simply asked, "Does it hurt? How does it feel to lose yourself?"

Despite the communication gap, Uncle Brodda did his best to answer. "It does not pain me. You notice, small small, that you are no longer the same. I can no longer cry. It is a part of who I am now."

It is part of who I am now.

I thought about the disappointment I'd become and listened as the language I had lost spilled from the windows. I heard my mother's laughter rise above the confusing hum. The entire village seemed to fill the house, welcoming us back home. They were so proud. They had all wanted me to go to America to "be better"; I was the first to be born among them and leave to be trained up in "the abroad."

Now that I had returned, I was too American. I was too different. I couldn't even tell them what I knew. I couldn't explain to them why I'd changed. How difficult it was when we first arrived. How my "otherness" lived on my skin. Why "forgetting" was survival.

That evening, after everyone had gone, I sat on the bed in my auntie's hotel in the village with a torch and examined my body. I searched for any hint of discoloration, anything that would grow into a patchwork on my skin. What story would I make up to explain my own? Would I tell people that I watched the brown slide off my face and crawl away? Would it just disappear one day? Would it be easier, then, to explain the kind of different I'd become?

After about an hour of searching with the torch, I found the dot on the back of my leg. This one is light, a reversal of all the other dots speckled on my body like black paint. I thought of Uncle Brodda and how this white spot could grow or show up on other places on my body. I told my mother the next morning. She said, "Don't worry. That one is your father's side." She said it as if I had somehow sprung whole from her. I have her mother's face, the one she gave us all, so it could have been the truth. I left it alone, checking every few years to see if the white spot had grown. It has been the same size since then. It hasn't moved.

When I think about these stars that litter my skin, when I think about the dot that defies all of those black marks, I recognize one thing—that even my body defies itself. My skin is a star-filled night of moles and marks, and there is one that chose to lighten. These collections of dots and marks tell a story of who I am. How I became. On the days when it feels like my skin is a prison filled with flaws and insecurities, I think of Uncle Brodda.

I returned to the village years later, on the verge of starting college. This time, the anxiety I carried came also with a threat of depression I couldn't name. I looked for Uncle Brodda. I had more questions about the way we change, but he wasn't around. He had left the village for some place that knew him as he is, that wasn't a reminder of how he'd changed. I think of how we both hid beneath the trees, that night, and how he spoke the language of acceptance.

It Doesn't Hurt, It Hurts All the Time
Jess Zimmerman

On July 4, 2019, I was bitten by a dog. I was on the beach in
Delaware with my family, and I asked for permission to pet
a sweet-seeming buddy who reminded me of my own pup.
His twentysomething chaperones told me to go ahead. As I
was reaching toward him and looking up to ask what he was
called, the dog—I never did learn his name—latched onto
my upper arm with what I now know was more than two
hundred pounds per square inch of force.

The details of what happened next elude me. I think his
people were screaming at him, though I still don't remember
what name they were screaming. I know I had to pry his jaws
off of my arm, that he seemed inclined to hang on until he
tore a chunk out. I know I staggered backward, shocked, and
that at the same time (maybe?) my family rushed forward and
someone shoved tissues into my hand, which I clamped to the
wound. I vaguely remember my mother hollering, "What's
your name? Does he have his shots?" as his people retreated
down the beach, saying "He's never done this" and "We're
not from around here." (They were from Arizona, and one

of them was named Miranda. The dog did supposedly have his shots. That's all I know.) The only part I recall clearly is lifting the wad of tissues I'd been holding to my arm, seeing glistening gobbets of blood and fat, and saying quietly, "I'd like to go home, but I think we should go to the ER on the way."

I knew where the ER was in this beach town, and it really was on the way home; I don't know if I would have insisted on going otherwise. It didn't hurt, but it didn't look right, either. Anyway, I spent the evening of Independence Day in the emergency room, getting stitches—only two, so you know it wasn't that bad, but two, so you know it was bad enough. The stitches were to repair the worst damage, a combined gash-puncture where the dog's top fang had penetrated. I also had a long scrape from his other fang, and—for months afterward, and still now if you know where to look—a perfect impression of every tooth from the front of his bottom jaw. After that initial glimpse of wet flesh, I was scared to look again until it was all stitched up and bandaged away, but a photo from the ER shows it was both better and worse than I thought: nothing torn open, but a good thirty square inches of lacerations and welling puncture wounds.

And still, I didn't feel it. I was stunned and bewildered— *How could a dog betray?* I texted my friends—and embarrassed, a fat middle-aged woman in the emergency room in my bathing suit and flip-flops. But I wasn't in pain. At the time, I thought it was the shock, that I had self-protectively shut down all nerve response in the area. I joked to the ER nurse that my brain was taking good care of me. In the weeks and months after, though, a hand-size (mouth-size) chunk of my upper arm remained numb. I could feel only pressure, and only very bluntly, like being poked through layers of padding. I kept waiting for the moment when my nerves would prickle back to life and the hurt would finally bloom, like the day after a tooth extraction when the novocaine wears off—I felt somehow that I needed this, that it would make the whole experience feel less surreal. But the pain stayed locked away, as unreachable as everything else.

This is not to say that it didn't bother me at all. Immediately following the bite, my worst suffering came from bandage adhesive, which made the non-numb parts of my arm flare up with a maddening, itchy rash. But for months, the bite itself also throbbed with a kind of sub-awareness phantom pain. It didn't feel the way a dog bite ought to feel—no lacerating sharpness, no throb. It was more like a sunburn, or maybe just the *knowledge* of sunburn: that sense, the day after an overexposure, of being more aware of your back and shoulders than is strictly normal. Not pain like a puncturing tooth, but pain like an allover inflammation, a diffuse and steady ache, just a notch above subliminal and yet unignorable. My arm had lost all feeling, and it also hurt all the time.

The pain of a wound is separate from the wound itself. Like everything you think you experience, pain must first be mediated by the brain—so in the same way that you see not objects but light bouncing off objects, you feel not the injury but the nervous system's reaction. Sensory neurons called nociceptors (literally "perceivers of harm") register unusual levels of stimulation—crushing, cutting, extreme temperature, chemical response. Above a certain threshold of activation, they send a danger message through the spinal cord to the brain. This process is very, very fast, but it's not instantaneous. There is room for interruption.

Ideally, the pain is a proportional response to the damage: as bad as it needs to be to make you stop what you were doing, sticking around no longer than it takes to heal. But it's possible to unhook the sensation from the cause. Any number of factors can influence your pain tolerance: cussing loudly can decrease your experience of pain (this has been tested in the lab), and being depressed can increase it. Some injuries hurt less when you see them coming; some don't hurt until you look at them.

And, of course, your ability to recognize pain can be impaired, by the wound itself or by other preexisting issues. There's nerve damage, like I had from the dog bite. There's episodic analgesia, which I initially thought I was experiencing, where a serious injury doesn't start to hurt for minutes or hours; the brain undermines its own pain response by releasing a flood of endorphins. Brain damage can disrupt your understanding of pain—you experience nociception but don't recognize it as unpleasant. There are even people who are born impervious to pain, lacking the pathways that signal damage from the body to the brain. These congenital analgesics are in grave danger all the time, needing constant vigilance to make sure they're not being mortally wounded. When you don't know something is hurting you, it can go on hurting you until you die.

There has been a fair amount of research done on pain with no obvious cause—chronic pain that comes, seemingly, from nothing, all the danger signals firing off without anything pulling the trigger. Lack of pain is less scrutinized. We want to understand and thus perhaps alleviate suffering, not its absence.

If a wound doesn't make you suffer, is it still a wound? It can still scar the same, if you're lucky. It can fester if you're not, infection or gangrene setting in because you have no warning signs. The pain is a reaction to damage, not the damage itself. They are linked, of course, but loosely; the worst hurts don't always hurt the worst. Sometimes the shallowest injuries cause disproportionate suffering. Sometimes, even, the injuries you don't feel are more dangerous than the ones you do. There are no nociceptors in the brain.

In mid-May, two months into New York's coronavirus lockdown, I tweeted: "The current situation and the need to keep living my life and doing my job have combined into a permanent experience of that moment when something terrible has happened but you just woke up and haven't completely remembered what it is yet." This was not a unique observation, which is why I put it on Twitter, a medium that generally punishes unpopular opinions but rewards people for saying the same thing as everyone else in a pithier way. Someone who had given himself the descriptive moniker "Socialist Self-Isolating Steve" responded, "That's trauma. You're describing a trauma. Look after yourself!"

This seemed, on the face of it, absurd. For starters, we're *all* going through it, *Steve*. (We weren't, actually, but it still felt that way at the time; it would be another week or so before it became painfully clear how much my experience, as a New Yorker staying pathologically home with my growing collections of masks and Chrome tabs of Covid statistics, was at variance with the experience of people who must already have been planning their Memorial Day beach vacations with friends.) But it also felt grotesque to class my perpetual unease as "trauma" when healthcare providers were spending sleepless nights placing nonstop emergency ventilators, when minimum-wage workers were being forced to choose between health and financial survival, when the sick were drowning in their own lungs, when their family members couldn't even say goodbye. Some of my own friends and family members were getting sick, sometimes very sick. By comparison with everyone directly affected, I was doing remarkably well.

In fact, I thought I must be doing better even than other people in my immensely privileged position, who were not sick and had not lost anyone and were not frontline workers and were not even trying to parent and teach and work at the same time. My social media feeds (which is to say, my entire social life) were crowded with monuments to the Before Time: lush reminiscences about mundane acts of social ease, rapturous details about favorite away-from-home meals, laments about missing family and friends. I, on the other hand, had snapped almost immediately into a kind of hibernation mode. I did think about my more carefree pre-pandemic life, but not about a recent routine I wanted to return to; instead I was flooded with random involuntary memories of much earlier times, as if watching my life flash before my eyes in excruciating slow-mo. The outside world, the ability to navigate it casually, already felt just as impossibly lost as youth, just as pointless to mourn. I didn't want this to be over, because "over" was meaningless. I wanted it never to have begun, and what was the use of longing for a disappeared past? We all wish, sometimes, that we could travel back in time, but we don't suffer from the lack of it.

And so I did not pine for diner pancakes, or drinks in bars, or the sound of the subway—or at least no more than I pined for video stores or smoking sections or thylacines. These were things that once existed and had stopped existing, and I had shut down fruitless longing for them like snipping a wire. Almost as soon as my office closed, my conceivable universe obediently shrank to fit within my 550-square-foot apartment. We have few windows, and no view—we're on the first floor, and our windows are partially papered over with translucent film—so I didn't even have to look at masked people or shuttered stores. I did feel a series of pangs as I watched the tree outside, the only thing we can really see, go from dead brown to full leaf, but beyond that tree the world did not exist. I naturally took on an attitude that reminded me of my dog getting a bath: *I guess this is my life forever now, and maybe it always was.*

I felt calm in isolation, even cozy. My husband and I cooked comfort food, burned indulgent candles, visited each other's islands in *Animal Crossing.* (We celebrated two birthdays and a first anniversary in quarantine, so now we suddenly own two Switches Lite.) But I knew that this calm was a thin glaze over unfathomable depths; it could be shattered not only by bad fortune, but by examination, the way ice melts if you breathe on it too close. I had curled myself into a complacent hibernation because thinking too hard would tip me into panic.

It's not that I didn't pay attention to the statistics or the news; like everyone else at first, I paid compulsive attention to them, cross-checking the reported death tolls against the projections, the projections against other projections, the reports against other reports, multiple times a day. I sobbed over firsthand accounts by ER doctors and Covid victims; every time my husband cleared his throat, I had a flash of him on a ventilator. But isolation and stasis let me keep that fear contained. I squirmed through the part of every video call, inevitable in the early days, where we all talked about how bad everything was, how scared we were; I didn't want to talk about it or analyze it or, god forbid, be encouraged to take a walk. I didn't want to connect with other people at all. I just wanted to be silent and impassive, aloof as an ascetic in a cell.

I was sure that the word *trauma* came from the German *Traum*, meaning "dream"; it seemed intuitively correct that disabling psychological damage bubbling up from your subconscious would be connected, etymologically, to nightmares. But of course, trauma was physical—as in *trauma ward*—before it was mental, and the word actually comes from the Greek for *wound*. It's still in use that way, especially in medical circles, but I would venture a guess that most people who hear the word *trauma* think first of the mind. This shift in primary connotation came late, late enough that my 1970s compact *Oxford English Dictionary* still contains almost no usage references for mental trauma. In the updated online edition of the *OED*, physical trauma is still the first definition, but it's been swamped by technical and figurative uses of *trauma* in the psychological sense. The clinical meaning dates back to the late nineteenth century—the first *OED* citation, from the *Psychological Review* in 1894, includes the beautiful phrase "psychic *traumata*, thorns in the spirit, so to speak." But the general usage didn't kick in until the late 1970s, when the concept of *post-traumatic stress* entered the general consciousness of an America inundated with psychologically wounded Vietnam vets. PTSD was finally enshrined in the *Diagnostic and Statistical Manual*, the registry of psych diagnoses, in 1980, after a long campaign by a group of psychiatrists working on behalf of veterans. And this idea, that the mind could sustain an invisible wound, also percolated outward to the general population—perhaps because people saw so much of it, in an era that featured not only traumatized American soldiers but traumatized veterans of the battle for civil rights.

Unlike physical trauma, psychological trauma was notable for its invisibility—not only because the damage was internal, but because it hid itself. There are several reasons why a physical wound might not hurt and reasons why even a serious injury might not be obvious. But for trauma, this self-erasing power is essential. The traumatized mind might understand that it had been through something harrowing; vets, for instance, were aware of how they'd spent their time, and I'm sure mostly understood how the ordeal of war might relate to the postwar nightmares. A defining characteristic of trauma, though, is the way it burrows like a tick into the subconscious, erasing the traces that might hold it accountable. You might not even know what's pulling your strings.

Like a lot of psychological terms, the clinical meaning of *trauma* remains much narrower than its public use. The *OED* general usage examples, which are from the late 1970s and early '80s, are about things like labor unions and the American rapid transit industry. Our current usage can include cumulative effects like neglect or racist microaggressions, which rarely rise to the level of notable damage in each individual instance but which build on each other to become complicatedly traumatizing. Meanwhile, though, the *DSM*, whose definition is imperfect but authoritative, limits trauma to ongoing effects precipitated by "actual or threatened death, serious injury, or sexual violence."

There is not, I think, any reason for me to class living safely through a global pandemic as a form of trauma in the clinical sense; while we are arguably all living under the shadow of possible death, it doesn't quite rise to the level of a threat. Being afraid of a virus is not the same as going to war. But a trauma also means a wound, and a wound has many forms. Some are abrasions, shallow but covering a lot of ground. Some are punctures, deep and sharp, or long lacerations, or internal bruises that don't even show right away. Some bleed; some are cauterized. Some go septic. Some you don't even feel.

Over the months of stay-at-home orders, which all felt like one long week, it became increasingly clear that while I was not supposed to go outside, and didn't want to go outside, I also couldn't. In the first week after my office closed, I was supposed to walk over and clear out the mail; instead, I had a hyperventilating panic attack. Once I stopped being expected to go out—once the prevailing sentiment became that, in fact, it was irresponsible to go out—the fear became quieter, less demonstrative, but still petrifying. It took a month before I could even go down the hall to the laundry room without crying, longer to go farther; I left the building twice in April and twice in May. I was still having stray flashes of memory—say, a sudden image of walking down a particular street in the Village where there was a pet shop—but instead of wistfulness, these were increasingly accompanied by a glacial sensation, like my bones and guts had turned to stone. I worried that I was inventing this fear to use as an excuse—I didn't want to go out, so I pretended I couldn't. But why wouldn't I want to go out? Everyone else did.

For a while, this didn't matter. When I mentioned, offhandedly, that I was perhaps *unreasonably* afraid to go outside, friends reassured me that it was actually extremely reasonable, even righteous. But at the same time, almost from the first days of lockdown, my Twitter feed was full of gentle admonitions to *get out, take a walk, just take one walk a day, my daily walk keeps me sane.* As states started lifting restrictions, even many of my most science-minded friends were so starved for normalcy that they started cautiously meeting for distance hangs or taking weird anxious road trips. Even the people saying, *I don't get it, is everyone else insane?* were posting that from the park, with masks on, at a safe distance from everyone else. And I was still inside.

When the Black Lives Matter protests started in the

last days of May, the switch of public opinion immediately flipped: now, instead of it being a moral imperative to stay in, it was (or at least it felt like) a moral imperative to get out and be in the streets. The cause was so much more important than my personal anxieties, and yet I couldn't make myself go to a rally a few blocks away—even seeing the ubiquitous masks, even when initial data suggested that protests were not big drivers of infection. My disgust with myself for my "excuses" intensified. Even if I was unable to overcome my anxiety to do my share of the grocery shopping, shouldn't I be able to set it aside for a critically important cause?

Maybe I would have judged myself less if the fear had been more dramatic. But it was more of a quiet freeze, a powerful and irresistible desire to stop thinking about it, stop thinking, stop doing anything. On a rational level, I knew I likely wouldn't get sick if I went outside, carefully, like everyone else. Marching or rallying while masked seemed relatively safe. Hanging out in a park with a mask on seemed extremely safe, in theory; the park near my house was a no-go in terms of distancing, but I could take one of those walks everyone was talking about. Except I couldn't. The apartment had become my planet, and going outside felt like going into space: vertiginous, airless, fraught with peril no matter how much equipment and preparation you had.

Technically, agoraphobia is not just a fear of leaving your home. It's a fear born of having a panic attack outside of your home—or in a subway, or at work, or any specific place where you are stranded or in danger. This fear feeds on itself, rebirths itself: Having been so vulnerable in an unsafe place, you are now more likely to panic when you try to return, which then scares you more. Eventually you fear a repeat of the badly located panic attack so much that it seems safer to avoid the location. This is one of the operations of trauma: it is self-replicating. It can even be self-originating. The immediate cause, the precipitating trauma, is something your brain did to you.

Agoraphobia also presupposes that there is nothing to *rationally* fear in the spaces you avoid—no war, no stalkers, no pandemic-level outbreak of a mysterious and unpredictable disease. Whatever was going on with me, it wasn't a phobia, that parthenogenetic fear that creates itself from nothing: the thing I'd been terrified of, initially, was out there and truly scary. But my immobilization still came from a fear of the fear, the instinct to shut down all pain pathways surrounding that initial wound. I did not want to acknowledge the danger, or look at it, or think about it applying to me, or fully process everything it would mean for the future. Unlike the people protesting for their right to mask-free shopping or haircuts, I didn't have the option to simply avoid or forget or resist the fear; I knew too much, and cared too much, and had paid too much attention. And so, the self-protective instinct: a radical numbing, interpolated between the wound and the pain it could cause.

This Fourth of July, I did nothing, of course. (I didn't much feel like celebrating this country anyway.) I wouldn't have thought I could top getting attacked by a dog, but that's the name of the game in 2020: things you didn't think could get worse get worse. My parents and my sister, brother-in-law, and nieces went back to the beach without me. They have cars and can get out of the city; they'd already crossed the streams of their households. I said we couldn't go because we don't have a car, and because my husband had to work, both of which were true. I was also scared, but I didn't want to admit that.

It seems unacceptable, somehow, to say something as simple as "I am in danger, so I am afraid." We have been blessed and cursed with access to cross-global communication, and it has in many ways overloaded our little primate brains: we are now constantly confronted with the suffering of thousands or tens of thousands of people at every moment, and for many of us, that knowledge comes with a sense of obligation. Social media's specialty is asking people why they're talking about this disaster but silent on this other one, why they're donating to this organization when they could have donated to that, why they're focused on their own tiny tragedies when the large ones are so large. All of these questions are righteous, the causes undeniable. We *do* owe it to each other to witness the suffering of the vulnerable, we *do* have a responsibility to do what we can, and the specific "we" I belong to—white, middle-class—should not be afforded the luxury of ignorance or inaction. But it gives you a new perspective on the smallness of your own suffering—and a sense of perspective, as Douglas Adams said, is the one thing living beings cannot afford to have. A glittering carpet of human misery is spread in front of us every day. Of course it feels obscene to say you're sad.

My fear of going outside, I think, was more like the opposite of a fear, the buffering negative space around it—an anti-fear. Like episodic analgesia, where the brain holds pain at bay, it was a protective nothingness, a shutdown. We are all so afraid. We are all so angry. We are all so lonely for our former lives and mourning the collapse of the future. We are genuinely in danger, from the virus. We are genuinely being endangered, actively, by a government that sees us as disposable or worse. It's too much: a black hole, all gravity and no light. At the same time, we are relentlessly, inescapably aware of how much worse it could be, how much worse it *is*, for someone, for many people. How do you let yourself feel that bolus of emotions at all? How, especially, do you feel it knowing that this is what *lucky* looks like?

If I gave in, if I truly faced things, I would be lost. I don't want that, and more to the point, I don't feel I deserve it. In the abstract, it seems like it might be uniting to suffer the same psychic blow as everyone else, but in practice it means that we're all trying to crawl into the same bed. How can I justify taking up space? Empathy, fellow-feeling, public-spiritedness seem to demand that I make way for people who have also suffered all the baseline traumas of this year, plus losing loved ones or being sick for months or having all the wounds of racism clawed open or getting their eyes shot out by "less lethal" police weapons. So I throw up these barriers to nociception: If I can't see damage, then I won't feel pain. If I don't think about pain, then I haven't been damaged. If I haven't been damaged, then what I feel is not pain. It doesn't hurt, it can't hurt, and it also hurts all the time.

What if we thought of emotional trauma the way we do physical: not as worthy injuries and unworthy ones, but as a wide class of wounds made in different ways, whose healing is unpredictable, whose scars take different forms? It is worse to die, to be grievously ill, to lose someone you love, to lose your job and fear for your survival, to not lose your job and be forced to risk your survival every day. But it is also terrible to fear the future, to be betrayed by your leaders, to see ignorance weaponized, to have your life treated as a bargaining chip by the powerful. It is terrible to hang suspended over the pit and try not to look down. The teeth of this year grind all of us. Maybe, in seeing each other's wounds, we can let ourselves feel our own.

Acknowledgments

We are grateful to every author in this anthology; to associate editor Alicia Kroell, editorial assistant Laura Gonzalez, editor in chief Megha Majumdar, and former publisher Andy Hunter; to Allisen Lichtenstein, Arriel Vinson, Eliza Harris, Gabrielle Bellot, Leah Johnson, Sarah Lyn Rogers, Stella Cabot Wilson, Tajja Isen, and all our digital editorial colleagues; to creative director Nicole Caputo and cover artist Sirin Thada; and to all the writers who have trusted *Catapult* with their stories.

About the Contributors

A. E. Osworth is the author of *We Are Watching Eliza Bright*, a novel about a game developer dealing with harassment (and narrated collectively by a fictional subreddit). They are part-time faculty at The New School, where they teach undergraduates the art of digital storytelling. They have an eight-year freelancing career, and you can find their work in *Autostraddle*, *Guernica*, *Quartz*, *Electric Literature*, *Paper Darts*, Mashable, and drDoctor, among other publications.

Andrea Ruggirello's writing appears in *Redivider*, *Gay Magazine*, *Bitch*, *Hobart*, *The Baltimore Review*, *McSweeney's Internet Tendency*, *Electric Literature*, *Catapult*, *Third Coast*, and elsewhere. Her novel manuscript was selected as a semifinalist for the James Jones First Novel Fellowship and was supported by the Tin House Winter Novel Workshop. She has an MFA in fiction from West Virginia University. Andrea was born in Korea and adopted as a baby. She was raised on Staten Island, New York, and now lives in Brooklyn.

Aricka Foreman is an American poet and interdisciplinary writer from Detroit, Michigan. Author of *Salt Body*

Shimmer, winner of the 2021 Lambda Literary Award in Bisexual Poetry, her poems, essays, and scholarship have appeared widely. She has earned fellowships from Cave Canem, Callaloo, and Millay Arts. She stewards as a publicist at Haymarket Books and serves on the board of directors for *The Offing*. She lives in Chicago—on the unceded homelands of the Council of the Three Fires: the Ojibwe, Odawa, and Potawatomi Nations—engaging poetry with photography and video.

Austin Gilkeson has written for Tin House, *McSweeney's, Foreign Policy, Vulture, The Toast*, and other publications. He lives just outside Chicago with his wife and son.

Bassey Ikpi is a Nigerian American writer, ex-poet, constant mental health advocate, underachieving overachiever, and memoir procrastinator. She is also the author of the *New York Times* bestseller *I'm Telling the Truth, but I'm Lying*. She lives in Maryland with her soccer superstar son.

Bryan Washington is the author of *Lot* and *Memorial*, which was a finalist for the National Book Critics Circle Award in fiction.

Callum Angus is the author of the story collection *A Natural History of Transition* (Metonymy Press), as well as managing editor of the journal *smoke and mold*. His work has appeared in *Orion, Nat. Brut, West Branch*, the *Los Angeles Review of Books, The Common*, and elsewhere; and in the anthology *Kink*, edited by Garth Greenwell and R. O. Kwon.

He has received support from Lambda Literary and Signal Fire Foundation for the Arts, and he holds an MFA from the University of Massachusetts Amherst. He lives in Portland, Oregon.

Destiny O. Birdsong's writing has appeared in *The Paris Review Daily*, *African American Review*, and *Catapult*, among other publications. She has received the Academy of American Poets Prize and the Richard G. Peterson Poetry Prize. Her critically acclaimed debut collection of poems, *Negotiations*, was published by Tin House Books in 2020 and was long-listed for the 2021 PEN/Voelcker Award for Poetry Collection. Her debut novel, *Nobody's Magic*, will be published by Grand Central Publishing in 2022.

Eloghosa Osunde is a multidisciplinary artist and the author of *Vagabonds!*, which will be published in 2022 by Riverhead Books and 4th Estate.

Forsyth Harmon is the author and illustrator of the illustrated novel *Justine* (Tin House, 2021). She is also the illustrator of *Girlhood* by Melissa Febos and *The Art of the Affair* by Catherine Lacey. Forsyth's work has been featured in *Granta*, *BOMB*, *Refinery29*, *The Believer*, and more. She received both a BA and an MFA from Columbia University and currently lives in New York.

Gabrielle Bellot is a staff writer for *Literary Hub* and the head instructor at Catapult. Her work has appeared in *The New Yorker*, *The New York Times*, *The Atlantic*, *The Cut*,

Gay Magazine, Tin House, Guernica, The Paris Review Daily, them, and many other places. Her essays have been anthologized in *Indelible in the Hippocampus* (2019), *Can We All Be Feminists?* (2018), and elsewhere. She holds both an MFA and PhD in creative writing from Florida State University. She lives in Queens.

Haley E. D. Houseman chases offbeat stories exploring communities of humans (and nonhumans). Passionate about nature and how we craft a relationship with the world around us, she cofounded an ongoing anthology called *HUMANxNATURE*, focused on unconventional nature writing. With a cohort of subscribers, writers, and naturalists, the anthology has released two volumes of essays, interviews, and exercises in imagining a new relationship with the natural world. She lives in Massachusetts and spend most of her time in the forest with her dog. Otherwise, find her in the garden, in the library, or sewing—just check the weather.

Hannah Walhout is a writer and a senior print editor at *Travel + Leisure*. She is also a founding co-editor of the process-focused lit mag *Headway Quarterly*, a 2019 finalist in the CLMP Firecracker Awards for best debut magazine. She has lived in Seattle; the Inland Empire; Rome; Abu Dhabi; and now, the greatest city in the world (Brooklyn).

Jenny Tinghui Zhang is the author of *Four Treasures of the Sky*. Her writing has appeared in *Ninth Letter, Passages North, The Cut*, and elsewhere. She received her MFA from the University of Wyoming and lives in Austin, Texas.

Jess Zimmerman is the author of *Women and Other Monsters* and *Basic Witches* (with Jaya Saxena). She is an editor at Quirk Books in Philadelphia.

Kaila Philo is a journalist based in Washington, D.C. She writes about justice in all its forms.

Karissa Chen is a writer who splits her time between Taipei and New Jersey. Her work has appeared in numerous publications, including *The Atlantic, Eater,* NBC News *THINK, The Cut, Guernica, Longreads, Gulf Coast,* and more. She is the recipient of a Fulbright Scholarship and a NJ Council of the Arts Individual Artist Grant and is a Kundiman fellow. She currently serves as the editor in chief at *Hyphen* magazine and is a contributing editor at *Catapult,* as well as a *Catapult* columnist. She is working on a novel.

Kayla Whaley lives outside Atlanta, Georgia, where she buys too many books and drinks too many lattes. She holds an MFA in creative nonfiction from the University of Tampa and is a graduate of the Clarion Writers' Workshop. She was named one of *Bustle*'s inaugural "Rule Breakers" in 2018. Among other venues, her work has appeared in *Catapult, Bustle, Michigan Quarterly Review, Uncanny Magazine,* and *Book Riot,* and in the anthologies *Here We Are: Feminism for the Real World* (Algonquin) and *Unbroken: 13 Stories Starring Disabled Teens* (Farrar, Straus and Giroux).

Maggie Tokuda-Hall has an MFA in creative writing from the University of South Florida. She is the author of the 2017

Parent's Choice Gold Medal–winning picture book, *Also an Octopus*, illustrated by Benji Davies. *The Mermaid, the Witch, and the Sea* is her debut young adult novel, which was an NPR Best Book of 2020. Her graphic novel, *Squad*, appeared on shelves in 2021. She lives in Oakland, California, with her husband, son, and objectively perfect dog.

Marcos Gonsalez is an author, essayist, and scholar living in New York City. Marcos's debut memoir, *Pedro's Theory*, came out in 2021. Marcos's essays have appeared in *Literary Hub*, the *Los Angeles Review of Books*, *Electric Literature*, and *Public Books*, among others.

Marisa Crane is a queer, nonbinary writer whose work has appeared or is forthcoming in *Joyland*, *No Tokens*, *TriQuarterly*, *The Florida Review*, *Passages North*, and elsewhere. Author of the forthcoming debut novel *I Keep My Exoskeletons to Myself* (Catapult, 2023), Marisa currently lives in San Diego.

Melissa Hung is a writer and journalist. Her essays and reported stories have appeared in NPR, *Vogue*, *Longreads*, *Jellyfish Review*, and *Catapult*, where she writes a column about chronic pain called Pain in the Brain. A former newspaper reporter, she is the founding editor of *Hyphen*. She grew up in Texas, the eldest child of immigrants.

Natalie Lima is a Cuban Puerto Rican writer and a graduate of the MFA program in creative nonfiction writing at the University of Arizona. Her essays and fiction have been published or are forthcoming in *Longreads, Guernica, Brevity, The Offing, Catapult,* and elsewhere. She has received fellowships from PEN America Emerging Voices, Tin House, the VONA/Voices Workshop, and the Virginia G. Piper Center for Creative Writing, and a residency from Hedgebrook. You can find her on Instagram and Twitter @natalielima09.

Nina Riggs received her MFA in poetry in 2004 and published a book of poems, *Lucky, Lucky,* in 2009. She wrote about life with metastatic breast cancer on her blog, *Suspicious Country;* her recent work has appeared in *The Washington Post* and *The New York Times.* She lived with her husband and sons and dogs in Greensboro, North Carolina. She is the author of the *New York Times* bestseller *The Bright Hour.*

Rachel Charlene Lewis is a writer and editor. Her work has been published in *The Normal School,* the *Los Angeles Review of Books,* and elsewhere. She exists across the internet as @RachelCharleneL.

Ross Showalter's stories, essays, and criticism have appeared in *Electric Literature, Strange Horizons, Catapult, Black Warrior Review,* and elsewhere. He lives in Seattle.

s. e. smith is a National Magazine Award–winning writer based in Northern California. smith's commentary and reported features, appearing in outlets like *The Guardian, Catapult* magazine, *In These Times, The Nation, Bitch* magazine, and *Esquire*, focus on life in the margins, social attitudes, and cultural assessments of worth.

Sarah McEachern is a reader and writer in Brooklyn, New York. Her creative work has been published by *Pigeon Pages, Pacifica Literary Review, Entropy*, and *The Spectacle*. Her reviews, interviews, and criticism have been published or are forthcoming in *Rain Taxi, Bookforum, The Rupture, Asymptote, The Ploughshares Blog*, PEN America, *BOMB, Full Stop, The Believer*, and *The Rumpus*.

Taylor Harris is the author of *This Boy We Made: A Memoir of Motherhood, Genetics, and Facing the Unknown*. Her work has appeared in *Time, O Quarterly, The Washington Post, Longreads, The Cut, Romper, Parents, McSweeney's*, and other publications.

Toni Jensen is the author of *Carry*, a memoir-in-essays about gun violence, land, and Indigenous women's lives (Ballantine 2020). Jensen received an NEA Creative Writing Fellowship in 2020, and her essays have appeared in *Orion, Catapult*, and *Ecotone*. She is also the author of the story collection *From the Hilltop*. She teaches at the University of Arkansas and the Institute of American Indian Arts. She is Métis.

About the Editors

NICOLE CHUNG is the author of *All You Can Ever Know*, a contributing writer at *The Atlantic*, and the former editor in chief of *Catapult* magazine.

MATT ORTILE is the author of *The Groom Will Keep His Name* and the executive editor of *Catapult* magazine.